The Bigger Tory Vote

by

Nick Toczek

AK Press

AUTHOR'S INTRODUCTORY NOTES TO FIRST REPRINT.

As this book goes into reprint, I'm just completing work on a much more detailed expansion of this whole text which will, I hope, run to at least 200 pages. It'll be fully indexed and will explore numerous other avenues for which there just wasn't the space in this slim volume. It should be available from A.K. Press in about a year.

Meanwhile, there are one or two staightforward errors in this book which I only noticed after it first appeared. Because these would be expensive to correct in the text, I'll do so in these introductory notes instead. There are also several points where in retrospect, either the tone or emphasis needs changing.

The research and follow—up work required for a book like this is so complex that a few errors are, I suppose, inevitable. Some you spot for yourself, others you only notice when they're pointed out to you. I'd like, in particular, to thank Martin Durham, Mark Taha and Robin Ramsey for taking the trouble to send me their very useful notes, criticisms and observations on the entire text.

On page six, line ten, Martin Webster gets called Colin. It's also worth mentioning that by the early '80s, if not before, Richard Lawson had rejoined the National Front. He proposed a motion at the November '84 AGM which was seconded by Michael Walker.

In the second paragraph on page seven, I link Gareth Light with Anna Bramwell via the young Monday Club. In fact, Bramwell was working there in the early '70's, while Light was a Committee member in the early '80's. And, as Bramwell quit the MC in '73 when G.K. Young went, this link is far more tenuous than I suggest. As it stands, it's just another indication that they moved in the same circles.

On page eight, line twenty four, I refer to Ray Shenston. His surname is actually Shenton. He later formed his own English National Party, which was authoritarian and far—right. It put up several unsuccessful electoral candidates and campaigned for the repatriation of all immigrants in England, including Welsh, Scottish and Irish.

On the penultimate line of page nine, I give '53 as the year in which Chesterton founded the League of Empire Loyalists. This was the year he founded his journal, Candour, but the LEL itself didn't come actually into being until the following year.

Likewise, on page eleven I say that Colin Jordan became World Fuhrer in '61. It was, in fact, '62.

On page eleven, in paragraph three I call the National Front After Victory a political party. It seems that this short–lived and elusive group, under A.K. Chesterton's leadership, was never more than a plan for post–war regrouping among some of the key figures on the far right. It didn't become a party, though it did enter into merger negotiations with John Beckett's British People's Party.

On page nineteen, paragraph four, I describe Birwood as having been involved in the British Military Volunteer Force in the late '70s. It was in the late '60s.

Near the top of page twenty, I imply that Ronald Bell followed Powell in opposing immigration. Not so. Bell had been speaking out against immigration since the early '50s.

Half way down page twenty two, I talk about Andrew Fountain's National Front Movement. This made it's brief appearance in the early '50s, not the late '50s.

On page twenty four, I lump together the International Freedom Foundation, Western Goals UK, the Salisbury Group and the Libertarian Alliance as if they're similar bodies. I didn't intend to give any such impression. The differences between them will be covered in some detail in my forthcoming expanded investigation.

On page thirty three, lines four and five, please drop the word parliamentary.

Near the foot of page thirty four, I say that the Adam Smith Club later became the Adam Smith Institute. Not so. The two exist entirely separately.

In the third paragraph on page thirty seven, I describe John Biggs–Davison's Friends of the Union as anti–Catholic. What I meant to say was that it was loyalist and anti–nationalist.

On page forty three, line seventeen, for Alan Sherman please read Alfred Sherman.

First published by
AK Press, 1991
this second edition, 1992

© Nick Toczek, 1992

ISBN 1 873176 20 1

CIP Data available from
The British Library

Cover design by Freddie Baer

AK Press, 3 Balmoral Place, Stirling, Scotland FK8 2RD

The Bigger Tory Vote

From '71 to '73, the Monday Club (MC) ran the Halt Immigration Now Campaign (HINC) from its London HQ. Those working there and involved in the campaign included *George Kennedy Young, Tony Vander Elst, Anna Bramwell* and *Harvey Proctor*.[1]

The HINC was run by *Ronald Bell* and G.K. Young. It had been founded by Young in '71, primarily as a means of side-stepping policy disagreements with other MC members (notably Harold Soref) in its less radical predecessor, the MC Immigration Committee. In September '72, following the Heath government's decision to admit Asian refugees expelled from Uganda by Idi Amin, a group of five individuals went to Downing Street to publicise their opposition to such a policy. Three of these were women — *Bee* (for Beryl) *Carthew, Joy Page* and *Lady Jane Birdwood*. The other two were Proctor and Young.[2]

The organisations and individuals which surface when we examine some of the political activities and loyalties of these eight right-wingers reveal a fascinating and remarkably intimate network. Moreover, it rapidly becomes obvious that what masquerades as a vast and diverse fleet of influential organisations is in fact crewed and very carefully steered by a tiny handful of single-minded (and sometimes narrow-minded) people. In truth, there is nothing exceptional about this particular example. On the contrary, what follows merely serves as a graphic, but absolutely pedestrian illustration of the way in which our political life functions.

Anna Bramwell

Leopards don't change their spots. On Saturday 25.10.86, at the Bonnington Hotel in London, Dr Anna Bramwell, Professor of History at Corpus Christi College, Oxford was one of six speakers at an international conference on 'Ecology: The Growing Dilemma'. Her contribution drew extensively on *Blood and Soil, Walther Darre and Hitler's 'Green Party'*, her recently-published hagiography of Darre, who was Hitler's Reichsbauernführer (National Peasant Leader) and Nazi Minister of Food and Agriculture from '33 almost to the end of

WWII. The conference was organised jointly by *Iona* 'an independent cultural society devoted to the study, revival, promotion, development and enjoyment of the islands of the North Atlantic' and the 'independent' magazine, *The Scorpion*, edited by Michael Walker who was himself one of the six speakers.

Iona was formed around '83 by Richard Lawson. Back in '73, Lawson had been editor of *Spark*, the journal of the National Front (NF) Students' Association. By December '73, he'd replaced Peter McMenemie as editor of the NF's newspaper *Britain First*. When the faction led by John Tyndall and Colin Webster ousted Kingsley Read's populist (and in some cases Strasserite) section of the NF at the end of '75, Lawson left with them. He then sat on the executive council of Read's ill-fated National Party, editing *Britain First* as that party's journal.[3]

The Scorpion's founding editor, Michael Walker, is also a former leading light of the NF. At the end of '81, he launched what was to become *The Scorpion*, under the title *The National Democrat* (which had G.K. Young as one of its contributors). He was then living at 50 Warwick Square in London, an address he shared with Nick Griffin, editor of the NF's theoretical journal, *Nationalism Today*. During Summer '83, the two editors were also co-running Heritage Tours. One of their tour guides was Roberto Fiore, notorious Italian terrorist and member of the neo-fascist NAR. Fiore himself lived with them for a while in the Warwick Square flat. According to another Warwick Square resident, a Young Conservative officer called Gareth Light, another NAR terrorist, Luciano Petrone, had also stayed in the flat. Petrone was at that time on the run from the Italian authorities for his part in the murder of two policemen. He was later arrested and deported to Italy where he was tried in '86 and given a 22-year sentence. In the flat below the Walker/Griffin home lived Nicholas Ridley.[4]

It's an odd coincidence that it was Nicholas Ridley, just before he quit the Thatcher cabinet, who granted the NF their sought-after limited company status. The front page of the June '90 issue of the NF newspaper, *The Flag*, celebrated the achievement with a picture of Ridley above the heading "Ridley OK on NF & Co".[5]

Gareth Light, Ridley's talkative Young Tory neighbour in '83, had curiously un-Conservative interests judging by his June '82 letter in historian David Irving's right-wing Focus Policy Group (FPG) journal, *Focal Point*. Writing from Westcliff-on-Sea, he begins: "I have spent several months drifting, politically, looking for a genuinely patriotic organisation putting forward positive views around which frustrated nationalists can rally." Having gone on to express his admiration for the ideas of Enoch Powell, he ends the letter with a request "to hear from individuals in the London/South-East area who would like to talk about a nationalist group". It would appear that his letter was answered and that it led to his residence in Warwick Square a year later.[6]

Searchlight, covering the Fiore/Petrone story, said that Walker and Griffin were actually sharing their flat with Gareth Light. This would explain his insider knowledge about visitors to the Walker/Griffin flat. Light was the Political Officer of Westminster Young Conservatives and a Committee Member of The Young MC. He'll therefore have known the woman who was the Young Members' Secretary at MC HQ. That was Anna Bramwell.[7]

Now here's a curious thing. We have a link between Gareth Light and G.K. Young (via Anna Bramwell). We have a link between Michael Walker and G.K. Young (via *National Democrat*). There's also a possible link, if *Searchlight*'s more recent allegations are true, between Roberto Fiore and G.K. Young via MI6. In '89, Home Secretary Douglas Hurd announced that the government would be taking no action to deport Fiore. This was an extraordinary decision.

Let's recap. Here was a known terrorist. He'd been living openly in Britain for nine years despite being wanted by the Italian authorities. He'd been living for part of that time in a flat shared by two extreme fascist activists and a leading young Conservative. According to the Conservative, a second Italian terrorist who'd murdered two policemen had also stayed there. Nicholas Ridley, a cabinet minister and a close personal associate of Mrs Thatcher lived in the same block of flats.

Furthermore, it turned out that Fiore had known links with a number of other active right-wing Italian terrorists and, in particular, that he had close connections with the NAR cell known to have carried out the Bologna railway station bombing (1.8.80) in which 85 people were killed and 200 injured. Indeed, Fiore became an important figure within the NF and is seen by some as having been the prime influence on its development during the '80s. He's specifically credited with having been behind the formation of the NF's 'political soldiers'. Why were Hurd and the British government apparently unconcerned about this man's continued presence? According to *Searchlight*, it was because Fiore, who'd trained in a Falangist militia camp in Lebanon before coming to Britain, had been working for MI6, gathering information and passing it on to them. G.K. Young, as we'll see, was a former second-in-command at MI6.[8]

According to the 23.11.81 edition of *Focal Point*: "Focus member Roy Bramwell has distributed hundreds of copies of a recent speech by Sir Ronald Bell MP, entitled 'This Sceptred Isle', to a meeting of the WISE group in London." Bee Carthew co-

> "goes deeper and further than the National Front"
> —*Joan Mason, describing WISE.*[10]

ran WISE (Welsh, Irish, Scottish and English) with its founder, Joan Mason. Harvey Proctor was an active member and spoke at WISE meetings, as did Bell, while Jane Birdwood attended several meetings including the one at which Proctor spoke (18.7.81) when Joy Page was also present.[9]

Roy Bramwell, a property developer, was Anna's husband. During the late '60s, he was active in both the MC and the Immigration Control Association (ICA), the latter organisation having been founded ('66-'67) by Joy Page in association with Racial Preservation Society (RPS) activist, Mary Howarth. In '70, he was one of the speakers at the ultra-right-wing Northern League's Pan Nordic conference in Brighton. He was there again the following year, when three former SS officers were also among the guests. By '72, he'd become chairman of the South-west London branch of the MC. Harvey Proctor, then the Conservative candidate for Hackney and Shoreditch, was a member of the same branch. Ray Shenston, who'd been recently expelled from Chelsea Conservative Association for canvassing on behalf of the NF in Battersea, was none-the-less admitted as a member.[11]

In Autumn '75, a 4-page pamphlet by D.R. (for Roy) Bramwell entitled *The White Man's White Paper on Racial Discrimination* was published in London by the Anti-Immigration Standing Committee (AISC). In Nov '76, the Inter-City Research Centre (ICRC) published a 44-page attack on the BBC for its multi-racial policies. Entitled *Blatant Bias Corporation*, it was written by Roy Bramwell with an introduction by JB (for Jane Birdwood). The same press went on to publish further pamphlets by Roy Bramwell: *Justice be Damned...* ('77), *The Death Tree* (Feb.'78) and *Public Ear* Nos.1 ('78), 2 (Dec.'78) & 3 (Feb.'79). The address for both the AISC and the ICRC was given as 100 Philbeach Gardens, SW5, which was at that time the home of Lady Jane Birdwood, who ran both organisations.

During the '80s, Roy Bramwell resurfaced as a member of the FPG,

founded (in '82) and run by that ubiquitous revisionist, David Irving.
Roy Bramwell died in late '88 or early '89.[12]

Bee Carthew

She was publicist for Enoch Powell in the late '60s. During the early '70s, she organised the Powellite Association (a.k.a. Powellight). Next, she was active in the MC, becoming the committee secretary in '71 of the HINC, which was run for G.K. Young by his protégé Geoffrey Baber. Their fellow HINC committee members at that time were G.K. Young, Gerald Howarth (son of RPS/ICA activist, Mary Howarth) and the Tory MPs Ronald Bell, John Stokes and Harold Soref. She continued with this work until she was expelled from the MC by Jonathan Guinness in Summer '73 following his acrimonious and damaging leadership battle with G.K. Young. Within a matter of weeks, Ronald Bell, Anna Bramwell, Geoffrey Baber, Roy Painter and others had quit in sympathy. Painter, a former Tory Candidate for Tottenham, promptly joined the NF. By late '75, Carthew was also working for John Tyndall in the NF as he fought and won his bitter legal battle with the Front's populist/Strasserite grouping of which Painter was a leading member. After that, she was for a while closely associated with the London Swinton Circle (LSC), before committing herself to co-running WISE.[13]

Joy Page

In mid-'65 Joy Page was running the London and Home Counties Housing Association. Despite its innocuous name, this was primarily an anti-immigrant organisation. The purchase of housing by non-whites was a major issue at the time. Against a background of all the standard fears and prejudices, many basically racist organisations were set up for 'concerned white residents'. Some chose their names carefully (a) to side-step the new Race Relations Act, (b) to have cross-party appeal, and (c) to enable their spokespersons to voice strong opinions without being easily categorised as extremist by their critics. The following year she teamed up with Mary Howarth of the RPS to set up an anti-immigration umbrella group, the ICA. They were quickly spotted by A.K. Chesterton who had been the propagandist and a key activist in Oswald Mosley's pre-war British Union of Fascists (BUF) and who was the founder (in '53) and chairman of the League of Empire Loyalists (LEL). He invited them to join his new project — a racist umbrella group to be called the National Front (NF, launched in '67 under A.K.'s chairmanship). The RPS was absorbed into the NF, though Page and Howarth elected to remain outside the NF proper, while maintaining a close campaigning relationship with many of its most active members.

Indeed, Joy Page not only marched with the NF during its Summer '72 campaign against the admission of Ugandan Asians, but personally delivered their letter of protest to Uganda House at the end of the 14th August march. Again, on 7th September, she was a key speaker at the pre-march rally (along with Martin Webster, Air Vice-Marshall Don Bennett and others).[14]

In March 1968, the first major trial under the Race Relations Act took place at Lewes Assizes. Five men had been arrested one Sunday afternoon in early '67 while posting copies of issue 5 of *The Southern News*, journal of the RPS, through doors in East Grinstead. A number of residents complained of finding some of the contents racially offensive. The five were charged with publishing and distributing written matter with intent to stir up hatred on ground of colour. All were RPS members. One went into hospital having suffered a coronary, but the other four appeared. Of these, Alan Hancock was a former member of the BUF. He and his family ran the deeply racist and anti-Jewish Historical Review Press. Another, Edward Budden was an active member of the NF. He still is, having his own column in their newspaper, *The Flag*. Joy Page and Professor R. Gayre (founder of the pseudo-scholarly racist journal *Mankind Quarterly*) were witnesses for the defence. Both concealed their racist pedigrees. Page appeared as a housewife and secretary of what was now called the London and Counties Tenants' Federation. She described at some length her past work as a nurse in Africa and listed a few of the good deeds of the 'non-political and non-sectarian Christian' LCTF. She then went on to plead for more sympathy for unfortunate white people driven out of their homes by massive local influxes of coloured immigrants who always live in overcrowded filth and squalor, making entire areas unfit for (white) human habitation. In the end, all five defendants were acquitted.[15]

A.K. Chesterton, the NF chairman, attended and reported on the entire trial. G. K. Young also attended, reporting events in *Freedom First*, journal of the Society for Individual Freedom (SIF). Young was Chairman of the SIF Executive Committee. But his involvement in the trial went further than mere reporting. He saw to it that the SIF provided free advice to the Free Speech Defence Committee, a body

10

set up to fund and run the defence of the five. Young was one of the signatories to the appeal for a fighting fund.

On 18.4.68, the SIF organised a public meeting at Birmingham Town Hall under the title 'Race Laws and Freedom'. Tory right- wing MPs Ronald Bell and Harold Gurden were two of the three key speakers. The third was Joy Page. *Freedom First* No.56 carries a full report of the event. From this we learn that "On the platform too was Mrs Mary Howarth whose hard work for the Free Speech Defence Committee has been crowned by the acquittal of the defendants in the Lewes Assizes...". Funding came in the main from the SIF National Council member Francis Willmott, a Birmingham industrialist. G.K. Young gave the closing speech. Later in the report, we learn of "Colin Jordan having been at the meeting". This is the man who, in '61, had been appointed 'World Führer' of the then newly-formed World Union of National Socialists, by US Nazi leader Lincoln Rockwell. Jordan was the man who'd been seen as too extreme to be allowed into the NF. In Spring '68, having just been released from prison for distributing his pamphlet *The Coloured Invasion,* Jordan was preparing to launch his own new organisation, the British Movement (BM). [16]

The SIF appears to have served two separate and ostensibly unconnected roles. In the late '60s and early '70s, it provided British racism with many of its prime movers. A decade on, it did the same for Thatcherism.

In '26 the populist author and publisher, Ernest Benn, opened The Individualist Bookshop. Out of this arose his Society of Individualists which, by '42, was functioning in tandem with a similar organisation called The National League for Freedom. The merging of these two during '42 resulted in the formation of the SIF. Founder members included Sir Ernest Benn, Lord Lyle of Westbourne, Col. A.V.G. Dower, Alderman Norman Tipstaff (a former Lord Mayor of Birmingham and the enthusiastic organiser of that April '68 gathering which the SIF dubbed 'Our Birmingham Rally') and Frederick Day (who was on the original Executive Committee).

Two notable organisations that have, over the years, developed links with the SIF are the Institute of Economic Affairs (IEA) and Aims of Industry (AOI), the latter founded in the same year as the SIF. Both receive support from a wide range of companies, trusts and individual businessmen. Both are run by committed and campaigning Tory Party supporters.

The IEA was established by Ralph Harris, now Lord Harris of High Cross, in '55 and began publishing in '57. It offers an extensive catalogue of books and pamphlets that present research and new thinking on social, political, educational, economic and moral issues. It's a much more academic body than AOI and, though it is broadly pro-Tory, it's not the propagandist anti-union, anti-Labour far-right soapbox that AOI has become under the unsubtle directorship of Michael Ivens.

In the early '70s, AOI was describing itself as having been "established in '42 by leading industrialists". That these had become "leaders of free enterprise industry" by the late '70s (with AOI undergoing a brief name-change to 'Aims of Freedom and Enterprise') gives an indication of the way in which the political climate was shifting. AOI, like the IEA, offers a wide range of booklets, but almost all are by committed Tories, many of them to the right of the Party, often writing with the prime intention of merely discrediting the Labour left rather than of presenting any fresh ideas.

Here are two curious side-lights. The first is that Ernest Benn was a regular columnist on the anti-Jewish magazine *Truth* during the late '40s and early '50s when A.K. Chesterton was its Deputy Editor and chief leader-writer. Benn and Chesterton were apparently jointly involved between '44 and '46 in an even more right-wing venture, a short-lived political party called the National Front After Victory that brought together a number of British pre-war fascists and former Nazi sympathisers.

The second side-light concerns the truth about *Truth*. Back in '36 this journal was secretly purchased by Joseph Ball, a devious and mysterious intelligence operative who'd been in MI5 since just after the end of WWI. In '36, Ball was personal advisor, closest friend and a ruthless fixer for the Prime Minister, Neville Chamberlain. For the next few years, as Chamberlain himself wrote in a letter to his sister in '39, *Truth* was "secretly controlled by Sir Joseph Ball". Basically, Ball had decided that the popular press was too ready to criticise the Conservative government and Chamberlain in particular. What Chamberlain therefore required was a popular, trusted and influential journal that could be 'persuaded' to serve as a covert propaganda arm of Tory policy. *Truth*, which had been in existence since 1877, fitted the bill perfectly. Following Chamberlain's downfall in May '40, the journal remained devotedly Chamberlainite, became very anti-American, bitterly anti-Soviet, and increasingly anti-Jewish, supporting the cause of those pro- German British citizens who'd been detained in prisons and camps under Defence Regulation 18b. Post-war issues repeatedly asserted that Communist espionage and Communism

12

itself were the result of a covert Jewish plot to take over the world, that WWI and WWII were caused by Jews and that 'World Jewry' was a major problem. Chesterton himself wrote copiously on these issues and the paper carried contributions from, among others, Andrew Fountaine (then a nationalist and anti-Jewish Tory, later a leading figure in the NF), Major J.F.C. Fuller (ex-BUF and NF after Victory) and Sir Charles Petrie (who had edited the *Fascist Review* and was associated with the BUF's 'respectable' front organisation, the January Club). In addition, publications by the pro-fascist British People's Party received very favourable reviews. *Truth* ceased publication in '55. Joseph Ball, long after his death, remains an enigma, not least because he systematically destroyed almost all the records detailing his work under Chamberlain.[17]

By the mid-'60s most of the old SIF leadership had gone. In '67, the ailing President Sir Louis Gluckstein, resigned and was replaced by Lord Lambton. Of the eight members of the Executive Committee, the three ascendant figures were John Paul, G.K. Young and Sir Ian Mactaggart. The SIF National Council included Dr Donald McI Johnson, owner of Johnson Publications, a prolific and influential right-wing political press. Throughout the '60s and '70s, *Freedom First* regularly carried enthusiastic reviews of Johnson books. Those published by the IEA got a similar treatment. And there was good coverage of the activities of AOI.[18]

In early '68, Sir Ian Mactaggart became chairman of the SIF National Council, replacing the aged Colonel Dower, while Michael Ivens (Director of AOI from '70 to date) joined Young and Paul on the SIF Executive. On 26.2.68, MC member Geoffrey Rippon was the speaker at a luncheon in the House of Commons organised by the SIF. The text of his speech appeared as an article in *Freedom First*.

With the Lewes Trial, race immediately becomes a very heated issue within the SIF. The very mixed press coverage given to the SIF following the Birmingham event brought matters to a head. At the year-end AGM, Mactaggart and Young came up with a cosmetic statement that the SIF should not become an anti-immigration society. However, they were not about to let such niceties deter them. Young proposed John Paul as the SIF Secretary, a post that carried with it the editorship of *Freedom First*. Mactaggart seconded and the proposal was passed.

John Paul was an oil company director and one-time chairman of South Kensington Conservative Association. A Tory candidate in two parliamentary elections ('50 and '51), he became a highly influential figure in Tory circles. In September '61 he'd founded the Anti-Common Market League (ACML), and become its first Chairman. The following year, Victor Montagu who for many years had been a Vice-President of the SIF, became the second ACML Chairman. Initially a Tory pressure group led by MPs, industrialists and academics, the ACML quickly became the key body in an amalgam of similar opposition groups, notably the Common Market Safeguards Campaign (CMSC). By '73, the ACML and the CMSC were both operating out of the SIF offices at 55 Park Lane (at a low rent, Mactaggart being the landlord). And it was in '73 that Montagu opened up another strong link between the SIF and the parliamentary Tory party when he took on the Chairmanship of the anti-EEC, anti-immigration and pro-free trade Conservative Trident Group. He still held both chairs in '80.

In '63, John Paul reportedly met with visiting anti-Jewish Australian nationalist, Eric Butler. Butler was opposed to British entry into the Common Market on the grounds that it would destroy the Commonwealth. In '70, shortly after the death of John Paul, the suggestion that a working deal had been struck between the two was given some credence by the arrival in the UK of another Australian, Don Martin. Martin was a Butler protégé who apparently came to the UK with the intention of pulling together some of the far-right and anti-market forces in Britain. Nothing like as influential a figure as John Paul, he still proceeded to set up (or in some cases to simply take over) several small right-wing, racist and anti-Jewish organisations. He also set up Bloomfield Books, a successful distribution company for primarily right-wing literature. Bloomfield's extensive catalogue is notable for its numerous anti-Jewish, anti-Communist and plain racist titles. Mainly through his own efficiency, he quickly became a central figure in far-right British politics.

By '87, the ACML had Bloomfield Books as the main distribution outlet for its publications. Now under the Chairmanship of Derek James, the ACML's leading supporters included obvious figures like Enoch Powell, Teddy Taylor and right-wing Powellite journalist T.E. Utley. From the parliamentary left came less likely figures such as Austin Mitchell and Bryan Gould. While from the far-right came leading conspiracy theorist Gordon Tether, former *Financial Times* columnist now working for American Willis Carto's Liberty Lobby as a contributor to their anti-Jewish journal, *Spotlight*. A second far-right supporter was Charlotte Horsfield, Secretary of the anti-immigration British Housewives League (BHL), another set-up controlled by Don Martin, with its publications in his Bloomfield Books catalogue.[19]

The abrupt death of John Paul a few months into '69 didn't appear to hinder the ascendancy of Young within the SIF. From the Annual Report we find that Gerald Howarth, having just graduated from Southampton University, was simply brought in as a replacement.

In the interim, John Radcliff stepped in to edit a couple of issues of *Freedom First*. Race relations and the views of those opposed to immigration featured heavily. In issue No. 60 for example, Ronald Bell contributed 'Race Laws and Freedom', having used the same title for a speech at a meeting of the SIF a year earlier (18.4.68). There were enthusiastic reviews of Enoch Powell's *Freedom and Reality* and of *Two Worlds — Not One* by Geryke Young (G.K. Young's wife), which purported to prove the impossibility of racial integration. Bell's fellow MC luminaries Teddy Taylor MP and Ian Greig both contributed articles; as did leading member of Powellite, Enoch Powell's publisher and ardent admirer, Andrew George Elliot (of Elliot Right Way Books). A speaker at a forthcoming SIF luncheon, booked by the President Viscount Lambton MP and Executive Committee member Sir John Rogers MP, was the SIF Treasurer, David Myddelton. The title of his speech: 'We're All Nazis Now.'[20]

Reginald Maudling had joined the SIF by '69. That year the MC published *Who Goes Home?* by G.K. Young in which he argued the case for mass repatriation of British non-whites. The UK Anti-Apartheid Movement, led by Peter Hain, was gearing up for their 'Stop The 70 Tour' campaign and the South African Bureau of State Security (BOSS) was preparing to counter them. Former BOSS operative Gordon Winter started a cautious collaboration with Gerald Howarth via the SIF's London office. His caution was prompted by the information, allegedly leaked from Special Branch, that two senior British intelligence operatives worked within the SIF. He was told that these were G.K. Young and Ross McWhirter and that the SIF was almost certainly a British Intelligence front.[21]

Some curious material crept into *Freedom First* around this time. For example, No.62 included contributions from both the Economic League (an anti-left information-gathering agency which has always been closely associated with both AOI and British Intelligence) and L. Ron Hubbard's Church of Scientology (which, as a world-wide force for Americanism, has been strongly linked with the CIA). More predictably, there were contributors like Milton Freidman, Anthony Lejeune, Rhodes Boyson and Maurice Cowling to herald the dawn of the New Right. (The first of five Black Papers on education appeared in '69 and the slow dawn fully broke in '78 with the publication of

Cowling's seminal anthology *Conservative Essays*. This was effectively the authoritarian manifesto of the ultra-Conservative Salisbury Group set up in '76 and centred on Peterhouse College, Cambridge). At the '70 SIF AGM, John Biggs-Davison MP, the man who'd brought G.K. Young into the MC, was voted onto the National Executive.[22]

As late as '66, the SIF had been happy to concern itself with campaigning on local issues and for the rights of particular individuals. Four years on, it was making a serious play for influence in government decision-making on major national issues. In '70, the SIF claimed to have nine members in the new Heath administration. In fact, there were eight: Reginald Maudling, Sir John Eden, Paul Bryan, Paul Dean, Edward Taylor, Nicholas Ridley, Walter Clegg and Jasper More. Of new MPs, Christopher Tugendhat and Peter Rost were both SIF members. That year the SIF set up a Parliamentary Group "with the intention of providing an active lobby in the House of Commons". It consisted of 24 MPs, all SIF members, under the Chairmanship of Sir Frederick Bennett, with Teddy Taylor as its Secretary.

In summer '70 there was one notable departure from among the SIF MPs. Viscount Lambton resigned as President following his appointment as an Under-Secretary at the MOD. Another MP, Sir John Rogers, took his place. Lambton was to make a much more abrupt departure from public life (and from his wife and children) just three years later. *Stern* and *The News of the World* brought down first him and then Lord Jellicoe in a sex-and-drugs scandal involving Lambton's relationship with prostitute Norma Levy.

The books reviewed in *Freedom First* Nos.63-66 included one by Air Vice-Marshall Don Bennett, one by Enoch Powell, an MC pamphlet, Lord Coleraine's *For Conservatives Only*, Rhodes Boyson's *Right Turn*, *Half Marx* by Sir Tufton Beamish MP and *The Soviet Threat to Europe* from Geoffrey Stewart-Smith's intelligence-linked Foreign Affairs Publishing Co., publishing arm of his Foreign Affairs Circle (FAC). (*NB* Stewart-Smith, who in '70 was elected Conservative MP for Belper, was the FAC Director; the FAC President was Lady Jane Birdwood).

Issue 64 carried a photo of a SIF stunt to protest against the success of the anti-apartheid Stop the 70 Tour campaigners. It shows Biggs-Davison, Young, Howarth and Ross McWhirter carrying an urn containing the 'ashes' of English liberty (an incinerated copy of the 1688 Bill of Rights).

Lady Jane Birdwood is the main contributor to issue 65. This edition also carried the news that Nigel Lawson had been elected onto the SIF

Executive Committee, while Kenneth Baker had hosted a SIF luncheon at the House of Commons. On the letters page, G.K. Young contributed a trenchant defence of white nationalists in South Africa and Rhodesia.

Issue 66 contained an attack on British race relations policy, a strongly worded defence of Australia's whites-only immigration policy *and* a four-page article by G.K. Young entitled 'To Be A Citizen...' in which he outlined his refusal to contemplate a multi-racial Britain and detailed his proposal for a "full repatriation programme". There was also a report on the '70 SIF AGM in which the adoption of the Society's Annual Accounts was seconded by none other than Roy Bramwell.[23]

Lady Jane Birdwood

In '55, Lord Birdwood made an unsuccessful application to the Foreign Office for funding to undertake (non-military) political warfare against Communism in Britain.[24]

About the same time, Lady Jane Birdwood was involved with the anti-Communist information-gathering organisation, Common Cause. Around '56, an acrimonious split resulted in the creation of two bodies called Common Cause. She was on the National Executive Committee of the faction led by one C.A. Smith. As the nineteen branches dwindled to six, she was appointed co-ordinator. This failed faction finally fell apart in '59.[25]

In '62, Geoffrey Stewart-Smith founded the Foreign Affairs Circle with The Dowager Lady Jane Birdwood listed as its President, a post she held until '71.[26]

Despite her extremist commitments, Jane Birdwood has long been (and remains) a member of the Conservative Party. She's also been a member of the MC. During the '60s, she became involved with the Festival of Light and campaigned fiercely against the mounting in the West End of the musical *Oh! Calcutta* (summer '70) and, a year later, against the staging of Oscar Panizza's play *Council of Love*. She later founded the London branch of Mary Whitehouse's Viewers and Listeners Association.[27]

In '71, Don Martin established the British League of Rights (BLR), with himself as National Director, Jane Birdwood as General Secretary and Air Vice-Marshall Bennett as Patron. Bennett, a committed right-winger, was also a fervent anti-marketeer in the Don Martin-Eric

Butler-John Paul mould, even standing as a parliamentary candidate on that particular ticket in '73.

BLR, as outlined in its own publicity material, opposed large-scale alien immigration, totalitarianism and Common Market membership, favoured 'the heritage and traditions of British peoples', supported law and order, advocated decentralised government, and was patriotic, nationalistic, Christian and individualistic. An indication of its undeclared but decidedly more extreme views was given in '80 by BLR membership secretary, Mary Downton. She was attending the annual international fascist rally at Diksmuide in Belgium as part of a British contingent that included members of the BM, Viking Youth, the League of Saint George, Column 88 and the NF. Interviewed by a reporter from *The News of the World*, she said: "I want to see a Fourth Reich and we all want the blacks and Jews out of this country". [28]

In '71, Martin made Birdwood a member of the National Executive of BLR offshoot, the British League for European Freedom (BLEF). When, in '74, Geoffrey Stewart-Smith withdrew his FAC from the World Anti-Communist League (WACL) because he took exception to its growing anti-Jewish and fascist links, Martin stepped into the breach by offering the BLEF as the WACL's British affiliate with Birdwood as the BLEF General Secretary. The two of them thus became the British WACL representatives. However, during the early '80s the WACL came under new leadership, headed by U.S. General John Singlaub (a patron of the London-based far-right Conservative group Western Goals UK and a central figure in the Iran-Contra scandal). He expelled many of the anti-Jewish affiliates, including the BLR.

During the '70s, Birdwood also became involved in the Law and Order Society, a Conservative group campaigning for the restoration of the death penalty.[29]

In '70, Lady Birdwood founded the anti-union Self Help Organisation (SHO), apparently with the assistance of Ross McWhirter. It seems it was his brainchild. Right-wing but not overtly extremist at the outset, it advertised widely in the press for volunteers. After the death of Ross in '75, the SHO moved steadily further to the far right. Others involved with the SHO included Edward Martell (whose previous ventures had included the Freedom Group, the *New Daily* and the National Party) and Air Vice-Marshall Don Bennett. It published the *British Gazette*, an occasional news sheet. Like the National Association for Freedom (NAFF), the SHO got involved in trying to break both the '77 Grunwick strike and the Randolph Hotel dispute in Oxford. It ran Operation Roadlift during the '81 rail strike. During the '84 Miners' Strike it tried to raise the funds to buy a small working mine in Wales, the plan being to incite the NUM to picket it so that the SHO could take the union to court and have its funds seized.[30]

In the mid-70s she was running the Inter City Research Centre (ICRC) and the Anti-Immigration Standing (or sometimes, Co-ordinating) Committee (AISC or AICC), in which Joy Page was also involved. It was as the AICC organiser that, on 30.9.72, Lady Birdwood was a speaker at a NF rally in Blackburn. Other speakers that day included the NF leaders John Tyndall and Martin Webster together with a leading local Conservative, John Kingsley Read, who was destined to join the NF before the year-end and would lead the Populist splinter group that broke ranks with the NF in Dec '75 to form the short-lived National Party.

> "One down, a million to go".
> — *John Kingsley Read on the death of a young Asian in Southhall.*

Soon after this, Birdwood became closely associated with Mary Stanton's pro-repatriation and anti-EEC National Assembly (NA) which campaigned for a parliament of hand-picked nationalists instead of elected MPs. Joy Page and Ronald Bell were also NA supporters, as was Geoffrey Hunt, a leading member of Young's faction in the '73 Young-versus-Guinness MC leadership battle.

At the end of the '70s, Birdwood was reported to have been involved in the British Military Volunteer Force, a British group working on sending mercenary forces variously to help the USA in Vietnam and to fight in Zaire, Biafra, the Yemen and Rhodesia.[31]

> "A woman wholly obsessed with 'the race question'"
> —*Ray Hill (former NF activist) talking about Lady Birdwood.*[32]

Since the '70s, she's been running an organisation called Choice, with local branches around the country and its own newspaper, called simply *Choice*. Unremittingly and proudly racist, it's written, edited, printed and published by her under the slogan 'Racialism is Patriotism'.[33]

In '82, she took part in the inaugural march of John Tyndall's new British National Party (BNP) and addressed a BNP rally in London in '88.[34]

In '85, Lady Birdwood attended the European launch of *Executive Intelligence Review*, house journal of the extensive publishing organisation run by controversial right-wing U.S. conspiracy theorist and intelligence disseminator Lyndon LaRouche.[35]

On St George's Day (23 Apr.) '89, she officially launched her latest venture, English Solidarity (Against Multiculturalism). This rivals Choice in the vehemence of its opposition to every form of racial mixing, but is even more narrow in that it's pro-English, not pro-British.

In June '89, Lady Jane Birdwood was one of the first to protest against the admission of non-whites from Hong Kong. She went to the Foreign Office with R.M. Harrison of the MC Race Relations Committee and Alan Plane, former chairman and patron of the LSC. There they had a meeting with John Hague, principal at the Hong Kong Department, in the course of which they detailed their objections to the admission of even one non-white or non-Christian person from Hong Kong.[36]

There were bitter complaints about "the current influx of new immigrants and 'refugees' in the United Kingdom" in a letter to the Home Office dated 12.10.90. Four days earlier, the authors of the letter had visited the Home Office in person to make the same complaint. The letter singled out "Iraqi Kurds and their Turkish brethren... 7,000 Somalis, huge numbers of Chinese and unknown numbers of Eritreans, Ugandans, Roumanians and Albanians, coupled with the threat of 40,000-50,000 East European and Russian Jews" and went on to express "very genuine fears about the continuing invasion of our country". The letter was signed by Alan Plane, Shirley Attree, Jane Birdwood and... Joy Page.[37]

Ronald Bell

The admitting of Kenyan Asians into Britain in '68 moved the simmering issues of race relations and immigration to the top of the British political agenda. It was the year in which Enoch Powell grabbed the headlines with his three immigration speeches in Walsall (9 Feb.), Birmingham (20 Apr.) and Eastbourne (16 Nov.). He then (3.1.69) went nation-wide with his views in an interview by David Frost on the ITV programme 'Frost on Friday'. Of these four public appearances, the key one was in Birmingham when he gave what became known as his 'Rivers of Blood Speech'. Perhaps co-incidentally, it was delivered on Hitler's birthday, a date that's much celebrated by neo-Nazis, most of whom were among Powell's more extreme fellow anti-immigrationists.[38]

Apart from a couple of very brief breaks, Ronald Bell was a Conservative MP from '45 until his death in '82. A leading right- winger, he rose to parliamentary prominence in the early '60s as a spokesman for the MC, as founder of the anti-Communist group Conservatives Against the Common Market and as leader of the parliamentary opposition to the Race Relations Act. His SIF speech, delivered just two days before Powell addressed the Birmingham gathering, placed Bell squarely on the Powellite bandwagon. As a founder-member of G.K. Young's MC immigration committee (out of which came the Halt Immigration Now Campaign), Bell continued his personal crusade for a white Britain. Through the seventies he was an active supporter of a number of other right-wing pressure

> "The House has lost one of its most distinguished members."
> — *Margaret Thatcher talking about the death of Ronald Bell (House of Commons '82).*

groups, notably the Selsdon Group and two organisations which were far more radical and reactionary, WISE and Tory Action. The latter, as we'll see, was another G.K. Young venture.

During '74, Enoch Powell, the faded hope of the far-right who'd at one time been so strongly tipped for the premiership, quit both the Tory Party and the Wolverhampton South West seat which he'd held for quarter of a century. He crossed the water and was narrowly elected Ulster Unionist MP for South Down. Following Powell's fall from grace, Bell came to be regarded in his final years as the leader of the old guard of right-wing Toryism.[39]

In '80, on the recommendation of Margaret Thatcher, Bell received a knighthood. At that time, he was leading the handful of MPs who backed Lady Jane Birdwood's Choice mass repatriation scheme, Homeward Bound. In fact, at the time of his death, he was due to take over the running of the project which involved the arranging of cheap one-way flights to the Caribbean. His death brought an abrupt end to the project which Lady Jane Birdwood has recently been trying to revive through English Solidarity (ES).

In '81, shortly after Harvey Proctor addressed a meeting of WISE, Bell announced that he was setting up a back-bench Conservative immigration group which would meet fortnightly.[40]

Harvey Proctor

In the Oct '74 General Election, the NF candidate for Hackney and Shoreditch won 9.4% of the vote, the highest percentage ever polled by the NF in any General Election. It's curious therefore to note that, in previous elections, the NF had not fielded a candidate in this highly fertile constituency. Had they done so, their candidate would have stood against a Conservative who fiercely promoted many of the policies embraced by the NF, particularly those on race and immigration. Harvey Proctor, who was not only a member of Roy Bramwell's branch of the MC but also an enthusiastic member of the SIF, had been Conservative candidate for this constituency. He worked at the offices of the MC, of which he'd been Assistant Director ('69-71), and was involved with G.K. Young's HINC. He became a Conservative MP in '79, serving first for Basildon and then, in the mid-'80s, for Billericay.[41]

Proctor, who's acted as Parliamentary spokesman for the Freedom Association, was frequently named in the Young Conservatives' controversial report on right-wing infiltration of the Conservative Party.[42]

An active and popular member of WISE, Proctor addressed a well-publicised and well-attended meeting of the group on 18.7.81. Joan Mason, Joy Page, Bee Carthew and Lady Jane Birdwood were all present. The vote of thanks at the end of the evening was given by Andrew Fountaine, himself a one-time Tory Candidate who'd been dropped on account of his overtly anti-Jewish stance. Fountaine had left the Conservative Party in the late '50s to, briefly, form his own National Front Movement. In early '60, he'd joined the original BNP (as opposed to Tyndall's '80s reincarnation) becoming its President and, in '67, had led the BNP contingent that became part of Chesterton's newly-formed NF. At the time of the Proctor speech, he'd quit the NF a year earlier and had set up his own splinter group, The NF Constitutional Movement (NFCM).

> "They don't know what lavatories are — they think they are something to swing from. Their very minds are different from ours. Close to the surface of a Negro's brain lie murder, witchcraft, hate, love, all mixed together — things that have almost ceased to exist in the white man's brain... We are not a fascist organisation. We expelled Colin Jordan from the party because of this."
> — *Andrew Fountaine, speaking as President of the BNP, 20th Century (No.1017, Spring '63).*

There were others, more sinister with strong neo-fascist and paramilitary connections, who also turned up to hear Proctor speak at this WISE meeting. Among these were Steve Brady (ex-NF, ex-NP, and from '78, International Affairs Officer of the League of St George), terrorist Tony Malski (BM, founder in mid-'82 of National Socialist Action Party) and Jimmy Styles (NF, NFCM). In a '81 MC pamphlet, *Immigration, Repatriation and the Commission for Racial Equality*, Proctor called for "a vigorous programme of repatriation for all of those who wish to take advantage of it, well financed, well publicised and well organised".[43]

At the 24.5.82 AGM of the MC, Proctor stood for the Chairmanship (rendered vacant by the retirement of Sam Swerling) but he was very easily defeated by his rival candidate for the post, David Storey.[44]

In the mid-'80s, K. Harvey Proctor MP was Chairman of the MC's Immigration and Race Relations Policy Committee, Vice-Chairman of its Northern Ireland Policy Committee, and a member of its Executive Council.[45]

A long-running controversy surrounding infiltration of the Tory Party by the far-right was sparked in Autumn '83 by a damaging report on the whole issue which was produced by the Young Conservatives. From the outset, Proctor featured strongly as a leading spokesman for the defence, despite being heavily implicated himself. The issue was still smouldering in '86 when the story that was to end his political career made gutter press headlines. In October of that year, he was named as the central public figure in a news story about gay sado-masochistic activities. There was the suggestion that children were involved. A raid on his flat in March '87 led to his arrest. Meanwhile, his constituency party had met to discuss his possible deselection. They passed a vote of confidence at their March AGM, but it made no difference. In April he was charged with gross indecency. He was tried in May and was fined after pleading guilty to four charges of gross indecency. He subsequently announced that he would be resigning as MP for Billericay and would not be seeking re-election. He then disappeared from public life.[46]

Tony Vander Elst

Tony Vander Elst was a young unemployed actor when G.K. Young brought him into the MC offices to work on repatriation proposals for the HINC. Adopted by the Conservatives as a candidate for Hampstead Council, Vander Elst attended the '72 conference of Movimiento Sociale Italiano (MSI), the Italian neo-fascist party. MSI paid the air fares and expenses for both him and Neil Hamilton (then involved with Bee Carthew's Powellight, later a Tory MP) to attend. Hamilton was at one time vice-president of the Federation of Conservative Students (FCS). The far-right of this body became such an embarrassment to the Tory Party that John Selwyn Gummer withdrew its Central Office funding for three months in '85. Following this action, it was Hamilton who, along with John Carlisle, Sir Alfred Sherman and others, ran a press conference at the Waldorf Hotel to defend the FCS. Controversy continued throughout '86. Harry Phibbs was forced to resign as editor of the FCS journal, *New Agenda*, after publishing an interview with Nicolai Tolstoy that included allegations that Harold MacMillan was a war criminal. Stuart Millson and James Coakley-Boyce caused a stir when they left the FCS to join John Tyndall's overtly pro-Nazi BNP. Two FCS members at Nottingham University, Neil Mason (vice-chairman of the University Conservative Association) and Miles Hempsall, were barred from the campus (and Mason forced to resign his vice-presidency) for painting Nazi slogans including 'Death to Jews'. In November '86, the Tory Party announced that the FCS was to be replaced by the Conservative Collegiate Forum. The FCS was duly closed down by Norman Tebbit in Spring '87 and formally disbanded that Summer. A number of its more controversial figures have since resurfaced in other far-right organisations like the International Freedom Foundation, Western Goals UK, the Salisbury Group and the Libertarian Alliance (which began as the Young Libertarians, the youth wing of the SIF).[47]

The right-wing and predominantly middle class pressure group, the Freedom Association (FA), currently produces a quarterly journal called *Freedom Today*. Its editor is Philip Vander Elst, Tony's brother. The FA began life as The National Association for Freedom (NAFF). The NAFF was officially launched on 2.12.75 at a news conference chaired by Lord De L'Isle, former Governor-General of Australia. It was apparently thought up by Ross McWhirter, one-time Conservative parliamentary candidate and a member of the Executive Committee of the SIF. G.K. Young is believed to have assisted and encouraged Ross McWhirter in planning the NAFF, though the extent of this involvement is not easy to gauge. Certainly, they'd worked closely during the early '70s (e.g. in the SIF, in opposing the Stop The 70 Tour campaign, in Walter Walker's Unison/Civil Assistance and in Lady Birdwood's Self-Help). Ross and his twin brother Norris jointly drew up the first NAFF charter. However, just a few days prior to the official launch of the NAFF, Ross was murdered outside his home, allegedly by the IRA. Norris was determined that the launch should go ahead. Other figures instrumental in the founding of the NAFF included Michael Ivens (Director of AOI and a SIF Executive Committee member) who apparently played the key role in realising the whole venture, Robert Moss (Australian author and journalist who'd succeeded Brian Crozier as editor of *The Economist*'s subscription-only *Foreign*

Report) and John Gouriet (who addressed a meeting of WISE in the early '80s). Moss became the NAFF's first Director (a post he held jointly with Gouriet) and, in March '76, was founding editor of the NAFF journal, *The Free Nation*.

The claim that the NAFF was a 'non-party political body' was simply not born out either by its activities or by the obvious affiliations of its active members.

When Moss moved on, the editorship of *The Free Nation* remained in committed Tory hands. Stephen Eyres held the post until '81, when it passed to Philip Vander Elst.

> " We have got to see that the Conservative Party, which we hope will be elected, does stand up for Conservative principles."
> — *John Gouriet at a NAFF meeting (Apr. '78)*

Eyres, who died in early '90 aged only 42, is an interesting figure. Back in the late '60s, still in his teens, he was already a keen Tory and early advocate of the policies which came to be labelled 'Thatcherite'. With others, notably Philip and Tony Vander Elst, he was a founder member in '73 of the influential Selsdon Group, a monetarist and free market think tank. The following year he became political secretary to Enoch Powell and ran the October '74 campaign which saw Powell elected Ulster Unionist MP for South Down.

In late '77, when he replaced Moss as editor of *Free Nation*, Eyres had just (Sept. '77) had a booklet published by AOI. *The National Front is a Socialist Front* was the first in a series entitled 'Studies of the Left'. The coincidental publishing of a letter (from 'C.A. Seymour-Burt') in the 2.9.77 issue of *The Free Nation* under the heading 'National Front left-wing' illustrates the way in which the NAFF and AOI co-operated. Both the letter and the booklet where crude attempts to smear the Labour Party by arguing that fascists were extreme left-wing socialists. Just four months later, the 6-19.1.78 issue of *The Free Nation* carried an advertisement for Don Martin's Bloomfield Books.

Moss and Crozier (who also joined the NAFF) had worked together on a number of projects and were both strongly associated with joint British and American intelligence agency covert operations. Notably, Moss wrote an anti-Communist book called 'Chile's Marxist Experiment' which, by arrangement with Crozier's covertly CIA-funded, London-based company Forum World Features (FWF), was published by David and Charles in late '73. A large number of copies of this propagandist book were bought up by the post-Allende Chilean junta who then distributed copies free of charge.

Six MPs were early members of the NAFF National Council. They were Nicholas Ridley, Rhodes Boyson, Sir Frederic Bennett, Winston Churchill, Stephen Hastings and Jill Knight, all Conservatives.

In '77, Margaret Thatcher attended a NAFF subscription dinner and was reported to have been much impressed with Robert Moss. It's also said that she read and enjoyed his sub-Orwellian anti-Communist political fantasy *The Collapse of Democracy*. Either way, the upshot was that he became one of her speech-writers. The NAFF changed its name to the Freedom Association (FA) in January '79.

Crozier, Moss, Michael Ivens and other leading members of the NAFF, were also on the Governing Council of Geoffrey Stewart-Smith's Foreign Affairs Research Institute (FARI, the successor to his previously-mentioned FAC). This, like FWF was a political publishing venture which proved to be an intelligence front when it was shown by *The Guardian* in '83 to have been funded for several years by the South African government.

In '82, Foreign Affairs Publishing Co. brought out the English language version of French author Suzanne Labin's whitewash job on the regime of fascist dictator General Pinochet and on its appalling human rights record. Once again, the Chilean government bought up a large number of copies for free distribution. The book (*Chile: the Crime of Resistance*), which carried an introduction by Brian Crozier, was extensively promoted and very highly recommended in several issues of the FA journal, *The Free Nation*. The editor of the journal first praised the book in '83, alongside an article on Chile by Crozier. In December '83, it topped the journal's list of recommended reading. In the January '84 edition, the same editor wrote a long and laudatory review of the book. That editor was Philip Vander Elst.

Crozier himself was a member of the editorial board of *The Free Nation*. In fact, until April '89, he was on the editorial board of *Freedom Today* and he continues to be a prolific and fervently anti-Communist contributor. Norris McWhirter remains Chairman of the FA. Michael Ivens is one of three Vice-Presidents of the FA. Ivens, McWhirter and Vander Elst are all on the five-man editorial board of *Freedom Today*. There are also several key figures from the SIF who crop up among the council members of the FA, notably Gerald Howarth and Rhodes Boyson. Philip Vander Elst has had an anti-Soviet book published by the IEA. He is married to Rachel Tingle. She writes 'Pulpit Watch', the religious page of *Freedom Today*. She has had a book published by AOI. More recently she's been the author of two books that have been widely vilified in the liberal and left-wing press. *Another Gospel* sets out to prove that the Anglican Church is a hotbed of far-left activists, while *Gay Lessons* is subtitled 'How Public Funds are used to promote Homosexuality among Children and Young People'.[48]

Some details now about Crozier's London-based research and publishing ventures. In '75 *Time Out* magazine presented evidence showing FWF to have been covertly CIA-funded. By then though, Crozier was trying hard to cover his tracks. What appears to have in fact been a joint UK-USA intelligence front had already been closed down by Crozier. He'd had plenty of time. Suspicions about FWF being an intelligence front had first become public back in '67. That year a detailed and damaging exposé by the U.S. magazine *Ramparts* of widespread covert CIA operations in the USA and Europe had strongly implicated Crozier's operation. The following year Crozier had launched his Current Affairs Research Services Centre. In '70, again with covert funding, this became the Institute for the Study of Conflict (ISC), allowing FWF to gradually fade from the scene. The *Time Out* revelations clearly showed the ISC to be simply an extension of the FWF operation. It wasn't hard to spot. Some of the staff and most of the files had simply switched offices. In addition, many of those involved in the ISC had worked in previous British or American intelligence operations. These included Michael Goodwin (who became the ISC Director after Crozier bowed out in '79), Peter Janke, David Lynne Price, Kenneth Benton, Leonard Schapiro, Fergus Ling and most of the members of the ISC's Council of Management, including Vice-Admiral Sir Louis Le Bailly who is currently a long-standing FA Council member. According to former BOSS agent, Gordon Winter, Crozier also carried out work for South African Military Intelligence in the early '70s. The ISC itself was finally closed down in 1990. In fact (surprise, surprise) its files and its entire back catalogue are still available and its extensive programme of publishing continues from new offices and under a new name. The whole operation of gathering a vast amount of information about conflict around the world and packaging it with an anti-Communist and pro-Western slant seems as healthy as ever. Even the house publishing style is virtually unaltered. The only difference is that it's now the Research Institute for the Study of Conflict and Terrorism (RISCT) which operates from 136 Baker Street, London, W1M 1FH. The RISCT Director is Paul Wilkinson, a leading authority on terrorism and a leading government advisor on the subject. He was very nearly killed at the first RISCT Annual One-Day Conference on Terrorism and Democracy held on 27.9.90 at the Royal Over-Seas League in London. The event grabbed all the headlines when a bomb, attributed to the IRA, was found and defused minutes before the conference was due to begin. It had apparently been timed to go off while Wilkinson was speaking.

The name RISCT arises from the merging of the ISC and The Research Foundation for the Study of Terrorism (RFST). Now watch the world shrink... The RFST was founded in the early '70s by Wilkinson in conjunction with Michael Ivens and Norris McWhirter. All three were trustees. It operated from 40 Doughty Street, the address of AOI. Ian Greig, an active member of the SIF and a co-founder of the MC, was a Council member of the RFST. The RFST publicity described him as a former senior executive of the ISC. Greig, who was an authority on Communist subversion, had worked as Geoffrey Stewart-Smith's deputy while the FARI was functioning as the British chapter of the WACL. A second MC and SIF luminary, G.K. Young's old friend John Biggs-Davison, was also on the RFST Council.[49]

G.K. Young

George Kennedy Young was born in Moffat, Dumfriesshire, Scotland on 8.4.11. He went to the University of St. Andrews and studied in Europe, gaining a first class honours degree in Modern Languages, then took his MA in Political Science at Yale. He joined the Labour Party and worked as a journalist with the *Glasgow Herald* ('36) and then with British United Press ('38). He married Geryke Harthoorn in '39 and joined the King's Own Scottish Borderers the following year. By '43 he was on the specially employed list (i.e. was working for British military intelligence), doing work against the Italians with General Staff Intelligence. Later he became chief instructor at the Command Intelligence School in Nairobi. Towards the end of the war, he joined a special counterintelligence unit in Italy and was responsible for rounding up what was left of the German intelligence service in Rome. Post-war, he returned briefly to his former job of journalism before accepting another intelligence posting, this time as head of Vienna station. He left there in '49 to become head of the economic requirements section in London. In '51, when Mohammed Mossadeq was elected Prime Minister of Iran, he was suddenly posted to take charge of the Middle East area. In this capacity, he was the Secret Intelligence Service (SIS) officer in charge of the British role in the Anglo-American intelligence operation which ousted the pro-Soviet Mossadeq and restored the exiled Shah. The Shah promptly executed thousands of Iranians suspected of having supported Mossadeq. Because the whole operation had never been authorised, Young resigned, but returned after all the Philby resignations to take the post of director of requirements. His job was to make SIS more efficient, with its efforts focused more effectively on priority targets. Rightly, as it later turned out, he suspected Soviet manipulation of a large-scale operation in which Baltic and Polish exiles were trained and then returned to the Eastern Bloc to gather intelligence. He stopped it (though it was later restarted), and concentrated instead on developing much better methods of analysing the vast amount of poorly assessed and badly collated information already in SIS archives. To help him in this work, he brought in Professor Leonard Shapiro (who would later be a key figure in Brian Crozier's ISC operations) and Professor R.V. Jones (currently a long-standing member of the FA's Council). In '56, when the Suez Crisis broke, Young was put back in charge of Middle East operations. He worked closely with Israeli intelligence, opposed Nasser as being pro-Soviet, and helped the Shah to build up his much-feared Savak intelligence service. At the end of '58 Young was appointed vice-chief of MI6. The information he gathered in a ten-week tour of

> "The NF could have had a very different future if it had not been so badly led."
> — *G.K. Young on 'Lunchtime Report',*
> *BBC Radio Scotland (Nov '80).*

MI6 stations in the Far East during early '59 helped to keep Britain from becoming involved in the Vietnam War. In '61, after 20 years in intelligence, Young resigned. He'd always been a cowboy figure in SIS/MI6, and accounts vary as to who did or did not approve of his methods and the results of his work. Did he choose to leave or did the then-head of MI6, Sir Richard White, actually ask for his resignation? Either is possible. The more important and unanswered question is whether he really severed all ties with the intelligence services in '61 and, if not, the extent to which his subsequent political activities were intelligence-related.

In '61, he became a merchant banker with Kleinwort Benson and was appointed President of Nuclear Fuel Finance SA in '69. He also worked as a professional writer, publishing six books between '62 and '84.[50] During the late '60s and early '70s, as we've already seen, G.K. Young and his associates gained control over the SIF. Much more remains to be said about the role of this organisation, its full history, and its links both with the intelligence services and with the far right of the Conservative Party. The organisation is still in operation. Professor David Marsland addressed a meeting at The Feathers, 20 Broadway, London SW1 on 26.9.90.[51]

In '28, Diana Mitford married Bryan Guinness. They had two sons, Desmond and Jonathan, and were subsequently divorced. In '36, Diana married again to become Lady Diana Mosley. Her new husband was Sir Oswald Mosley, leader of the BUF. During much of WWII, Sir Oswald was interned under Defence Regulation 18b. After the war, he launched his pro-European Union Movement which later became the Action Party. He died in '80. In Sept '89, Lady Mosley was the guest celebrity on an edition of BBC Radio 4's Desert Island Discs. In '90, the Friends of Sir Oswald Mosley organised Lady Diana's 80th Birthday celebration in London. This gathering of young and old fascists (including former BUF members and current members of extreme fascist organisations like the League of St George) heard the unrepentant octogenarian talk of their British and European future.

In June '72, when MC membership was at its highest level (then or since), one of Lady Diana's sons, Jonathan Guinness was elected chairman. He was immediately faced with the problem of what the media was beginning to describe as ultra-right-wing or fascist infiltration, namely the growing presence of a large NF contingent at public events organised by the MC and the fact that a number of activists were apparently members of both the MC and the NF. Because the MC was a Tory organisation with about three dozen MP among its members, this ultra-right faction was becoming an embarrassment not only to the MC, but to the Conservative Party as a whole. However, when Guinness made moves to clean up the MC image and oust some of its more obvious NF sympathisers, he clashed with G.K. Young, who chaired the MC's vital fund-raising body, the Action Fund, as well as being its HINC organiser. The result was a bitter and dirty '73 leadership battle between the two of them. Young's views on race and his commitment to repatriation were well-known through his '69 MC pamphlet, *Who goes home?* It emerged that he'd also helped to produce a racist anti-immigration film called *England, whose England?* (It was written and directed by Tony Bastable of Thames TV and made by Counterblast Films, an organisation apparently set up by Young and funded through him. The film was made for the British Campaign to Stop Immigration, an organisation which was manned and supported in part by the NF. Part of the film was shown on BBC TV's Open Door in '76, though plans to turn Counterblast into a wider-ranging communications group never materialised).

Young was by now felt to be too extreme even for the MC and Guinness retained the chairmanship by a comfortable 625 votes to 455. Following his defeat, G.K. Young and some of his supporters quit.

Others were expelled by Guinness in an attempt to restore the reputation of the MC by being seen to purge it of 'undesirables'. However the public damage had been done and MC membership plummeted. The following year, '74, G.K. Young set up Tory Action (TA), a covert far-right body that functioned for five years before its existence was made public by *Searchlight*.

There were several other organisations in which Young is believed to have had a hand.

It was during '73 that General Sir Walter Walker, who'd just retired after having been Commander-in-Chief of Allied Forces in Northern Europe ('69-72), began to set up his Unison Movement (later also known as Civil Assistance). This was a private and covert paramilitary organisation intended to take over essential services in the event of massive civil unrest in Britain. It was one of several such groups set up around the time that the unions brought down the Heath government and Wilson led the Labour Party back into power for his second term. The blimpish Walker saw the changes in Britain as symptomatic of a Communist plot for world power. An ardent anti-Communist and anti-Marketeer, Walker was also active during the mid-70s (with Air Vice-Marshall Don Bennett and others) in the New Britain Party (NBP). However, it was '73 (before he'd joined the NBP and while Unison was still being planned) that he addressed Brent East Conservative Association. The constituency's election candidate was G.K. Young. Their association at this time adds some weight to the suggestion that Young actively participated in the creation of Unison. Anthony Cavendish, the former MI6 officer and a great admirer of Young, is understood to have been a strong supporter of Unison. Ross McWhirter is also believed to have been involved in the founding of this secretive body. Indeed, according to Walker himself, he and McWhirter jointly set up Unison at the invitation of Young. Walker also claims that Civil Assistance was his own (completely separate) venture which came about in '74 following some kind of difference between himself and Young. Apparently Walker had begun to question Young's objectives with regard to Unison and had found that this only made Young more secretive than ever. Thus Civil Assistance appears to have been Walker's attempt to continue his own efforts while distancing himself from Young.

Ross McWhirter, incidentally, is also said to have been involved around this time in 'secret negotiations' with John Tyndall, then Director of the NF (and currently leader of the BNP). To see how such a liaison might fit into the scheme of things is far from easy. We do, however, have a couple of intriguing threads. There's Young, the Tory candidate, making a racist film for a group that's apparently strongly NF-linked. We also know that Young was simultaneously trying to form some kind of umbrella group linking members of the MC, the NF and the HINC. Could McWhirter have been acting as Young's delegate? It wouldn't be the first time that the McWhirter name has been linked with the far right.

By August '74, Walker was claiming a nationwide volunteer membership for Civil Assistance of 100,000 and predicting three million by October. It never happened and Walker's set-up soon fizzled out amid a welter of ludicrous press stories about it campaigning for legalised brothels and the banning of pornography. In October '76, following the collapse of protracted linkage negotiations between Civil Assistance and the newly-formed NAFF, Walker sent a final note to Civil Assistance members announcing the demise of the body. Walker later resurfaced as a patron of Western Goals UK and attended the '83 WACL confererence.

> "We all have a high regard for Walter Walker. Unfortunately, the public impression of Civil Assistance is that it is a 'private army'... the left did a good smear job on it when it started, and we do not want to attract similar adverse publicity. Therefore, while we welcome individual members to join us and encourage local co-operation, we are not in a position to announce a merger."
> — *John Gouriet, on behalf of the NAFF ('76).*

In '75 the HINC, reduced to operating without its former MC resources, merged with parts of other shrinking groups such as the ICA and the Powellite Association to form the Nationalist Alliance.

In April '81, Young was a founding member of Joan Mason's relaunched white separatist and pro-repatriation umbrella group, WISE. (Mason had been trying to get WISE going since '74 when she'd taken out an advertisement in the *Daily Telegraph*. However it only really took off in July '81 when activists from a variety of fascist and neo-Nazi groups were among those who attended the meeting addressed by Harvey Proctor). WISE went into eclipse following the exposure of its sympathies and connections on national TV in a Panorama programme in Jan '84.

> "It's a marvellous organisation."
> — *Joan Mason referring to the NF (Oct '81).*

In November '80, Young had received extensive media coverage when he publicly defended Andrew Moffat, the 21-year-old who'd been expelled from the Coldstream Guards for his membership of the NF.[52]

TA is not an independent body. It's an active part of the parliamentary Conservative Party, describing itself in a recent issue of its members-only newsletter, *Round Robin*, as a "pressure group within the Party". According to Edward Frostick, TA's current National Organiser, anyone wishing to be considered for membership must have been "an active member of the Conservative Party for more than two years" and must obtain a reference from someone known to TA.

Much of its membership was and probably still is drawn from MC ranks. In the *Daily Telegraph* (10.4.81) G.K. Young claimed that TA had the backing of at least 25 Tory MPs. How many of these were actual members was unclear. Elsewhere it's been claimed that over two dozen MPs are members of TA and that it has representation in over a hundred Conservative Associations around the country. Given the ultra-right racism so often vented in the pages of *Round Robin*, the apparent reluctance of any MPs to admit having links with TA is understandable.

According to 'Maggie's Militant Tendency', a January '84 Panorama documentary on BBC TV, MPs involved in TA included Gerald Howarth (denied) and Harvey Proctor (denied). The programme linked several other Tory MPs with TA, among these were Roger Moate, Nicholas Winterton and Neil Hamilton (denied). Howarth and Hamilton took the BBC to court and, on 23.10.86, won an out of court settlement. The following day, the BBC's defence lawyers got a list of TA 'correspondents' (TA's name for its members). Both men were on it. They also got documents suggesting that the two MPs had backed G.K. Young's '73 candidacy for the chairmanship of the MC, that they supported his stand on an end to coloured immigration and on the introduction of a programme of repatriation, and that they were among those expelled from the MC following the Guinness victory. Hamilton's response to his expulsion from the MC was a letter notifying them that he would appeal against it. He wrote on Eldon League notepaper, signing himself Grand Prior of the group. Both men were later reinstated. Also in the possession of the BBC's lawyers were photos of Hamilton and Young together at functions of the Eldon League during the mid-70s. Howarth, of course, had worked closely with Young (in the SIF, the HINC, etc.) since the late '60s.

TA claimed that it was launched with the support of Edward Du Cann (denied) and of Airey Neave, the man said to have engineered the rise of Thatcher. Neave was to die in March '79, allegedly at the hands of the INLA, in a car-bomb blast outside the House of Commons. Another MP predictably associated with TA from its inception was Ronald Bell.

We can be more certain of the identities of some members of this secretive organisation. In the earlier issues of *Round Robin* and later in letters to TA members, the names were given of all those serving on the management committee of TA. The committee in early '79 was listed as being Simon Bird, Robin Davies, P. Warren Hawksley, Eric Langcaster, Dr C. Michael-Titus, Steve Patriarca, Lt. Cmdr. Noel Paulley, Philip Rankin, Ken Wooton and G.K. Young. Of these, we already know about Young who was TA's founder and Director. Robin Davies was working in '83 as secretary to the historian David Irving, helping him to run his far-right Focus Policy Group and to produce the racist, pro-fascist and pro-nationalist journal *Focal Point*. He was also the editorial secretary of *The Anglican Catholic*, the journal of the Anglican Society. In the Autumn of that year, he was flat-sharing with *Scorpion* editor Michael Walker and all the others at the notorious 50 Warwick Square address in Victoria. Philip Warren Hawkins has been MP for Wrekin since '79 and, despite being listed as a TA committee member for three years, has denied any connections with the body. Philip S. C. Rankin who was involved in Bee Carthew's Powellight in the early '70s had a letter defending the NF in the August '78 issue of the anti-racist journal *New Equals*. He signed it as a spokesperson for Liverpool Scotland Exchange Conservative and Unionist Association.

By Autumn '85, only Robin Davies, Rankin & Young remained. The newcomers were John Andrews, Geoffrey W. Bevan, G.R. McKay and Michael R. Wheddon (who became TA's Treasurer).

By Summer '87, Merrie Cave, Adrian Davies and Colin J. Grant had replaced Robin Davies and Bevan.

In Spring '90, G.K. Young retired due to ill-health and National Organiser, Ted Frostick, took over as TA's Director.

We can identify four more TA supporters from a book published by TA around '81. Entitled *Neither Up Nor Down*, it contained essays by five 'dry' Tories. One of these was G.K. Young himself. Another was Barry Bracewell-Milnes who was also a member of the Selsdon Group (apparently set up by Philip and Tony Vander Elst in the mid-70s as a grouping of disaffected ex-members of the MC), of the Adam Smith club (later Institute) and of the SIF. A third was Brigadier Michael Calvert (ex-SAS) who was a military historian and expert on unconventional warfare. A fourth was Sir Charles Pickthorn of the Salisbury

Group. And the fifth was Sam Swerling, then chairman of the MC, who had been an active supporter of the HINC in the early '70s, marching with them and attending their meetings.

Given the lack of publicised information about TA and its membership, all we can do is speculate about which other Tory MPs might be covertly involved with the group. *Round Robin* is helpful here. It is critical, if not dismissive, of most politicians. However, it does go out of its way to single out and praise a few MPs. It would be fair to assume that among these are a few who return some of that fulsome admiration and approval.

Since '86, TA approval has been voiced in the pages of *Round Robin* for, amongst others, Julian Amery, Timothy Renton, Malcolm Moss, Tony Marlow, Enoch Powell, John Biffen, Peter Brooks, Sir Philip Goodhart, Terry Dicks, Viscount Cranborne, Jeremy Hanley, John Carlisle, John Biggs-Davison and Harvey Proctor.

We can be more certain about the involvement of another MP. On 14.3.90, John Taylor was both host and key speaker at a House of Commons TA meeting. Other (unnamed) MPs attended.

In '87, TA supported Sir Alfred Sherman for inviting the anti-Jewish and racist French NF leader, Jean-Marie Le Pen, to address a Western Goals UK fringe meeting at the Tory Party Conference in Blackpool. There was a strongly-worded defence of Sherman in *Round Robin* which stated that "we congratulate Sir Alfred for his brave stand for free speech". Sherman, a one-time Communist who's written at least ten books for AOI over the past twenty years, has been a personal advisor and speech-writer to both Margaret Thatcher and Keith Joseph. The three of them co-founded the Centre for Policy Studies (CPS) in '74 — Sherman becoming its first Director, Joseph its first Chairman, Thatcher its first President. His is another Thatcher-recommended knighthood. His son, Gideon, who is a Director of Western Goals UK was once a leading right-wing member of the FCS.[53]

Sherman, whose extremism was already proving to be an embarrassment to many in the Tory Party, left CPS in early '85 to set up his own research body. However, if a further indication is needed of how deeply the far-right was able to enter into mainstream Tory circles, the CPS provided it in '86. In the Autumn of that year, it acquired a new Director of Studies. Despite her political affiliations and only weeks before she was due to speak at the Scorpion/Iona conference, this CPS job went to Anna Bramwell. Here we have a woman with long-standing and currently active neo-Nazi affiliations being appointed Director of the think-tank which Margaret Thatcher had set up and from which she had drawn and was continuing to draw many of her speech-writers and personal advisors. It furnished her government with numerous policy initiatives and programmes. Anna Bramwell's tenure was brief. It seems that there was a quick rethink. The post became vacant again almost immediately and by early '87 the current holder, David Willetts, was in place. These changes must have been very delicate. They took place with the minimum of media attention. A situation that could so easily have produced sensational headlines linking Thatcher with the NF was quietly defused. This is probably the first published account of it.[54]

The June '89 issue of *Round Robin* carried a lengthy article in support of Roy Painter's legal battle following his refusal to buy a TV licence as "a personal protest", claiming that "The BBC is telling lies after lies" and that a lot of BBC programmes were "nothing but left-wing propaganda". The article described Painter variously as "A former Conservative candidate", a "Barnet businessman" and "a Free-man of the City of London". For an article so concerned about the lies after lies and biased reporting, *Round Robin*'s omission of the most obvious description of Painter is a remarkable one.

In '74, Roy Painter's proven track record as a reliable activist within the NF was such that he was not only elected onto the NF Directorate, but also onto its Executive Council. The following year he was the main organiser of the attempted Populist coup against John Tyndall's hard-liners. When this failed and the Populists were expelled from the NF, Painter and Kingsley Read together founded the National Party (NP). This damaging split deprived the NF of some of its best organi-sers and key figures (including Denis Pirie, Dave McCalden, Mike Lobb and Richard Lawson, plus Painter and Read) and the NP looked set to be a powerful alternative to the NF. However, the NP never had more than a couple of hundred members. There were too many would-be chiefs and not enough indians. Within a matter of months, its failure became obvious. By June '76, Painter was apparently mak-ing overtures to the Conservative Party again, in the hope of being re-admitted.

'Jokes' in recent issues of *Round Robin* have included the sugges-tions that Stockwell was part of Jamaica, that the Tandoori chickens were coming home to roost in Bethnal Green, and that a large propor-tion of the 30,000-strong U.S. force based here in Britain were "preg-nant negresses". A report on the '87 Notting Hill Carnival appeared under the heading 'Masque of the Black Death' and called for the banning of the Carnival, repatriation to the Caribbean of black British citizens, and for "white people, particularly local residents... The Police, too" to participate in next year's Carnival by picking pockets and by assaulting and mugging people. On one page of another issue, readers were offered these two catchy headlines: 'Mongo Bongo from the Congo' and 'Nigger in the Woodpile'. In the December '87 issue, G.K. Young supported the suggestion that "black people stay away from the streets, so white people can really have a white Christmas".

It's hardly surprising, therefore, that it was a TA group that played host in London to three leading South African white supremacists in Britain for a speaking tour in June '89. The trio, apparently invited over by Western Goals UK, were Conservative Party (CP) leader Dr Andries Treurnicht, Clive Darby-Lewis who was a leading CP MP and CP spokesman Carl Worth.

> "What you don't realise is that I'm a National Socialist at heart. Only I am careful."
> — Roy Painter to Martin Webster.[56]

TA also uses *Round Robin* to voice its support for such organisations such as Jane Birdwood's ultra-racist Choice and the overtly anti-Jewish BLR in which she's also involved; John Biggs-Davison's right-wing, anti-Catholic Friends of the Union (now run by his daughter, Lisl) and the similar Ulster Unionist Council; the fanatically anti-Communist Common Cause; Bernard and Avril Smith's reactionary and often racist-linked Christian Affirmation Campaign; former anti-immigration campaigner and Powellite supporter Victoria Gillick; and even to defend the NF (several times) in the name of free speech.[55]

> "A former Conservative candidate more to our readers' liking" [than Lady Olga Maitland! — NT] "is our old friend, that stalwart campaigner Roy Painter."
> — G.K. Young .[57]

In Spring '90, it was announced in *Round Robin* that Young had been compelled to resign from the committee of Tory Action due to ill health. The brief note ended with the committee's wish that he make a speedy recovery. It wasn't to be. George Kennedy Young died in May, aged 79.[58]

Sources

1. Martin Walker, *The National Front*, p.126.
2. *Searchlight*, No.75, September '81. Also Stuart Christie, *The Investigative Researcher's Handbook*, p.124.
3. *The Scorpion*, No.11, Summer '81. Also Ciaran O Maolain, *The Radical Right: A World Directory*, pp.306-7. Also *Spark*, No.1, Summer Term '73. Also *Britain First*, No.16, December '73. Also Martin Walker, *The National Front*, pp.186-90.
4. Ray Hill with Andrew Bell, *The Other Face of Terror*, pp.189-94. Also *National Democrat*, No.1, Winter '81.
5. *The Flag*, No.43, June '90.
6. *Focal Point*, 5.6.82.
7. *Searchlight*, No.99, September '83. Also Martin Walker, *The National Front*, p.126.
8. *Searchlight*, No.168, June '89. Also Anthony Cavendish, G.K. Young's Obituary in *The Scotsman*, 11.5.90. Also Geoffrey Harris, *The Dark Side of Europe*, pp.109 & 117-119.
9. *Searchlight*, No.81, March '82. Also Paul Gordon & Francesca Klug, *New Right New Racism*, p.67.
10. David Edgar, Kenneth Leech & Paul Weller, *The New Right & the Church*, p.33.
11. Martin Walker, *The National Front*, pp.99, 125-6. Also *Searchlight*, No.47, May '79.
12. Roy Bramwell, *The White Man's White Paper on Racial Discrimination, Blatant Bias Corporation, The Death Tree, Public Ear* Nos.2 & 3. Also early issues of Birdwood's journal *Choice*. Also *Searchlight*, December '87 & June '89. Also a letter from Jane Birdwood dated 1.2.91.
13. Martin Walker, *The National Front*, pp.126, 130, 189. Also Paul Gordon & Francesca Klug, *New Right New Racism*, p.64.
14. Martin Walker, *The National Front*, pp.59, 64, 99, 135-6.
15. A.K. Chesterton, *Not Guilty*, pp.17-19, etc. Also two different editions of *Southern News*, No.5. Also *The Flag*, Nos.40-50. Also Michael Billig, *Psychology, Racism and Fascism*, pp.11-13.
16. A.K. Chesterton, *Not Guilty*. Also *Freedom First*, No.55, Spring '68. Also No.56, Summer '68. Also Martin Walker, *The National Front*, pp. 41,77,etc. Also Colin Jordan, *The Coloured Invasion*.
17. Sir Ernest Benn, *More Murmurings*. Also various AOI pamphlets

from the '70s. Also assorted AOI & IEA publicity leaflets. Also several issues of *Freedom First* ('67-'71) & of *Truth* ('46-'51). Also Richard Thurlow, *Fascism in Britain*, pp.236, 241 & 257-258. Also A.K. Chesterton, *The New Unhappy Lords*. Also R.B. Cockett, 'Ball, Chamberlain and Truth', *The Historical Journal*, Vol.33, No.1, '90. Also G.C. Webber, *The Ideology of the British Right 1918-1939*, pp.150-151 & 159.

18. *Freedom First*, No.50, Winter '67. Also No.53, Autumn '67.

19. *Freedom First*, No.54, Winter '68. Also No.55, Spring '68. Also No.56, Summer '68. Also No.58. Jan/Feb '69. Also Paul Gordon and Francesca Klug, *New Right New Racism*, p.61. Also Martin Walker, *The National Front*, p.118. Also R. Hugh Corbet, *Britain, not Europe*, p.52, etc. Also various '71-'73 ACML leaflets. Also, anonymously, *Monday Club — a Danger to British Democracy*. Also Don Martin's journal *On Target*, various editions from '70 & '71. Also Derek James, *Bound to Fail*. Also Conservative Trident Group leaflet & Newsletter, Summer '78. Also *Who's Who 1980*, p.1788. Also issues of *Spotlight*. Also Bloomfield Books '90 catalogues & leaflets. Also British Housewives League leaflet. Also letter from Charlotte Horsfield, 25.7.90.

20. *Freedom First* No.60, Summer '69. Also Enoch Powell, *Freedom and Reality*. Also Paul Gordon and Francesca Klug, *New Right New Racism*, p.32.

21. *Freedom First*, No.61, Autumn '69. Also Paul Gordon and Francesca Klug, *New Right New Racism*, p.65. Also Martin Walker, *The National Front*, p.117. Also Gordon Winter, *Inside Boss*, pp.382-3.

22. *Freedom First*, No.62, New Year '70. Also Martin Walker, *The National Front*, p.117. Also C.B. Cox & A.E. Dyson, *Fight For Education — A Black Paper*. Also Maurice Cowling, *Conservative Essays*. Also *Searchlight*, November '82.

23. *Freedom First* Nos.63-66, May/August/November '70 & February '71. Also D.G. Stewart-Smith, *No Vision Here*. Also *Who's Who 1980*, pp.1459 & 2440. Also *Daily Mail Year Book 1986*. Also Nigel Blundell, *The World's Greatest Scandals of the 20th Century*, pp.29-39.

24. D.G. Stewart-Smith, *No Vision Here*.

25. *Lobster*, No.12, '86.

26. D.G. Stewart-Smith, *East West Digest*, Vol.3, No.12, December '67. Also Vol.6, No.11, November '70. Also Vol.7, No.6.

27. John Sutherland, *Offensive Literature*, pp.98 & 149. Also John

Tomlinson, *Left, Right*, p.54. Also Labour Research Dept., *The National Front Investigated*, p.26. Also Paul Gordon and Francesca Klug, *New Right New Racism*, p.11.

28. D.A. Martin, *On Target*, Vol.2, No.14, 9.1.71. Also Donald A. Martin, *Objectives of the British League of Rights*, 24.3.73. Also Ciaran O'Maolain, *The Radical Right: A World Directory*, p.296. Also John Tomlinson, *Left, Right*, pp.50-51. Also Air Vice Marshall Don Bennett's Anti-Common Market election leaflet.

29. Ciaran O'Maolain, *The Radical Right: A World Directory*, pp.300, 321 & 325. Also Alan Moore & Bill Sienkiewicz, *Brought To Light, Shadowplay — The Secret Team*, p.13. Also *An Introduction to Western Goals*.

30. *Lobster*, No.11, April '86. Also Ciaran O'Maolain, *The Radical Right: A World Directory*, pp.318. Also John Tomlinson, *Left, Right*, p.54.

31. Ciaran O'Maolain, *The Radical Right: A World Directory*, pp.328. Also *Searchlight*, August '75, August '82 & April '83. Also *The New Daily*, 21.7.66 & 8-14.1.67. Also Dr Kitty Little, 2 ICRC pamphlets. Also Roy Bramwell, ICRC & AISC pamphlets. Also Martin Walker, *The National Front*, p.136. Also Derrick Knight, *Beyond the Pale*, pp.40-42 & 46.

32. Ray Hill with Andrew Bell, *The Other Face of Terror*, p.168.

33. *Choice*, No.10, January '81. Also No.19, '88.

34. Ray Hill with Andrew Bell, The *Other Face of Terror*, p.168. Also *Searchlight* October '89.

35. Ciaran O'Maolain, *The Radical Right: A World Directory*, pp.299. Also copies of *Executive Intelligence Review*.

36. Jane Birdwood, *English Solidarity Newsletter*, 9.6.89.

37. *Choice* No.21, 1990.

38. Bill Smithies & Peter Fiddick, *Enoch Powell on Immigration*, pp.43,etc.

39. *Who's Who 1980*, p.186. Also Paul Gordon and Francesca Klug, *New Right New Racism*, p.32. Also Martin Walker, *The National Front*, p.117. Also *Secession*, Vol.6, No.2, August '83. Also *Focal Point*, 8.3.82. Also *Daily Mail Year Book 1986*.

40. David Edgar, Kenneth Leech & Paul Weller, *The New Right & the Church*, p.36. Also *ES Newsletter*, September '89.

41. Martin Walker, *The National Front*, p.126. Also *Who's Who 1980*, p.2071. Also various *Daily Mail Yearbooks*, '79-86.

42. John Jennings, *The Enemy Within*, p.24.

43. John Tomlinson, *Left, Right*, p.49. Also *Stuff It*, No.5, Summer

'85. Also *20th Century*, No.1017, Spring '63. Also Ray Hill with Andrew Bell, *The Other Face of Terror*, pp.141, 188- 9, 233, 239. Also David Edgar, Kenneth Leech & Paul Weller, *The New Right & the Church*, pp.33-4.

44. *Focal Point*, 1.7.82.

45. Various MC policy papers, '84-86.

46. Various issues of *The Times*, September '83-May '87. Also *Searchlight* June '87.

47. Martin Walker, *The National Front*, p.126. Also Paul Gordon & Francesca Klug, *New Right New Racism*, p.44. Also Ciaran O Maolain, *The Radical Right: A World Directory*, pp.303-304. Also Matthew Salusbury, *Thatcherism Goes To College*, p.38. Also *Searchlight*, February '84 & April '86. Also various Western Goals, International Freedom Foundation, Salisbury Group and Libertarian Alliance publications. Also *Freedom First*, August '70.

48. David Edgar, Kenneth Leech & Paul Weller, *The New Right and the Church*, pp.4-5. Also John Jennings, *The Enemy Within*, p.4-9. Also various issues of *Freedom Today* and *Free Nation*. Also *Searchlight* December '85. Also Roger King & Neil Nugent, *Respectable Rebels*, pp.76-100. Also Rachel Tingle, *Gay Lessons*. Also Rachel Tingle, *Another Gospel*. Also Rachel Tingle, *Housing and Mobility in Scotland*. Also Philip Vander Elst, *Capitalist Technology for Soviet Survival*.

49. Brian Freemantle, *CIA*, pp.188-190. Also Jonathan Bloch & Patrick Fitzgerald, *British Intelligence and Covert Action*, pp.98- 99. Also Gordon Winter, *Inside BOSS*, pp.168-171, 543-544. Also Philip Agee & Louis Wolf, *Dirty Work: The CIA in Western Europe*, pp.204-210. Also John Jenning, *The Enemy Within*. Also various issues of *Lobster*, *Freedom Today* & *Free Nation*. Also various ISC, RFST and RISCT information and promotional leaflets. Also Geoffrey Harris, *The Dark Side of Europe*, p.53.

50. Anthony Cavendish, G.K. Young's Obituary in *The Scotsman*, 11.5.90. Also *Freedom Today*, Vol.15, No.6, December '90. Also Jonathan Bloch & Patrick Fitzgerald, *British Intelligence and Covert Action*, pp.109-113. Also Stuart Christie, *The Investigative Researcher's Handbook*, pp.123-125.

51. *Freedom Today*, Vol.15, No.4, August '90.

52. Nicholas Mosley, *Rules of the Game*, p.268. Also *Who's Who 1980*, p.1823. Also *League Sentinel*, No.9. Also Paul Gordon and Francesca Klug, *New Right New Racism*, p.67. Also Derek

Knight, *Beyond the Pale*, p.51. Also Martin Walker, *The National Front*, pp.117-118, 127-131 & 212. Also *Lobster*, Nos.11 & 19. Also David Leigh, *The Wilson Plot*, p.214. Also Roger King & Neill Nugent *Respectable Rebels*, p.97. Also *Searchlight*, June '87 & August '89. Also Stuart Christie, *The Investigative Researcher's Handbook*, pp.124-125. Also Ciaran O Maolain, *The Radical Right: A World Directory*, p.327 & 328.

53. Two letters from Edward Frostick, 21.4.90 & 5.6.90. Also TA leaflet: *Aims of Tory Action*. Also various TA letters to members. Also assorted copies of *Round Robin*, February '79-May '90. Also *Focal Point*, 30.10.81. Also phone conversation with Philip Vander Elst, 1.2.90. Also Ciaran O'Maolain, *The Radical Right: A World Directory*, p.319. Also Paul Gordon and Francesca Klug, *New Right New Racism*, pp.9, 44 & 67. Also *Searchlight*, September '81, May '82, April '83, November '83, February '84 & December '86. Also Dennis Kavanagh, *Thatcherism and British Politics*, pp.89-90 & 111-112. Also Kenneth Harris, *Thatcher*, pp.307 & 311-312. Also letter from Western Goals UK dated October '88.

54. *Salisbury Review*, October '86. Also CPS, *Exertion and Example*, annual address '89.

55. Assorted copies of *Round Robin*, Autumn '88-May '90. Also Western Goals UK press release. Also Martin Walker, *The National Front*, pp.137, 174 & 193. Also letter and Friends of the Union publicity material from Lisl Biggs-Davison, dated 13.2.90.

56. Martin Walker, *The National Front*, p.194.

57. *Round Robin*, June '89.

58. *Round Robin*, May '90. Also *The Independent*, 13/5/90.

Author's note

Throughout this text I've deliberately replaced the commonly used 'anti-Semitic' with the more accurate 'anti-Jewish'. However, this in itself is inaccurate because (a) there are shades of prejudice and 'anti-Jewish' is a cover-all that leaves the precise degree of prejudice unspecified, and (b) I should have at least distinguished between 'anti-Zionist' and 'anti-Jewish'. Please therefore bear in mind that you need to decide for yourself, through further reading, which of the people and organisations described as 'anti-Jewish' are actually racist, which are simply opposed to Zionism (Jewish nationalism) and which occupy the middle ground. In a similar vein, I'm unhappy about my repeated use of adjectival descriptions like 'right-wing','far-right' and 'ultra-right'. I've opted for them because they suggest certain sets of political tennets which are commonly held to be of the political right. In fact, it's become increasingly clear to me that the holding of extreme and/or unpopular political views is better seen as general outsider-ism. The remarkable ease with which many activists switch, during their political lives, from one extreme to the other (Alan Sherman, Oswald Mosley and G.K. Young himself being among them) indicates that these outlying territories meet, encircling the norm rather than occupying either flank. Outsiders, though they'd be reluctant to admit it, often have far more in common with their extremist opponents than they do with the moderate or apolitical mass. They not only share commitment to a struggle and a sense of alienation, but have means and method in common even though their aims may be diametrically opposite. Thus a terrorist, for example, is perceived as simply that by non-terrorists. Whether the terrorist's politics are left-wing, right-wing, anarchist, nationalist or whatever is usually of little interest to the broad public... but of great interest to anyone else involved in terrorism.

Glossary of abbreviations*

ACML Anti-Common Market League (John Paul/Victor Montagu)
AICC Anti-Immigration Co-ordinating Committee (Lady Birdwood)
AISC Anti-Immigration Standing Committee (Lady Birdwood)
AOI Aims of Industry (Michael Ivens)
BHL British Housewives' League (Don Martin)
BLEF British League for European Freedom (Don Martin)
BLR British League of Rights (Don Martin)
BM British Movement (Colin Jordan).
BNP British National Party ('60s incarnation, Andrew Fountaine/current incarnation, John Tyndall)
BOSS Bureau of State Security (South African intelligence)
BUF British Union of Fascists (Oswald Mosley)
CIA Central Intelligence Agency (United States intelligence)
CP Conservative Party (of South Africa)
CPS Centre for Policy Studies (Margaret Thatcher)
ES English Solidarity (Against Multiculturalism) (Lady Birdwood)
FA Freedom Association (Norris McWhirter)
FAC Foreign Affairs Circle (Geoffrey Stewart-Smith)
FARI Foreign Affairs Research Institute (Geoffrey Stewart-Smith)
FCS Federation of Conservative Students
FPG Focus Policy Group (David Irving)
FWF Forum World Features (Brian Crozier)
HINC Halt Immigration Now Campaign (G.K. Young)
ICA Immigration Control Association (Joy Page)
ICRC Inter City Research Centre (Lady Birdwood)
IEA Institute of Economic Affairs (Lord Harris)
INLA Irish National Liberation Army (pro-Catholic & paramilitary)
IRA Irish Republican Army (pro-Catholic & paramilititary)
ISC Institute for the Study of Conflict (Brian Crozier)
LCTF London and Counties Tenants' Federation (Joy Page)
LEL League of Empire Loyalists (A.K. Chesterton)
MC Monday Club (G.K. Young)

* With key figures in brackets.

MI5/6	Military Intelligence (MI5 is the British Security Service) (MI6 is the British Secret Intelligence Service) internal/external.
MOD	Ministry of Defence
MSI	Movimento Sociale Italiano
NAFF	National Association for Freedom (McWhirters/Ivens)
NAR	Armed Revolutionary Nuclei (Roberto Fiore)
NF	National Front (A.K. Chesterton)
NFCM	National Front Constitutional Movement (Andrew Fountaine)
NP	National Party (John Kingsley Read/Roy Painter)
NUM	National Union of Mineworkers
RISCT	Research Institute for the Study of Conflict and Terrorism (Paul Wilkinson)
RFST	Research Foundation for the Study of Terrorism (Paul Wilkinson)
RPS	Racial Preservation Society (Mary Howarth)
SHO	Self Help Organisation (Lady Birdwood)
SIF	Society for Individual Freedom (G.K. Young)
SS	Schutzstaffel (Hitler bodyguard)
TA	Tory Action (G.K. Young)
WACL	World Anti-Communist League (Stewart-Smith/Don Martin)
WISE	Welsh Irish Scottish and English (Joan Mason/Bee Carthew)
WWI/WWII	World War I ('14-'18)/World War II ('39-'45)

Useful addresses for those interested in parapolitics and related topics...

Lobster, 214 Westbourne Avenue, Hull, HU5 3JB. (0482-447558). It's the essential journal. Subscribe and order back copies.

Covert Action Information Bulletin, P.O. Box 34583, Washington, DC 20043. (202-331-9763). American CIA-watchers and reporters on international covert operations, right-wing networking, etc.

Searchlight, 37b New Cavendish Street, London, W1M 8JR. (081-534-6445). For a long time the leading and best British journal (un)covering the activities of fascist and other far-right organisations. Two caveats: (1) The Gable memorandum is a notorious letter from *Searchlight* editor Gerry Gable which seems to show that he compiled information on left-wingers and passed this on to the South African government-funded, right-wing FARI run by Geoffrey Stewart-Smith, whom he describes as having 'strong CIA links'. Sent confidentially on London Weekend Television note paper on 2nd May '77, it concerns associates of Young Liberal anti-Apartheid and pro-Palestinian campaigner Peter Hain. Gable also seems to have been feeding the information to the British and French intelligence services and seems to have contacts in the Israeli Foreign Office. All very strange. (2) In '90, Gable and co. were at the centre of a second controversy which resulted in a complete split with the Campaign Against Racism and Fascism, their longtime associates on *Searchlight*. It arose when two anti-fascists were refused entry to a *Searchlight* meeting on anti-Jewish activity in Britain on the grounds that their support for Palestinian rights made them anti-Jewish.

AK Distribution, 3 Balmoral Place, Stirling, Scotland, FK8 2RD. Send for a catalogue of their books, comics, journals, fanzines, second hand publications, etc. Most of the material on offer is political, much of it not easy to find elsewhere.

Other journals which often carry useful information include: Black Flag, Private Eye and Maximum Rock'n'Roll.

Lastly, you can contact me c/o the publisher.

Nick Toczek
March 1991

Also available by Nick Toczek:

A collection of quirky short stories, *The Private Crimes of Nick Toczek*, The Amazing Colossus Press, 1989. (£1.50)

Also, a collection of lyrics and performance poems, *The Meat Boutique*, P.B. Publications, 1991. (£4.50)

Write to: AK Distribution, 3 Balmoral Place, Stirling, Scotland, FK8 2RD.

Praise for *Business Leadership Under Fire*

'In the digital era, where technology is viewed as the driving force in delivering corporate success, it is easy to overlook that business requires the basics of informed leadership, well-crafted strategy and undiluted human endeavour if it is to survive and thrive.

This concise and entertaining book by Pepyn Dinandt and Richard Westley provides welcome food for thought in providing an important reminder of what it takes to manage and transform business performance in an increasingly complex world.

I have great respect for their down-to-earth approach, which seeks to cut through the noise of business commentary and settles on the fundamentals, which are clearly encapsulated in nine steps.

Perhaps the greatest strength of the book is the fact that the advice and guidance it gives is rooted in the hard-edge, real-life experience of the battlefield and boardroom, where both authors have excelled in their chosen careers.

I hope that those who read this book enjoy the experience, are inspired by the content and use the advice given as a practical guide to strengthening their leadership skillset, broadening their operational mindset and honing their competitive edge.'

— **Sir Roger Carr**, Chairman, BAE Systems

'Once in a generation or so, you get to read a book that discusses what you know and deal with every day as a leader but makes you see, understand and then confront your challenges anew. Pepyn Dinandt is that author and *Business Leadership Under Fire* is that book. Its nine simple steps can be applied by anyone to any organization. It is essential reading. Read this book to go from the hard shoulder to cruising in the middle lane to warp speed in the fast lane in nine easy lessons.'

— **Holger Engelmann**, CEO, Webasto SE

'The stories, lessons and recipes for success offered in *Business Leadership Under Fire* are drawn from the authors' hard-won experience, tested on the frontlines of the military and business worlds. Dinandt and Westley's concise book is inspirational boardroom reading in times of transformational change.'

— **Johannes Huth**, Head of KKR EMEA

'No matter what business or industry you are in – or, indeed, your position – transformative change is the order of the day everywhere nowadays. Whatever flavour of challenge faced, those who fail to adapt are destined to be left behind or consigned to the slow lane. Now more than ever, leaders really need to lead as well as inspire confidence, loyalty and motivation from their staff and customers alike. Dinandt and Westley's pithy but thoughtful new book *Business Leadership Under Fire* offers a handy guide to leadership excellence along with a checklist of tried-and-tested steps to help almost any manager or leader survive, thrive and be successful. If you only read one business book this year, make sure it is this one.'

— **Joanne Bennett**, Chief Business Officer, PizzaExpress

BUSINESS LEADERSHIP UNDER FIRE

BUSINESS LEADERSHIP UNDER FIRE

Nine steps to rescue and transform organizations

Pepyn Dinandt
with Richard Westley OBE MC

LONDON PUBLISHING PARTNERSHIP

Published by London Publishing Partnership
www.londonpublishingpartnership.co.uk

ISBN: 978-1-913019-42-6 (hbk)
ISBN: 978-1-913019-43-3 (ePDF)
ISBN: 978-1-913019-44-0 (ePUB)

A catalogue record for this book is available
from the British Library

Typeset in Adobe Garamond Pro by
T&T Productions Ltd, London
www.tandtproductions.com

Printed and bound by TJ Books Ltd, Padstow

CONTENTS

Foreword by Colonel Tim Collins OBE   ix

Preface   xv

Introduction   1

Step 1. Burning platform: establishing leadership   21

Step 2. Analysis and determination of the mission targets   41

Step 3. Comprehensive evaluation of the environment/theatre of operations   59

Step 4. Who Dares Wins/strategy and tactics   75

Step 5. Determining the best course of action   91

Step 6. Building and managing an excellent leadership team   109

Step 7. Team and organization structure/maximizing business impact   127

Step 8. Campaign delivery   143

Step 9. After-action review   159

Afterword   175

Acknowledgements   179

Endnotes   181

Index   183

Skillful pilots gain their reputation from storms and tempests.

— Epictetus

FOREWORD BY COLONEL
TIM COLLINS OBE

The sheer number of leadership 'do it yourself' books on the shelves of bookshops would normally make me shy away from such a topic. There is room, however, for a good book on leadership that can inform and educate. *Business Leadership Under Fire* is one such book because it is entirely grounded in tried-and-tested strategies that span military and civilian leadership.

I find it relevant because my own experience of leadership encompasses both the military and civilian life. My career included twenty-three years in the military followed by fourteen years at the head of a private company. This taught me that, while the consequences of getting decisions wrong in the army are far more serious than they are in civilian life, getting it right still matters, whatever the environment. In the former, people may die due to poor decision making; in the latter, a business could fail and livelihoods could be lost. There is an argument that in some cases leadership in the army is easier, because people tend to do as they are told (though this is not always the case). In civilian life, people want to be guided, not barked at. Generally, though, individuals from all backgrounds just want to do the right thing. And therein lies the rub. If there is no clear direction from the top, the system fails before any form of actual leadership can even begin to take effect.

I was in a leadership position for most of my career in the army: first as an infantry platoon commander, then as an SAS troop commander on many operations, then as a company commander on operations, and finally as a staff officer in the SAS and at the Headquarters Special Forces. Yet, despite this experience, as well as the benefit of attending the British Army Staff College (and having a spell at the US Staff College at Fort Leavenworth), nothing prepared me for leading a battalion of 700 men in the Air Assault Brigade. At least, that is how I felt in January 2001 when I stood before the soldiers of the First Battalion, the Royal Irish Regiment in Canterbury. Six years later I would be making my way to Colebrook Castle in County Fermanagh to speak to the first 'on-boarding' (or induction) course of my own company, New Century, whose contractors would shortly deploy to Iraq in support of the United States Marine Corps. I had the very same doubts then too. What would these people like me to do? What do they want (need) from me?

Some people have told me that they find it hard to believe that I would find myself stuck for words, but it was true, albeit briefly. In the first instance, I was to lead an infantry battalion who had experienced the trauma of having had men taken prisoner on operations. Even months later, they had the sullen air of a defeated organization and were also haemorrhaging manpower as people opted to leave and no one was joining. In the second case, I was addressing contractors who were a mix of retired policemen and linguists. What did I, with little experience of the civilian world at that time, have to offer?

On both occasions I resorted to the same resource for inspiration: the leadership of an old boy of my regiment, Field Marshal Sir Gerald Templer. He had distinguished himself as the leader of the British clandestine special forces in World War II and, most notably, as the man that saved Malaya when it looked like it had been lost to the Communists. Templer ultimately delivered a free and independent new nation of Malaysia three years ahead of the planned schedule. Having studied the Templer approach, I noted a number of strategies that were relevant to leadership style in both the military and corporate worlds.

It is crucial to figure out what exactly your organization stands for. What does it do? That would seem like an obvious starting point, but military and corporate history is littered with examples of where that was simply not the case. One of the most notable examples from the military side is the Royal Navy's victory, in May 1916, at the Battle of Jutland (or Skagerrak if you are German). It was a chaotic engagement and, at the time, the Royal Navy failed to understand that they had won, mostly thanks to a lack of understanding of the basics of the available technology. The Royal Navy had a culture of firing their guns as quickly as possible and hoping for the best, because that was what they believed Nelson would have done. The Germans, on the other hand, with a very new navy, had a deeper understanding of the available technology and sought to sink the enemy's ships. Both sides did what they set out to do on the day. The Royal Navy triumphed (even though they did not immediately realize it), but little was said about the loss of two British ships to every German ship lost, not to mention the fact that twice the number of British sailors were lost. The German High Seas Fleet, having declared victory, returned to harbour leaving the North Sea to the Royal Navy and never left port again. It fell to the US newspapers (the US was still neutral in 1916) to point out that, despite the devastating losses inflicted on the Royal Navy, all the Germans had essentially done was assault their jailer and then go back to jail.

What made Templer successful was that he made sure that whatever he did was in accordance with the main plan. Indeed, he refused to deploy to Malaya until he had obtained precise instructions from the government about what they wanted to achieve, which was, it transpired, making Malaya independent by 1960. With this clear aim in mind, he was able to bend the colonial administration to that purpose as well as defeat the Malayan Communist Party. All of this despite significant pushback from the old 'Malaya hands' within his own system.

Another key lesson is that leaders need to create, or modify, their organization to fit the purpose of the aim. In Templer's case he needed to race to train and include Malays in every aspect of the administration from early on. Many of the experts told him that, because he was in the country for the first time, he did not understand all the subtleties. He responded by asking how many times the country had been made independent and then sacked the experts. For my purposes, I interpreted this as showcasing the need to think independently and instil a sense of operational purpose that leads to a new sense of confidence. When my battalion was warned to be ready to take part in the invasion of Iraq, we still had the problem of being down on manpower. I addressed the situation by looking closely at where we drew our recruits from. I listened carefully to what the experts within the Army recruiting organization had to say on the matter and then did the exact opposite of what the experts advised. To my delight we went from 300 soldiers understrength to fully recruited.

All of which brings me to the need to get the *right* people into any organization – something that will often mean cutting out some dead wood and replacing it with talent. What both Templer and I discovered along the way is that not everyone will share in your vision. Some people like things just the way they are. These people are the change resisters. They have to go. All organizations benefit from the loyalty of their people but teams can get set in their ways. Both Templer and I can speak for the benefits of an influx of new talent to gee up the gene pool and create a team that shares the vision and has good ideas of their own on how to achieve it. Key to this is getting the right spirit into an organization. This is where everyone on the team feels a sense of belonging and ownership of the task. This means leaders need to be willing to delegate: individuals derive deep satisfaction from taking responsibility, and, in doing so, they enhance the team, instilling the same emotions in their subordinates. Getting the right spirit into your people is what I call the 'factory floor' of leadership.

For this to work efficiently, a leader needs to get their instructions to their people right – but this is also a two-way street. Leaders need to listen carefully to what their teams are telling them and understand their viewpoint if they are to give them effective instructions. When I reflect upon why things go wrong, one of three reasons is usually in the frame.

The first, and by far the most common, reason for failure is that individuals were not told what they had to do in order to succeed. That is the fault of the leader. Sometimes leaders do not really know themselves. It is for this reason that we in the army rely on models such as the combat estimate, which is a process to discover what the task actually is. This model is covered in *Business Leadership Under Fire* (along with others) and it is a crucial part of the process of mission analysis. It is only once you have answered the question, 'What have I been asked to do and why?' that you can tell your team how you, as a unit, fit into the overall big plan.

The second reason for things going wrong is that situations change. In the military it may be as a result of enemy action; in business it may be market fluctuation or the unanticipated actions of a competitor. That is everyone's and no one's fault, and, once again, following the careful checklist presented by a model will stop you getting caught out.

The third reason things go wrong is that a subunit knows what they have to do and has the resources to achieve it but fails to do so. Here, there is either a problem with the team or a problem with the leadership. In either case, a leader needs to intervene and fix it.

One of the final, and arguably most important, leadership lessons that resonates in both a military setting and a civilian one is: let them get on with it! When the team knows what they have to do and they have the resources and talent to do it, there is a fair chance that they will perform even better than you could ever have imagined. This does not mean a leader can completely walk away. Sometimes, when a problem hits or the unexpected happens, a leader does need to step in. Guidance at this stage should be just that, though: guidance, or a steadying hand. Some leaders like to see activity verging on hysteria in the face of a crisis. Rather like the German Admiral Reinhard Scheer at the Battle of Jutland, I would always be inclined to ask whether we were just firing the guns really quickly or actually aiming at a specific target for a specific reason.

To summarize, successful leadership in both military and civilian life starts by having a clear idea of what you want to achieve. Surround yourself with the best team you can find and afford, tell them clearly what it is you would like them to achieve and by when, and then let them get on with it and watch them exceed all expectations with ease. Finally, you take all of the credit for the success! All jokes aside, this has been my experience, in both military and civilian life. Well-motivated teams, acting on clear guidelines and instructions, unfailingly succeed beyond all expectations. My battalion went from a badly understrength, demoralized one to a fully manned and, arguably, the best trained in the Army. As a result, it was the first battalion selected by Land Command for the order of battle for the planned invasion of Iraq in 2003.

I thoroughly recommend *Business Leadership Under Fire*. It is a valuable guide to dealing with the unexpected challenges that can stall the growth of even the most successful firms. Leaders setting out on their journey will be presented with an inspiring, helpful guide packed full of strategies that they can try, but even the old hands will find that there is plenty that can be learned here – after all, it is never too late to succeed.

PREFACE

Running a business well has always been difficult. There are winners and losers. There will always be some new kid on the block waiting to steal your lunch, and developments in technology mean this can often happen at a dizzying pace. One minute you are at the top of your game, and the next a disruptor swoops in and scoops up your entire market, seemingly overnight. Alternatively, a completely unexpected event – a pandemic, say – changes the trading environment in a heartbeat, threatening the survival of tens of thousands of businesses.

My thirty-year leadership career has been based on leading turnarounds and transformations of once-healthy businesses that have seen a downturn in their fortunes – often a dramatic one. I have worked in a wide range of international companies, in industries from building materials to household goods. I am the person that is usually parachuted in at the time when an organization realizes it is in real trouble. What each of the businesses across the almost two dozen transformation projects I have led had in common was that everything had been going well, but then they had gone into rapid reverse.

I started to write this book just as Covid-19 began its destructive journey around the globe. While I had not yet helped any companies recover from the aftermath of a pandemic, it occurred to me that I had many valuable lessons I could pass on. The virus has had a devastating impact at a personal level for millions of families, but it has also struck whole economies and individual businesses too. There is no business anywhere that has not now, in some way, been impacted by the global health emergency, and many have suffered severely. The time certainly seems right to articulate a process to help businesses get out of trouble.

My style of working and the strategies I prefer are very pragmatic, and they have often been inspired by military tactics, not least because the military comes into its own in complex and challenging situations. Although Sun Tzu's classic work *The Art of War* was written more than 2,500 years ago, it is uncanny how pertinent the strategies it describes are for business today. The great Chinese strategist outlines faults in leadership that I have seen examples of time and time again. Down the years, I have developed this line of thinking and worked with modern military experts to find ways to apply some of their knowledge and experience in a business setting. The first expert I consulted was Colonel Tim Collins, the renowned British Army officer famed for his rousing speech to the 1st Royal Irish Battlegroup on the eve of battle in Iraq in March 2003. It was Tim who introduced me to my co-author Colonel Richard Westley. Richard, who served in Northern Ireland, Kosovo and Afghanistan, was awarded the Military Cross for his command tour of Bosnia in 1995 and an OBE for unswerving and courageous leadership in Helmand Province, Afghanistan, in 2007. Richard and Tim had come to very similar conclusions to my own and had been using the lessons gained from their military background to advise business leaders. Again and again, when working with these military leaders, I found parallels between what I had been doing in my work with failing corporates and the techniques used in the military to rapidly recover when things do not go as planned.

One of the first stories Richard relayed to me showed me that I was on the right track. Richard explained that when he works with business leaders he likes to do an exercise in which he throws executives into very unfamiliar circumstances that may or may not have direct relevance to their particular line of business. The goal is to see how good they are at problem solving, giving clear instructions, contingency planning and (finally) putting what they know into action. Invariably, the executives flounder because of the unexpected circumstances.

During the review at the end of the exercise, the feedback from the participants invariably includes that it would have been a lot easier if there had been a model to work from to assist them in the decision-making process to get from A to B. Richard's next step is to take them through a simple structured model in which the executives first focus on the aim of the exercise, then look at the factors that might affect it, investigate the possible courses of action that are open to them, and, finally, make a plan to move forward.* The result of introducing this discipline, Richard says, is like seeing a penny drop. Suddenly, the executives can see a clear way forward.

There are dozens of models like this in the military: there is a model for just about any course of action. As well as Richard's AFCP model, there is the six-stage estimate, the seven-stage combat estimate, the strategic estimate, the OODA loop – the list goes on. The UK's much-respected Special Air Service (the SAS) has a very succinct model known as the Mission Success Cycle. Here, the stages are plan, brief, deliver, debrief. These basic frameworks are all there to ensure that when soldiers are under pressure – often in addition to being tired or frightened or dislocated – they do not miss anything. They will have a complete understanding of the environment, the resources that are close to hand, the enemy's intentions and their own capabilities.

They all follow a similar path:

- What is the current situation?
- What do we need to do?
- What resources have we got in order to be able to do it?
- What constraints are we operating under?
- What are the options for doing this particular mission, and which is the best of those options?

Once the right path is decided upon, you are into the delivery of orders, which are pretty rigid in the way they are written and disseminated. After that, it is into rehearsals and delivery.

Each model also has two other crucial points in common. The first is that they all tacitly accept the mantra first voiced by Prussian commander Helmuth von Moltke in the nineteenth century that 'no plan survives beyond first contact with the enemy'. The armed forces have to be willing to constantly adapt and change, according to the situation, because circumstances frequently change, often in very

---

* The plan is known as AFCP – aim, factors, courses open (available), plan – and is often informalized by instructors at RMA Sandhurst to 'Any Fool Can Plan'.

unexpected ways. The second point is that no mission is complete without a full and thorough debrief, done as quickly as possible after the completion of the action, with everyone involved. It is crucial to understand what went wrong and what went right, so that these lessons can be drawn on in the future.

All of these models informed the development of the nine-stage, step-by-step model envisaged for businesses that this book proposes. It seemed logical to work through these various broadly similar stages to synthesize them in order to help any business in crisis understand their position and then decisively solve their problem. After working through several iterations of my step-by-step model, I asked Richard to collaborate with me as I reasoned that, to get things right, the best way forward would be to work in close conjunction with a military expert. We therefore combined the best bits of thinking from the business world and the armed forces in order to come up with the most effective model. *Business Leadership Under Fire* is the result. It is a template, recipe and model in nine steps that, we think, combines the best thinking of military and business leadership to help transform any organization, institution or business in crisis.

INTRODUCTION

In July 2020, Tesla celebrated its seventeenth birthday by becoming the world's most valuable car company. The electric vehicle maker's valuation of more than $208 billion represented more than the *combined* value of many of its rivals, such as Fiat Chrysler ($20 billion), Ford ($24 billion), Ferrari ($32 billion), General Motors ($36 billion), BMW ($41 billion), Honda ($46 billion) and Volkswagen ($74 billion).[1] Just how did this upstart speed past its rivals, with their decades of experience and business models that were once the envy of the world?

To many observers it seems astonishing that the world's once-mighty car giants had completely missed the opportunity represented by electric cars. While Elon Musk, Tesla's charismatic, visionary and driven CEO, has an unconventional approach to business, he did not get the idea out of nowhere – in fact, he was an early investor in Tesla, not the company's founder. The concept of electric cars dates back to 1832,[2] although it was not until the early 1990s that the push for clean air and energy put them back in the spotlight. Yet, even then, the major manufacturers only made half-hearted attempts to produce mainstream electric models. They appeared to reason that the driving public were more interested in the then-fashionable gas-guzzling sports utility vehicles, so why rock the boat? Besides, they were hampered when it came to innovation because they were not really set up to buy hardware and software components from a range of different sources. Then, along came Musk, who looked into the future, saw the way things were headed and drove his developers hard. Tesla resolved some innate issues with electric cars, most importantly the restricted battery life and the need to manufacture all the complementary components in-house. With almost fanatical attention to detail, Tesla created a car for the future that ran off one central 'brain-like' computer that can be updated at the click of a mouse. One could even say that Tesla's cars are like smartphones on wheels. And now the results are in: it turns out the public does want electric cars after all. Unsurprisingly, other car businesses are now falling over themselves to play catch-up.

Tesla is not the only company that has turned an established industry on its head. In recent years, we have seen a rapid succession of disruptors. The hospitality industry has a new lease of life after Airbnb introduced homeowners to the opportunity to rent their houses out to travellers at a reasonable price. There's Uber, which super-charged the taxi business, making transport more accessible and affordable while at the same time spawning a whole new gig economy. Netflix is another textbook example, with their movie and TV show streaming model becoming an everyday essential in millions of homes. And then there is the tech giant of them all, Amazon, which has changed the way we shop for everything from aspirin to lawnmowers.

While everyone equates disruption with technology, the concept is nothing new. Businesses develop, grow and succeed by inventing something new or by markedly improving upon what came before. Despite all the many failings of the human race, we are, at heart, inventors. We see a problem and we ponder: wouldn't it be great if …? Then we go on to make our idea a reality. This has been happening since the day we swapped rocks for spears and carried on from there. In every case, there were winners and losers. Far back in time, when the first army appeared with a newly invented chariot, it is pretty certain that the foot soldiers on the opposing side could see that their days were numbered. And this is the key point: for every Tesla, Airbnb, Uber, Netflix and Amazon, there are millions of businesses that fall by the wayside, superseded by the new.

My lifelong career in major transformation projects has shown me that there are many reasons for a company's change in fortunes. Some businesses that I have been brought into have had no outside forces disrupting them at all: the problems are all of their own making. Poor leadership has simply failed to spot changes in customer demand. The competition is not particularly dynamic, but the firms that called me in were simply doing the same thing badly. At other times, the problem was all about a flood of products from abroad, turning a market on its head. Again, not particularly disruptive in the traditional dramatic sense of bringing in the new, just disruptive because the imports were much cheaper. The various experiences I have had have taught me many lessons about turnarounds and transformations.

One of the first things I noted is that the status quo does not simply change because another business comes along with something a lot better. There is a big element of culpability on the other side too. The incumbent businesses in the sector have often passively allowed things to drift. Like the major motor companies referenced above, these companies were content with what they were doing and saw no reason to change even when their customers were. In doing so, they left the way wide open for something better. What puts Musk and his ilk out in front is that they are not constrained by a lengthy past in their respective industries. They can be quick on their feet because they do not carry any of the baggage of previous platforms. In Musk's case, while the established players basked in their long-term success with petrol and diesel models – models their teams knew and understood inside out – the entrepreneur was able to start with a blank sheet of paper. Tesla's team was not held back by legacy technology: they could look at anything and everything, including things that may never have been considered when putting together the various components of a car. Meanwhile, while assessing their markets, Tesla could look forwards, backwards and sideways at the developing concern around environmental issues and the gathering initiatives to meet CO_2 targets. At the same time, they were able to see the changing appetites of the car-buying public.

There is a lovely expression that perfectly encapsulates the way established companies seem to stall so spectacularly: the racehorse phenomenon. Consider the rough and tumble of a professional horse race, as the competing horses hurtle around the track towards the finishing post. If a jockey failed to pull up their charge once they had galloped past the finish line, their horse would storm on and on, without hesitation. Racehorses are motivated and energized to run and run. Yet, we humans seem to stop immediately on achieving our goal. I have seen it time and time again. When a business reaches number one, it quite rightly celebrates that attainment. *We are number one!* And then they stop right there, at the metaphorical finishing post. Meanwhile, across the competitive market, rival horses are just building up a head of steam to chase down, and then pass, the number one. You cannot blame – or stop – them. That is what businesses are set up to do. The runners who are at numbers two, three, four and five in your sector are constantly plotting and scheming about how to beat you.

Nokia is a fantastic example of this phenomenon. The Finnish company was once the recognized giant of the mobile phone market. It supplied 40% of the world's phones in the early 2000s and boasted record revenues and profits year after year. Everyone in the business, from top to bottom, thought Nokia was the king of telecoms. It could walk on water! Unfortunately, this inbuilt confidence meant that the organization was unable to fathom the threat posed to them by a new entrant to the mobile phone market from Cupertino, California, which had produced this funny looking device called the iPhone. Nokia's business model focused on small phones, with long battery life, and they were completely certain their customers loved them. They scoffed at the larger iPhone, with its new touchscreen and a battery that needed charging every day. How could you sell that to a customer, they asked? Nokia's chief executive, Olli-Pekka Kallasvuo, shrugged off any danger: 'rivals had come and gone,' he said.[3] Despite having ample time to react to counter the threat – as well as plenty of resources, since Nokia was the leader in the mobile phone industry – they did not. They just failed to get it. Clearly, as we all now know, Apple customers did. In fact, the iPhone became iconic, with cult-like followers that would even camp overnight outside Apple stores to snap up the latest smartphone releases. Nokia tried to play catch-up, releasing its own smartphone in 2008, but it changed tack too late. It had completely lost its dominant position and exited the mobile phone making business in 2014, selling the division to Microsoft.

Nokia fell into a trap that has snared numerous once-successful businesses by neglecting what I call the four Cs.

- It neglected the Customer's true wishes.
- It neglected the Competition.
- If fell into a Comfort zone.
- It became Cowardly, failing to do what was really necessary to deal with the problem.

TRAP OF NEGLECTING THE 4 CS

→ **C**ustomer

→ **C**ompetition

→ **C**omfort Zone
(falling into)

→ **C**owardice
(failing to make the tough decisions
required to fix problems caused by the
first 3Cs)

The four Cs. (© Pepyn Dinandt.)

The four Cs

There is a German saying that is very apt when it comes to my second important lesson from turnarounds: *Erfolg hat viele Väter, Scheitern ist eine Waise* – success has many fathers, failure is an orphan. This is especially true in larger corporations. When everything goes well, people cannot wait to put their hands up and point out what a fantastic job they did to contribute to the great result. But when things go badly, there is silence. No one wants to take responsibility. Ultimately, though, there can be only one conclusion when things go wrong: there has been a failure of leadership. While bad luck sometimes has a part to play in failure, when businesses start to falter it is a sure sign that the person at the top of an organization has made a bad call or a tactical error, has failed to properly communicate their strategy, has failed to see a huge opportunity or has just completely failed.

Kodak is a prime example of the latter point. The company, whose name is synonymous with film and photography, actually pioneered digital camera technology back in 1975 but then completely missed the boat with it. They could – indeed, they should – have been the innovator and brought in the next big thing in photography. Yet, the organization was unwilling, or unable, to follow through.

There are plenty of theories about why organizations are so reluctant to change. In Kodak's case, the most relevant one would be the 'theory of architectural innovation'. Here, a business does not want to accept or adopt anything new because they are comfortable in the old way of doing things. (We saw the same thing with the established motor businesses at the start of this chapter.) Kodak, under its then-president and CEO Walter Fallon, conducted a study into digital in 1981, at around the time Sony introduced its first electronic cameras. The study concluded that digital photography had the capacity to replace Kodak's established film business but that the company probably had at least a decade to adapt and prepare for that eventuality. History proves both of the study's conclusions to be accurate. Unfortunately, in that crucial ten-year period, during which Colby Chandler took over as CEO, Kodak did little to prepare for the digital disruption, preferring to focus its attention on improving the quality of its film. Even after the extent of the mistake was laid bare, the company continued to spectacularly fail to make its mark on digital, despite a subsequent succession of new CEOs promising to do just that. In 2012, Kodak filed for Chapter 11. It has since emerged from bankruptcy but it is a shadow of its former self.

It is worth noting that this strategy of ignoring new innovations can have even more devastating consequences. You may be familiar with the word *Blitzkrieg*, meaning lightning war. Despite the German name, it was not a German invention. It was developed in 1918 by J. F. C. Fuller, a brilliant British officer, who saw it as a revolutionary way to make best use of the latest development in military technology at the time: the tank. The British Army completely failed to see the merit in Fuller's idea, leaving it to the Germans to take it up. Sure enough, a little over twenty years later Hitler's tanks thundered across Europe, achieving the kind of rapid victories Fuller had predicted.

Perhaps the most useful theory about why organizations fail to see what is coming is the 'theory of disruptive innovation', which was defined by American scholar Clayton Christensen in 1995. A disruptive innovation is one that creates a new market and value network, eventually displacing what came before. The new upstarts are frequently overlooked for a variety of reasons. Sometimes, it takes time for the new order to build up steam and for the disruptor to make a significant impact on its market. In other cases, the business models may be so different that incumbents do not see the threat until it is too late. And, of course, there is the fact that new innovations are not always successful, with the subtext being: why not wait and see? In the early 1990s, countless internet retailers pursued disruptive paths, but very, very few succeeded.

Clearly, companies should not begin dismantling what might be a very profitable business at the mere threat of disruption. If and when new competitors appear on the horizon, existing companies should strengthen relationships with their core customers and invest in new innovations. (Arguably, they should be pursuing this strategy all the time.) But if the threat seems real, that is the time to change something.

My greatest revelations about strategic reorganization come from outside the corporate sphere altogether: the military. Oddly, since we are all brought up to value the new as though it is the best word on any matter, my prime source has been a book that was written more than 2,500 years ago. Sun Tzu's classic work *The Art of War* has quite rightly become one of the world's most influential books on military strategy, studied by academics everywhere. I have read and reread the book many times because this master strategist has outlined lessons that are just as applicable to business, and particularly businesses that are fighting to survive. Lessons such as 'know your enemy and know yourself, and fight a hundred battles without danger' seem entirely relevant to the types of organization I deal with. A big part of why they had lost their way was because they no longer knew what they stood for and they completely misread their position in the markets they operated in and the competition they were up against. Another example is when Sun Tzu says that 'you do not win in battle in the same way twice'. How many companies find one way of doing things and stick with it come what may? It is hardly surprising that other organizations – leaner ones – fly past them.

Sun Tzu has plenty to say on the culpability of leaders too. Indeed, he notes five dangerous faults that may affect a general.

- Recklessness, which leads to destruction.
- Cowardice, which leads to capture.
- A hasty temper, which can be provoked by insults.
- A delicacy of honour, which is sensitive to shame.
- Over-solicitude for his men, which exposes him to worry and trouble.

As a seasoned observer of leadership and, in particular, failed leadership, I can attest to the fact that I have witnessed each one of these faults many times over. We all have experience of, or have observed, impulsive, verbose or micromanaging leaders. Any one of these characteristics is bad enough for a leader, but a combination of all three is terrible.

Exploring further, I came across the interesting acronym VUCA, based on the theories of Warren Bennis and Burt Nanus,[4] which describes the volatility, uncertainty, complexity and ambiguity of general conditions and situations. It was first used by the US Army War College to describe the conditions resulting from the end of the Cold War. The military is used to operating in a much more active and kinetic situation. Fighting units are constantly trying to outthink and outmanoeuvre the enemy. Every action and event is subject to analysis from day one and is thoroughly checked against established models. This way of working is drummed into new recruits from the first day of training because military leaders know that doing the right thing is not always the same as doing the easiest thing. Staged processes force troops to go through every eventuality and look at all of the available options to find the best one for each circumstance. Having done so, they may still arrive at the same solution they did last time – but at least they will have checked it and will know they are covered. The mental process of going through a checklist stops complacency in its tracks.

Ordinarily, even with the constant rise of the disruptors, most businesses are uncomfortable in a VUCA environment. The majority of corporations thrive on structure and normality. Conversely, the military is there precisely because we live in a VUCA world. Today, though, in one of the toughest trading environments for generations, there is no doubt that we all live and work in a VUCA environment. It therefore makes more sense than ever to learn from the military, an organization that has to thrive on stress and change, and to be responsive and agile. We need our businesses to be like that if they are to get through this.

My explorations into links between military strategy and business leadership are what led me first to Colonel Tim Collins and then to my co-author, Colonel Richard Westley. It was my work with these two modern military strategists that helped develop my thinking to its logical conclusion.

The goal was clear: how could we use the clear-cut techniques espoused by military models to succeed in a corporate turnaround challenge? What are the mental processes that a business leader needs to go through from the moment they arrive on the scene in a failed company, through to quickly establishing a leadership position, and then working through exactly what needs to be done? Setting down a clear structure seems to be the best way forward in a challenging environment with many variables.

To explain how the thinking developed, it may be helpful to go into more detail about what you might find in one of these processes. Below, I have outlined the seven-stage 'estimate process' used for battle planning. It is a logical and sequential process, and it also allows the people on the ground to use their own intuition and initiative.

The seven stages of the estimate process are listed below.

(1) *Review of the situation.* This involves considering as much of the background information as possible, including determining threats, understanding the available resources and evaluating previous experiences.
(2) *Mission analysis.* This is where the mission is determined. It is the 'what' and the 'why', or the task and the purpose.
(3) *Evaluation of factors.* An outline of tasks, constraints and points for clarification that will underpin the more detailed future planning.
(4) *Commander's guidance on courses of action (COAs).* Here, the person in charge gives clear, concise instructions that the team are to develop, based on what he/she thinks is viable and what might

prove to be critical. The team is not precluded from thinking and questioning; indeed, everyone involved should play an active role.

(5) *Development and validation of COAs*. Following the guidance given in stage (4), a planning team develops a series of COAs for consideration and validation.

(6) *Evaluation of COAs*. A cost–benefit analysis takes place for each COA.

(7) *The final decision*. The person in charge decides which option – or which combination of options – to choose, based on logic and intuition, and this forms the road map for the way ahead, where plans are completed and the action embarked upon.

This model and others like it are the foundation for the nine-step model that Richard and I have designed for failing businesses, i.e. the model outlined in this book. Our model clearly lays out the processes required to keep businesses on track or, most pertinently to me, restore organizations that have drifted off the mark. The act of running through very familiar processes, marking each stage off one by one, is the perfect way to address the problem with structured analysis. By 'stepping back' you will see much more about the situation than anyone else. The value of this brief pause cannot be overestimated when you want to see what is really happening. When a business is in crisis, you need to take time to detach yourself from it and take a good, honest look at what is really going on. You may be very surprised by what you see.

Giving structure to these recovery processes makes sure that leaders do not miss anything. It sets the work pattern and the rhythm to meet the objectives, even in a tough and constantly changing environment. After all, when a business is in crisis mode, it will be coming up against entirely unexpected, unexplored circumstances. This is the basis for our nine-step model to help business leadership in crisis.

As you will see from the outline below, Richard and I were not looking to reinvent the wheel. Each of the steps has a direct correlation with the leading military processes. Our nine-step model is as follows.

Step 1. Burning platform

This is where leadership is established.

Leadership is not always effective. This is why a good leader achieves success and a bad leader fails. It is the role of a leader to help everyone recognize that there is a problem and that change is required. For a new leader, this means getting to know an organization from the inside. Although it may be blindingly obvious that a business is in deep trouble, many people within the organization may be unwilling to admit this because doing so inevitably leads on to an obvious conclusion: something needs to be done. Doing something means change. This is why one of the early challenges in any transformation process is to get people to recognize and accept that there is a problem that is an issue for them personally, as well as for the business, and then to get those people to change their behaviour.

Step 2. Mission analysis

Here, the full extent of the mission is evaluated. This involves a review of the business and how it has arrived at its current position. How has the situation changed? Or how might the situation change? This is something that needs to be thoroughly interrogated at the beginning of the nine steps and then again and again throughout the process. Many businesses seem to fall at this first hurdle. In the aftermath of the UK's Brexit referendum to leave the European Union, for example, many businesses immediately raced to open divisions in Ireland and mainland Europe, in order to protect their future interests. Amazingly, though, many other businesses still had not made any concrete plans even two years later. They may have been in denial, or paralysed with indecision, but in either case this was unforgivable. There is zero point in beginning contingency planning *after* the worst has happened. Some people may question why mission analysis comes after the burning platform. To explain why I would use the analogy of a restaurant hiring a top chef. This talented individual will always want to inspect the state of the kitchen before they start thinking about what to cook.

Step 3. Environment/theatre of operations

No businesses, especially established ones, want to admit they have weaknesses. They are all strong! Even if they are losing market share, it is not their fault: it is down to a particularly strong competitor or fickle customers, or it is because of an unfavourable economic environment – anything might be blamed, but the solution is never close to home. There is an innate (and very human) tendency to refuse to admit that products are not actually as good as those of one's competitors, or that R&D has been a bit stale for five years or more. Who wants to admit that they are not doing a good job? Yet, you need to do this before you can move on to the next stage.

Step 3 involves a full evaluation of *all* factors that the business is up against, taking into account the competition and the operating environment. Key here is understanding what customers want both today and in the future. You also need to know your competition, or your 'enemy'. It is crucial to measure yourself against them. What is the enemy trying to do and why? What do we have to do to outfight them?

This process forces you to think through all the variables. It stops you from just taking the easy option. It will not let you withdraw into your comfort zone of continuing to do what your business has always done. (In the military, this would be the equivalent of attacking on the right-hand side because that has worked the past three times. It is highly likely, of course, that the enemy has spotted that too and has put all their guns there!)

Step 4. The 'who dares wins' strategy

In a nutshell, successful strategies have the following characteristics. First, you leverage your strengths against the weaknesses of your competitors – assuming that your business has actual objective tangible strengths (God help your business if it does not). Second, the simpler and more understandable the strategy is for those that need to implement it, the higher the likelihood of success.

Protecting your weaknesses and playing to your strengths, while seeking out your enemy's weaknesses, is the way to success. This is how to create a tempo that a competitor can never really recover from. Indeed, they will have to switch their efforts towards trying to work out what you are doing, which means they are not looking to their own issues. Those who 'dare' to make a logical, clear and simple strategy are often very successful.

Step 5. Plan

This is the formulation of the what, where, by whom and when. The plan must be analysed and interrogated in order to fully understand its complexities and predict all possible barriers to success and any potential side effects that it has.

It is very easy to get carried away in a crisis situation, putting out one fire after another, doing your level best to hold it together – but this often means you lose sight of the one thing that is most likely to bring your company down altogether. I gained some inspiration about this from another military source: Jocko Willink, the author of *Leadership Strategy and Tactics*.[5] Willink writes about a training exercise in which a unit that had become bogged down in front of a large building were being shot at with paintballs from multiple directions. Some of the men were 'wounded' and there were many 'innocent civilians' in the vicinity, who were, quite understandably, scared. To add to the mayhem, the leader had lost track of some of his men. Willink describes the chaotic scene, with the leader trying to undertake a head count, evacuate civilians and the wounded, and simultaneously work out where the shots were coming from. As Willink wryly notes, this leader really had only one priority: to find and stop the enemy. All of the other problems were merely academic otherwise, since everyone would be dead. This is why having a coherent plan, with all team members knowing what their tasks and priorities are, is so important.

Step 6. Management team

The challenge in step 6 is all about the key people within an organization because this is something that may prevent you from being able to deliver. Any new leader entering a transformation situation might believe that a substantial clearout of the old guard is applicable, so that a clean break with the past can be made and the business can 'start again'. However, while bringing in an entirely new leadership team might seem like a decisive early action, it would also be very disruptive and might in fact make a bad situation even worse. While some senior people will, indeed, have to go, it would be a mistake to lose the many good people within the firm – they will hold a great deal of vital knowledge.

It is impossible to lead a company out of a crisis if you do not know the strengths and weaknesses of your team, both as a group and on an individual basis. As military leaders often say, it is really important to know your people well when things are going well, but it is vital to know them well when things are not. It is essential to know the limitations of your team. Your planning process cannot put you in a situation where you start writing cheques that your organization is unable to cash.

Step 7. Organization: units and subunits

Here, leaders explain to the team what is going on. That is very different from a CEO sitting in a boardroom and telling their ten direct reports the plan. To change things, it is crucial to take *everyone* with you. Everyone from the top of the organization to the bottom has to understand that there is a burning platform and that things need to really change. It is not an option to simply pay lip service to change.

When briefing and organizing the team, instructions must be clear, concise and constructive. Team members have the opportunity to comment on, and potentially refine, the plan, but the leader has the final say.

This all means that leaders need to be present in their organizations. This may require a different organizational pyramid from before – one in which the leader is very visible and, more importantly, one that puts the organization into a state where it can deliver.

Step 8. Execute and achieve the plan

The previous steps have all been about laying the foundations for rebuilding things and getting the business back on track, and these need to have been completed correctly and thoroughly in order to move on to this step. Step 8 is where the new strategy is implemented: the turnaround and transformation of the organization. Here, a leader will move from the building stage into the growth stage, and it is this step on which the entire mission will be judged and by which a leader will be measured.

No plan will survive first contact with the enemy, so the delivery of the plan must allow room for strategies to be constantly reviewed and changed according to circumstances. Good lines of communication are essential here, so that changes to the operating environment can be quickly noted and reported. Similarly, it is crucial that the team feels empowered to speak up and that it makes shifts in strategy according to the overall intent. It is useful to break down the overall goal into 'bite-sized chunks', so that progress can be measured against defined success criteria.

The British military has a number of 'principles of war', which help focus attention, but one thing that is paramount is the 'selection and maintenance of the aim'. It is inevitable that soldiers will get distracted by things that need to be urgently dealt with, but this cannot detract from the main objective. Having selected the mission, do not allow yourself to be pulled away from it.

Step 9. After-action review

The last, crucial step is to evaluate the mission, discuss and record any lessons learned, and gather input for next time. Businesses are constantly evolving, and so is the competitive environment. Turning around a crisis-stricken company is not a one-off task that – if it succeeds – allows everyone to pat themselves on the back for a job well done. The nine-step process is an ongoing one. Even hugely successful entrepreneurs such as Elon Musk need to bear in mind a model like this. If the market changes again, which it will, he too would end up in a bad place if he failed to react.

The success, or otherwise, of a transformation plan will always come down to leadership, and any after-action review should be set up to fully scrutinize the leader's efforts. As Napoleon once said: 'There are no bad soldiers, only bad officers.' A leader is at the top of the pyramid, with the organization stretched out beneath them. Sometimes, they will simply be the wrong person for the job. It is a tough thing to say, but when stupid instructions are given or bad plans are made, there is only one person who can take the rap: the leader. The consequences are not as bad as, say, the famed Charge of the Light Brigade, where British commander Lord Raglan foolishly sent his light cavalry up against a well-prepared Russian artillery battery, but for a business that is already on a shaky footing, the outcome of a poor strategy can be severe. Our nine-step process is about helping a leader organize themselves and the business they head, as much so that they do not miss the threats or fail to see the opportunities as to show them the way to recover if they do. It is about helping a leader be in touch with every part of the process. It is vital that any action is followed by a comprehensive review, to ensure all lessons are learned. It is not always easy for a leader to subject themselves to this sort of scrutiny, but without doing so important lessons will be lost.

⌒⁓

The rest of the book looks in detail at the specifics of each of the nine steps to achieve the goal of rebuilding a sustainable, growing business, with each step laid out in full in its own chapter. The steps are sequential, but you need to be aware of what is coming next because there will be a large element of preparation for the next step as you work through each one, and often you will need to work on two or more in parallel. For example, while you are working through step 4 (designing the strategy), you will also be keeping one eye on step 6, thinking about who in your team will be responsible for working on and delivering the individual parts of the strategy, and one on step 7, where you will be considering if a different organizational structure will be necessary to implement the plan. If you are a new leader, brought in to revive an ailing business, you will be dealing with an inherited team, so you need to quickly get to know individual strengths and weaknesses. Alternatively, if you are an incumbent who has been working with the team for a number of years, this is the moment to start asking yourself if particular individuals are the right people to continue this journey. Arguably, the incumbent leader faces a tougher job because they will need to reinvent themselves as a leader in the eyes of their organization and make sweeping changes – something that everyone will be very resistant to.

There is no such thing as a perfect leader. Whatever our training or background, we are fallible human beings who are, in large part, governed by our emotions. In a situation like this, many tough decisions will need to be made, but decision making is, by definition, a cognitive process, and very often our emotions get in the way of rational decisions being made. It is inevitable that we will become stressed or anxious, or that we will suffer from low self-esteem at this time. No matter how good a leader you perceive yourself to be, if you were really honest with yourself you would realize that there have been certain points in your career when you have been overtaken by events on the ground and may not have reacted as you should have done. All leaders, at one time or another, find it difficult to work with extremely competent colleagues, or realize that they have not properly questioned what they have been told because of some deeply felt insecurity about their position.* I would certainly admit to being in situations where emotions have got the better of me during the decision-making process. Our nine steps go a long way towards helping you discard those emotions and be extremely rational and effective in solving the core problems your organization faces.

Whatever the situation – whether you are an established leader or someone new to the business – you have to start at step 1. If you do not create a burning platform and effectively establish your leadership credentials, acknowledging that things have changed and that you are going to reverse that change (or certainly herald a new era), you are going to have a tough time turning things around. This is not an easy position to be in, of course. I have frequently found myself in a situation where I am the third person to have been brought in to sort things out in as many years. The first new

---

* If you are not convinced that even well-known and much-feted military leaders get it wrong, do read *On the Psychology of Military Incompetence* by Norman Dixon (Pimlico, 1994). It is a fantastic book on explaining the concept of military incompetence – and in my opinion, it is equally applicable in the business world.

leader failed and number two did not do the job either, so now it is my turn. I know, before I have even got my feet under the desk, that everyone in the organization will be leaning back and thinking: so, they are sending us another one. *Let's see what this guy does.* This is not an inspiring starting point. This is why step 1, establishing leadership, is so crucial.

Establishing leadership is a delicate balancing act. You need to show who is in charge from the off while also making sure there is good and positive interaction between yourself and the rest of the organization. You will not get anywhere unless everyone is behind you, adding value to the work you are doing. At the same time, though, it is highly likely that jobs will need to be cut and that the people who are left will see some changes to their roles. Individuals may well find themselves having to do 80% of the work they once had to do but with only 50% of the previous resources. They may have produced product X before but now need to produce products X and Y. No one likes change. No one likes to step into unknown territory. But that is part and parcel of a turnaround situation. Everyone will need to change their way of operating on a daily basis.

Some companies already instinctively use many of the processes contained in the nine steps. Many large defence and security companies bidding on multimillion- or multibillion-dollar contracts conduct a detailed initial prospect review or use a phased gate process, for example. Many organizations even go as far as 'wargaming' potential outcomes. They will Red Team or Black Hat* proposals, using teams to actually test the vulnerabilities of a business plan before it is started to manage the risk. Unsurprisingly, these companies tend to be quite successful at what they do thanks to the intensity of these cross-checks. By going through the process of understanding their market, their clients and the competition they are able to design and deliver the products and services that their customers want. Experience also tells me that leaders who founded their businesses tend to

---

* Red Team: put together a team of subject-matter experts to challenge your business plan, proposal or bid. This is also used in battle procedure by the military. Black Hat: similar to Red Team but here participants role play your specific competition with the aim of improving your strategy in order to win.

be more instinctive and consistent when it comes to adopting and pursuing rigorous processes. Perhaps this is because they have more skin in the game. Overall, though, this type of behaviour is rare. In fact, it is far more common to see businesses limping along, sticking with the status quo, often until it is too late to do anything.

I am fully aware that no one likes process for process's sake. Similarly, processes are traditionally the preserve of management, not leadership, and CEOs do not generally like administration. In a crisis situation, though, there is no substitute for a structured thought process, whether you are working through a plan to turn around a business or looking to succeed in a military operation. The very worst thing that can happen is suddenly being brought up short and realizing that you have forgotten a crucial detail just before you launch a merger and acquisition plan or embark on a military operation. This is not simply a case of 'oops, we didn't think about that' – it could have dire ramifications. If you do not have a checklist in your mind, things will get missed. The potential outcomes in the military and business contexts are quite different, of course: if something goes wrong in the field of battle, people will die; if a company fails to hit its revenue targets, or misses out on a deal, it is not life threatening. But if a business goes under, it will have a severe impact on every employee, and there is a big knock-on impact on jobs, mortgages and family life.

As time goes on and you become familiar with the nine-step process, you will find it becomes second nature. Certainly, very experienced businesspeople and military generals have reported being able to cut right through these processes because they are familiar with the sequence of events and they tend not to forget things. Interestingly, though, Richard says that even after twenty-five years in the military, where he has undoubtedly got to the stage where he could use his intuition and experience to cut corners where needed, he still always goes through the relevant process checklist in his mind before he commits to actually giving orders to his people. He says he wants to make absolutely sure that he has not missed anything because, when the pressure is on and the environment is tight, there is no room for mistakes. There is always a danger of missing something.

I appreciate that there are hundreds of books covering every aspect of being a leader, and I am certainly not in the business of reinventing leadership. *Business Leadership Under Fire* is simply a handbook laying out a structured process for leading a business through a crisis. It matters little if your starting point is as a great leader or an average one. The clearly defined steps that I outline will shore up your natural abilities and help you to help your organization make it through troubled times. The nine steps cannot turn you into the perfect leader – if indeed there is such a thing – but if you apply the programme to the best of your ability, you are probably going to significantly reduce the odds of failure and be the best version of yourself. Likewise, this book will not help you figure out what the right strategy is for your particular organization; only you can do that. But the nine steps will lead you towards finding the best strategy and assessing the risks around it.

This book does not advocate reinventing either yourself or your business; it simply takes the best from military and business practices and shows you how to apply them. You will still make some mistakes, and that is fine. As they say in the SAS, how we learn from our successes and failures is what allows us to improve. Or as Vince Lombardi once said, 'If you are not making mistakes, you are not trying hard enough!' Making a mistake is OK – just do not make the same one twice.

Most importantly: do something. Act now. And when speed is of the essence, it is very good to have an intuitive step-by-step process to work with. As Richard says: 'Good decision, great. Bad decision, regrettable. No decision, unforgivable.' Think through the problems that your organization is facing today and then do something. Doing nothing is not a solution, and 'hope' is not a mission verb.

STEP 1. BURNING PLATFORM: ESTABLISHING LEADERSHIP

In the military, it is always fairly obvious when there is a 'burning platform': that is, an unusual and threatening situation that needs to be dealt with pretty smartly or the results will be catastrophic and quite possibly lead to loss of life. In a corporate situation, the scenario is often more nuanced. Those within the organization may be aware that something is wrong and see that profits are a bit off, but it may not yet seem like a desperate situation, and certainly not one that warrants drastic changes in behaviour. It often takes someone from the outside to see that the (metaphorical) platform is on fire and that urgent action is needed.

In fairness to business leaders, the parallels with their military counterparts are generally not always as clear-cut in this situation. The military is cyclical. There is a period in which battalions will warm up for a tour with pre-deployment training. The group will then go out to the theatre of operations for the duration of the tour, where the objective is clearly defined, and when it is over they will return. Then it is on to preparing for the next tour. In business, you are out on the equivalent of operations *the whole time*. There may well be persistent gossip on the shop floor, rumours among suppliers and stories from disgruntled customers, but how do you really know that this is the burning platform that requires immediate action?

The short answer is that, even without explicit data, most people on the senior team will be acutely aware that something is not quite right. (And for a leader that should go doubly, or triply, so.) Yet, what usually happens is that everyone is just too busy working their eight hours a day to really bother trying to understand the issue, much less do something about it. Plus, of course, there is the scenario where it is always someone else's problem. There is no need to get involved.

(Nothing to see here!) Any organization, whether it is 5,000 strong, 10,000 strong or 20,000 strong, acts as a passive mass. It is unusual for people to step forward and volunteer to get out of their comfort zone or do anything too radical. When the proverbial hits the fan, it is far more likely that they will sit there and watch it happen.

If you would like a taster of the consequences of ignoring the burning platform, consider the following tale of two bookstore chains. Back in 2007, when online giant Amazon produced the original Kindle, the majority of book retailers, including Borders (one of the leading booksellers in the US), barely gave the clearly smouldering platform a second glance. But rival chain Barnes & Noble did, and it moved quickly on multiple fronts. It aggressively reduced costs and reorganized stores to make them more customer friendly. At the same time, it invested in development of an e-reader of its own, debuting the Nook in 2009. The Nook was a worthy competitor to the Kindle – indeed, it was better than it in certain key ways. It was good enough to capture nearly a third of the e-reader market and, most importantly, to save the company. Borders did not fare so well: it filed for bankruptcy that same year. Ignore a burning platform at your peril.

Naturally, it is ultimately the responsibility of a leader to say: this is not right, something has to change. This is why it is so often the case that it takes a new leader coming in to highlight the extent of the burning platform, having observed it dispassionately from the outside. He or she has to take the first step in making everyone aware of the fact that things are going to have to be done differently. This is not to say that an incumbent cannot do the same job. In fact, the nine steps are designed for exactly this scenario: to help existing leaders stand back, view the burning platform from afar, then start the process of making the necessary changes.

For clarity, it should also be noted here that the burning platform does not always need to indicate looming meltdown, where a company is on the brink of insolvency. A burning platform could be as simple as what transpires when a company is bought by private equity and the new owners expect improved performance in order to realize their investment in a timely manner. I have certainly been brought into businesses in these circumstances and in each case have used the burning platform as my starting point. It is the ideal way to be very open with the team about the current state of play and to indicate that everyone needs to work towards improving performance. A burning platform is an indication of hard work to come, but it is not a negative message. Quite the opposite, in fact.

The point of the burning platform is for a leader to begin a conversation with their team. There is a need for a change/transformation programme. This is the 'why', and it signifies the time for telling everyone that they all need to step up.

Getting the situation under control

If you are a new leader, this first step is your opportunity to introduce yourself and tell everyone a little bit about what you have done previously and about how you like to work. For an incumbent leader, the burning platform is an opportunity to re-establish your leadership credentials. *Things are going to change and this is why I am the right person to lead you through that change.*

Richard's take on this from his military career, inspired by the times when he took over as a commanding officer and was faced with an entirely new battalion, is that there is a finite period of time in which to impose your personality on a situation. This applies both to the optimum amount of time available to deliver the message and to how soon a commander delivers it after being put in charge of a particular group. As for the latter, the new leader should speak as soon as possible. In the case of the former, twenty minutes is often all that is available when it comes to keeping the attention of the average soldier, who may then quickly switch to thinking about their next meal or engagement with the enemy.

If morale is not high because of what came before, or what might come next, these twenty minutes are the best opportunity a new commander will get to win everyone over to their side and their way of thinking. In terms of delivery, military leaders prioritize finding a short, punchy way to help everyone understand what they are about and what their values are. They also need to communicate that they have an understanding of the situation and are very clear about what they want everyone to do. In Richard's case, one of the key points he always prioritized was to ensure that everyone knew that he was a leader who would reward good behaviour, but one who would also firmly deal with any bad behaviour.

Richard found a powerful way to achieve this when he took over a battalion in Afghanistan in the middle of a tour of duty. To add an extra layer of challenge, the new assignment meant he was now leading a large battle group of 650 men, split between two separate locations. He therefore had to get people together as best he could to deliver his message while accepting that not everyone could be there.

Richard did not want to sugar-coat the task ahead. This was during his second tour of Afghanistan and he was already well aware that the Taliban were the toughest enemy he had ever fought. The fighting force had a natural warlike character, a vehement dislike of foreigners on their land and an enduring belief that, if they died, they would go to a better place. He needed to convey all this to his battle group and prepare them for what lay ahead. His solution was to produce one single sheet of paper that outlined his values, his working ethos and what he wanted from his battle group. The focus was on keeping things both succinct and meaningful. His message, which was conveyed in a session lasting no more than twenty minutes, was boiled down to three key points, which he announced as follows:

> You're infantry men and we are on operations. I require you to do three things. I need you to shoot straight, run fast and drive on.

Now that he had their complete attention, he continued:

> Shooting straight means more than just the obvious. It also indicates that I require complete honesty. That's being honest with yourself, honest with your men and honest with me. Run fast doesn't mean in a physically fit sort of way. That is a given. It means being faster than the enemy in everything we do. Finally, driving on is saying there will be tough times, but you have been well trained and you will be well led.
>
> What I require of you now is to exercise that determination to defeat the enemy and achieve our objectives.

Richard ended his short speech on an upbeat note:

> In my twenty years, I have never lost a firefight yet, and I don't intend to do so now with you alongside me. I will make sure you have the right resources and equipment, clear instructions and that I will be leading you and with you.

There is a lot that can be learned from this concise, clear message, much of which is applicable in a business setting too. Although the speech was brief, everyone immediately learned a lot about their new leader and his values. Equally importantly, they could see that Richard was not going to commit them to anything while he was sitting in a command post twenty kilometres away.

Both Richard and I agree that it does not matter if you are from a military background or a civilian one, if you do not get this initial address right, you will be playing catch-up from there on in. The burning platform presents a window in which every new and incumbent leader has the opportunity to introduce themselves and set out what they intend to achieve. It is the time to take extreme ownership of the situation, where everyone can see that you are there to get the job done.

Something every leader does have to be aware of at this stage is to not go too far with their rallying cry. If you stand up and say that a business is in deep, deep trouble and there is a danger it might not survive, there is a real possibility that the message will go far further than intended. Use the wrong words, or words that can be misinterpreted in any way, and you could easily end up in a worse situation than you are already in. You might find your suppliers taking it upon themselves the next day to tell the purchasing department that they are no longer delivering unless they get payment up front. Customer-facing staff may speak out of turn, alerting loyal customers to the fact that they might soon need to seek alternative suppliers. Soon, everyone, customers and competitors alike, will be fully apprised of the situation, and rest assured that the competitors will be having a field day. When you are already starting from a position of weakness, this would be a terrible development. The goal of this initial stage is therefore to shake up the organization, to explain that things are going to have to change in order for things to get better, but to not go overboard with the projections of imminent failure if people do not all pull their weight. Put the changes into context and give staff as much of a positive spin as you can; explain that the company is losing money, or market share, or has cash flow issues, but make it clear that it *can* make a recovery. Tell people that, in order to do so, something needs to change and that a plan is being worked on right now to turn things around. It will require a lot of effort by everyone, but the results will be good for all.

Likewise, if it is highly likely that there may be a reduction in headcount, I articulate this fact early on in this initial meeting. It is the first thing anyone will be thinking about at a time like this. There is nothing more dispiriting for a team than to leave that possibility hanging, yet unsaid, only for the CEO to announce a wave of redundancies six months down the line. Normally, I initiate the cost-takeout exercise as quickly as possible in order to get it done and out of the way. This creates the necessary breathing space for the business to execute the recovery via the transformation plan. If you ignore the potential for job losses, there is a very real possibility that everyone will be too focused on whether or not they might need to leave and/or will begin actively polishing their CV. One thing is for sure: you will not have their full attention for the task ahead. If there is a possibility of redundancies, give as accurate a picture as you can according to what you know at this stage. Indeed, as a general rule, always be clear and honest in everything you communicate during this initial talk. People will catch you out if you lie, and that could cause problems further down the line. You can, of course, communicate in an economic fashion. In other words, you do not have to say too much at this point because it is early days. However, do not make any promises you cannot keep.

I use a colour-coding method to manage any short-term restructuring programme – to make sure I get it right while also adhering to the principle of getting bad news out, up front. The aim is to take out cost without compromising future growth while also ring-fencing sales, and I find that the following system helps me work through what it is prudent to do at this early stage. My four-colour system is as follows:

- Project white: white collar cost takeout.
- Project blue: blue collar cost take out, preferably without shutting factories down permanently if it is important to keep capacity for recovery.
- Project green: purchasing and supply chain management savings and efficiency.
- Project red: sales force effectiveness, efficiency and pricing. This might be a short-term measure ahead of the strategy being changed later in the process, and it should only be done if there are obvious and concrete benefits to doing it at this early stage.

The objective of the burning platform is to galvanize people into action. The way to do this is not to inject terror but to give hope through good leadership. The situation is bad, but it is not unrecoverable.

I am reminded of another Sun Tzu quote here:

> Soldiers in desperate straits lose their sense of fear. If there is no place of refuge, they will stand firm. If they are in the heart of a hostile country, they will show a stubborn front. If there is no help for it, they will fight hard. Thus, without waiting to be marshalled, the soldiers will be constantly on the alert, and without waiting to be asked, they will do your will; without restrictions, they will be faithful; without giving orders, they can be trusted.

If a bad situation is presented in the right way, it can be highly motivational. By the same token, if you lead poorly, you cannot pretend that things will be OK, come what may. Sun Tzu is helpful once again on this subject:

> If, however, you are indulgent, but unable to make your authority felt; kind-hearted, but unable to enforce your commands; and incapable, moreover, of quelling disorder; then your soldiers must be likened to spoilt children; they are useless for any practical purpose.

When you are planning your burning platform approach, do so from a standpoint that prioritizes the injection of an aura of good leadership.

Leading the transformation

My preferred way of working during this initial stage is to meet with the executive team as a large group. This will usually involve up to twenty or so people, from across operating and staff units, and, just like the military approach used by Richard and his colleagues, this is where I outline who I am and what is important to me, alongside my initial reading of the situation.

MY VALUES, ETHOS & EXPECTATIONS	**MY VALUES**	1.	Leadership is humility, service & ownership
		2.	People are key
		3.	Experience and knowledge are great assets, but key is to continue to learn
	MY WORK ETHIC	1.	Listen and learn
		2.	Decision making on basis of facts, facts and facts
		3.	Embrace change and act on its needs
		4.	Always try to be the best version of you
	MY EXPECTATION OF TEAM	1.	Of your job/role: Set priorities and focus
		2.	Our relationship: Don't disobey but if disagree come forward
		3.	If something is unclear, ask
		4.	Bad news upfront

My values, ethos and expectations. (© Pepyn Dinandt.)

It is not an extensive meeting that outlines the precise strategy for the way forward, but rather an opportunity to acknowledge that something is not right and that there will be changes ahead.

Following this meeting, which is generally held in the company headquarters, I will go out and visit each of the organization's satellite branches and factories to deliver a more nuanced message to the rest of the team below executive level. The communication concerning the depth of the problem will be less explicit than it was with the people at management level, apprising everybody of the situation but in a less detailed manner. The message is, essentially: things need to change, but we have a plan.

Ideally, these follow-up meetings will be face to face, as far as possible, which is the most effective way to spread the word. Depending on the numbers in the organization, it may not be possible or practical to speak to everyone in this way, and sometimes it might anyway be more appropriate (particularly post Covid-19) to speak via webinars or video links. A curt email explaining that change is afoot is far too impersonal though. The aim is to speak in person or online with a good proportion of the organization to ensure your message has enough momentum to get to everyone else.

Ensuring that *everyone* gets the message properly is key. This is why it is crucial to make sure that the nub of what is said is also written down, otherwise you may end up with a bad case of the 'broken telephone game'. In the military they deal with this not simply by taking note of the intentions of the commanding level and the one just below, but also by looking intently at how messages have been received two levels down. Richard always made a point of sitting down with people to whom he had just given orders to get their feedback, and then, after that, he would go one level down to speak to those that the orders had been passed on to. This was to make sure they did not have a situation where messages became vastly distorted as they were disseminated down the ranks.*

It is important to get into the habit of 'walking the ground' with your people and saying: 'OK guys, this is the mission, what do you see as your part in it?' This is the only way for a leader to be sure in their own mind that the message has filtered down properly. If it has not, that needs to be addressed. At this stage, as I move around making sure the burning platform scenario is widely understood, I re-emphasize that we recognize that there is a problem in the business and that changes will need to be made but that right now there is no concrete plan. We will be working on that in the coming weeks. My goal is to make myself highly visible as the leader of an

---

* As Richard jokes, he did not want his message of 'send reinforcements, we're going to advance' to morph into 'send three and fourpence, we're going to a dance'. That interpretation would clearly lead to a very different outcome!

organization as well as explain the direction of travel. After telling everyone that you are about to take them into a hostile environment, you need to be there with them. The military spends a lot of time assessing the best place for commanders to be at any given time, making judgements about where they will have the most influence. The ability to be close enough to your people for them to understand that you share the risk but far enough to be able to get an overview about what all the various groups are doing is a perpetual balancing act, and one that it is crucial to get right. You do not want to be what they call a seagull leader: one who hovers overhead doing nothing and then flies in, shits over everyone, and flies off again!

It is not a given in business that we all arrive fully formed, with a complete range of leadership abilities. Indeed, very often, people find themselves in charge following a series of promotions without having had any formal training for each stage, let alone for the top job. This is the opposite of what happens in the military, where people are selected for leadership and then put through a vigorous period of training before being put in charge of anything. It is for this reason that, with a tough assignment ahead, you must grasp the opportunity at this stage to take stock of your own leadership style and your abilities, perhaps canvassing some of your trusted colleagues for this exercise. A great deal of your opportunity for establishing leadership at this initial stage is based on your strengths and weaknesses. Are you someone who is highly articulate and well versed in clear instructions? Are you confident and charming? Can you summarize complex topics in a clear and engaging way? If the answer to any of these questions is no, or perhaps 'not as much as I could be', then you may need to consider how you will shore up these skills while dealing with this crucial – burning platform – opener ahead of the mission. One of the advantages of the nine-step programme is that it is a perfectly designed framework for ensuring that if there are any weaknesses they are immediately addressed, so you can focus on the task in hand. Thus, whatever your abilities, whether positive or negative, if the framework is applied properly it will lead you and your organization to the goal. The starting point, though, is to recognize the aspects of leadership in which you may not be as agile as others.

The most successful leaders, whether in the military, business or sport, are the ones with a heightened sense of self-awareness. Part of the way they get to understand their weaknesses is to work with others and act on their feedback. It is unlikely, however, that subordinates will ever directly say: 'that was a terrible decision' or 'you've made a real mistake'. The hierarchy of business rarely allows for such direct criticism. People are much more likely to say 'yes' and then get on with things even if they patently disagree with a decision. For this reason, a leader needs to actively listen to their audience and watch them too, in order to pick up those additional nuances indicated by body language. They listen to understand too, rather than simply to respond. This is a crucial part of step 1. While you are delivering your short, well-considered speech, or visiting satellite offices introducing yourself and the plan for change, watch what effect your words are having on your audience. This will give you many clues about how receptive, or otherwise, the team is to the task ahead. It will also indicate which skills you will be most heavily reliant on.

At the beginning of this book, I introduced the idea that we are, of course, only human – subject to the vagaries of our emotions and insecurities. I gained a lot of inspiration about incompetence in leadership (a harsh term, but a necessary one) from the work of Norman Dixon, who coincidentally, was one of Richard's tutors at Sandhurst.

Dixon describes three dangerous incompetencies, or weaknesses, or neurotic disabilities, that are as applicable to business leadership and decision making as they are to military leadership.

- *Pontification.* When those in authority are threatened by the facts, pontification is often used to preserve their omniscience rather than accept a new truth.
- *Cognitive dissonance.* The less justified a decision is, the greater the cognitive dissonance. The inability to admit that one has been wrong (and, in doing so, compromise one's self-esteem) will be greater the more wrong one has been, and the more wrong one has been, the more bizarre will be the subsequent attempts to justify the unjustifiable.

- *Neglect of risk.* Individuals who become anxious under conditions of stress, or who are prone to be defensive and deny anything that threatens their self-esteem, tend to be bad at judging whether the risks they take are justified and rational. This means they usually end up taking far too much risk in light of the situation and its challenges.

To be truly effective in this nine-step approach you need to make a genuinely honest and objective assessment of yourself in the context of such neurotic disabilities, understanding your weaknesses as much as your strengths. As Sun Tzu said: 'If you know ... yourself, you need not fear the result of a hundred battles.' Our nine-step approach works best with the highest degree of self-awareness and rationality possible.

Establishing a rhythm

The acknowledgement of the burning platform also marks the time where a leader begins to establish a rhythm in the way they work with their team. An assessment will need to be made about how often you need to speak with various departments and the individuals within them. It would be entirely self-defeating to burden everyone (and yourself) with too many meetings at this stage; indeed, it is never a good idea to do so at any stage of a company's lifecycle: they just get in the way of getting things done. But, by the same token, there need to be open lines of communication. You need access to up-to-date information, and the team needs a platform where they feel comfortable in offloading and making you aware of looming problems.

There is another useful lesson to be learned from the military in this respect: do not be selfish with time. Time is the critical information requirement for any commander. Whenever there is a problem, commanders immediately look at the time they have available. The rule is to take one-third for yourself and give two-thirds to your people. Once you give them orders, they have to think about what they have been told and then they have to give their orders.

Being unselfish with time plays a big role in ensuring that everyone on the team is left with the very firm impression that their boss is someone who listens. They are someone who will actively enquire about the opinions of others and are open to hearing better ideas. I would like to think people would say about me: tough boss, but he listens. Many of the solutions for problems within a business invariably lie within the company. A great number of team members will be very smart indeed and will have first-hand knowledge of the issues that blight an organization, but all too often no one even bothers to ask them what they think. Time and again, we see CEOs begin the work on the turnaround and transformation process by bringing in consultants to look at a business and tell them what is wrong. I spent three years working at McKinsey, where I learned a lot (I like to refer to this period as my paid period at 'business school'). Much of what we did was to go out and speak to people within organizations and then, often, we would rewrite their ideas into presentations that were illustrated with numerous charts. It makes a lot more sense for CEOs to cut out this stage, and the huge expense that goes along with it, and set a precedent that shows they value speaking to their people themselves. They can use consultants to supplement their own investigational activities and fact finding into the existing problems and issues, but the leadership must be in the middle of the action: they should never delegate this very important part of the first step.

For this culture of openness to work properly, there needs to be an environment in which people feel comfortable to voice their true opinion – this is something that is easier said than done, though, particularly when everyone is fearful for the future. The best way to foster this culture is to actively show that people's contributions do make a difference. At Sandhurst Royal Military Academy, part of the training that is relevant in this respect is nicknamed 'slate a mate', which sounds rather like attacking a friend but actually has some real merit in teaching the value of speaking out and constructive feedback. Every few weeks, following an exercise, a group of eight officer cadets are asked to mark each other on their strengths and weaknesses. Richard recounts how, early on, the remarks are endearingly polite: 'he tried really hard', 'he's a great team player'. Unsurprisingly, a group that lives and works together are reluctant to criticize one another. Then, under encouragement from instructors, the comments begin to become more robust. Indeed, they can often go to the other extreme and become positively spiky: 'he didn't put in the effort', 'he's too lazy'. Since the comments are then shared around the group, the spiky comments escalate for a while, in a sort of tit-for-tat style. But eventually everyone realizes that this is not a satisfactory state of affairs and, most importantly, that it is not a very effective exercise if no one is being fair and honest. At this point, slate a mate comes into its own. Everyone begins to make pertinent observations that can make a real difference to the development of the individuals in question and the group as a whole. It becomes a really useful exercise in self-awareness. If, say, someone does not perform as well as they might on an exercise, it is helpful to know and work towards understanding why. This type of honest discourse is a useful way to begin to shore up any weaknesses. If you know what you are not good at, you can do something about it.

Creating an open and honest environment in a business setting requires this type of self-awareness, not just from individual team members but from leadership too. It also requires humility, since the team needs to understand that the person at the top is prepared to listen without criticism and is open to seeing if anyone else has a better idea.

If you look back at any big business failure you will most likely see a glaring lack of humility or ownership from leadership. Somehow, despite all the evidence to the contrary, when a business fails it is rare for anyone to put their hands up and say: 'I screwed up.' There is still less chance of an apology. This is despite the fact that a complete lack of humility can make a bad situation a whole lot worse. Perhaps the most famous recent example of this comes courtesy of BP CEO Tony Hayward, who offended millions with his glib statement: 'I'd like my life back.' This utterly thoughtless comment came in the wake of the 2010 Deepwater Horizon explosion, which killed eleven men and caused untold damage to the Gulf of Mexico. To compound the gaffe, Hayward initially grossly underestimated the damage caused by the 4.9 million barrels of oil that eventually gushed out of the stricken rig, claiming that the spill was 'very, very modest' and 'relatively tiny'. He was later forced to revise his statement to admit it was an 'environmental catastrophe'.

Hayward is by no means alone in lacking humility. One cannot help thinking that the lack of this character trait must have contributed in some large way to the fall from grace of ThyssenKrupp, which was once a towering symbol of German industrial prowess. Industry and City commentators were baffled by the firm's 2007 decision to spend $12 billion on building two of the most modern steel mills in the world in Alabama in the US and in Brazil. It was not just that Brazil is a notoriously difficult market to operate in; it was also mystifying why the company's board decided they had to undertake *two* such ambitious projects simultaneously. Even to a casual observer, the somewhat grandiosely titled Steel Americas project had to be a tremendously risky decision. And so it proved to be. The world steel industry peaked in that same year, and a year later the financial crisis hit. ThyssenKrupp lost $11 billion on the two plants, which sold steel at below the cost of production. The company subsequently admitted that Steel Americas was a sign that leadership culture in the company had failed.[6]

Contrast this with what can happen when a leader does admit that he or she is fallible and has screwed up (as we all do now and again). This is what happened in 2008, when Maple Leaf Foods in Toronto was faced with a disastrous listeria outbreak in some of its packaged meat plants. After meat became infected, there were nine confirmed deaths and eleven further suspected ones connected with eating the tainted products. Against the advice of his lawyers and accountants, CEO Michael McCain immediately stepped up and said: 'It's our fault and we're going to fix it.' His message, on TV and YouTube, was sincere.

'It's not about money or legal liability; this is about our being accountable for providing customers with safe food,' McCain said in his broadcast. 'This is a terrible tragedy. To those people who became ill, and to the families who have lost loved ones, I want to express my deepest and most sincere sympathies.'[7]

McCain's *mea culpa* has been widely praised for saving the company's reputation – even securing its future. Indeed, the stock price, which had initially taken a hammering, actually rose on the back of McCain's quick and appropriate response. As one newspaper opinion piece noted: 'I actually trust the man!'

Interestingly, humility is another of the skills that is taught very early on at Sandhurst, where the motto is 'Serve to Lead'. In fact, the first six weeks of training have earned the nickname of the 'beat-up'. This is the period during which a bunch of raw recruits who will have mainly come straight from university, where they have been living a fairly self-centred life of looking after themselves while they get their degree, are worked as hard as humanly possible. No matter how fit, capable and positive they are when they arrive, they will be entirely changed in a matter of days. The aim is not to 'break' the new recruits, but rather to teach them that their new career is not all about them. Each new recruit needs to learn to lean on their fellow recruits and, more importantly, put others first at every opportunity. Unsurprisingly, Sandhurst graduates often say that some of their strongest and most enduring lifelong friendships are made during those first six gruelling weeks.

In a similar fashion, David Stirling, the founder of the SAS, included humility as a significant part of the regimental ethos when he defined its culture. Success in the military is never about you, the leader, it is about your team, and that requires empathy, self-aware-ness and, above all, humility. When things go really, really well, it is for the leader to stand up and say it is all down to the team. Likewise, when things go badly, they should personally take the blame.

If your leadership style is not traditionally one associated with humility, the nine steps can be a useful reminder that will help shore up the skill and help you organize your thinking. Having explained that there is something wrong in the business, the team will be wait-ing for the leader to do something. This is the moment to briefly outline the steps that you will be going through, which will involve listening to others to understand the extent of the problem. Listen-ing and accepting input is, of course, a key aspect of humility.

It is important to add that humility is not the same as appearing to be everyone's best friend. Machiavelli, the Italian diplomat, philosopher and writer, who also wrote a book entitled *The Art of War*,[8] differenti-ates between being loved as a leader and loathed as a leader. He argues that being feared as a leader is OK, but it must never turn into loathing. You cannot be everyone's buddy, and you cannot be too humble. You are still the boss and everyone needs to think of you in that way.

This is a point that Richard wholeheartedly agrees with. There is a natural tendency to want to be close to people when you have shared hard times with them and have seen them take huge risks under your command. A military commander also needs to seem approachable. Yet, soldiers have to view their leader with respect, rather than as a great bloke and one of the lads. Thus, although Richard socialized with his officers, none of them would have dreamed of calling him by his Christian name, and he never invited them to do so. He was always on his guard for seeming to be too chummy. This practice has continued into his career in corporate life, where he is always wary of being over-friendly with the chairs of the firms in which he has worked.

Business leaders need to make some very tough decisions, particularly in a situation like this, and this means they cannot in any way be subjective. They must always be objective. If a leader is consistently powerful and assertive, the team will have confidence in their ability to get the job done. There will be a tacit understanding that the leader will make the right decisions and will not be swayed by individual relationships. Although the leader listens and is humble, he or she has a plan and knows how to make it work. The tough calls will be made where they need to be made.

And what if it all goes right?

It may seem a little premature to be planning a victory lap right at the beginning of the nine steps, but this is the time when you should be doing just that. Failure to plan for success could put you right back where you started – it could even lead to a worse situation than you find yourself in now. Again, this is a scenario that is highly familiar in military planning, although the military do not, as we will see, always get it entirely right.

When planning a campaign, there are three main priorities. The first is situational awareness. When things get to the status of a burning platform, it is a very clear indication to commanders that they have missed something. It shows that there has not been enough assessment prior to this point, and that has left an opening for a threat to evolve. Everyone now needs to be made aware that something new has to happen, or that something is going to change. This leads on naturally to the second stage: contingency planning. This is where leaders set out what they are going to do about the new situation. If you kick off a restructuring programme early on in this process, one of the topics to be aware of is that your initial cost-cutting exercise does not compromise your ability to recover volume if the current business model is still in any way relevant. As you move through the various steps, the subsequent plan will look at the most likely scenarios but also at the worst possible outcome, which will lead to a completely new course of action. The final, important stage, which runs concurrently, is to plan for 'catastrophic success'.

For a prime example of the consequences of not getting this third stage right, we need look no further than the Iraq War of 2003, when a coalition led by the US invaded Iraq, deposing the country's authoritarian president Saddam Hussein. It was, as many readers will vividly remember, an emotionally charged event, culminating in chaotic scenes as Iraqis toppled statues of their leader in the capital Baghdad in an unprecedented show of contempt. The US Brigadier General, Vincent Brooks, who was the Central Command spokes-person in Qatar, said at the time: 'With every day that passes, we are breaking the grip of the regime.' Yet, inexplicably, little thought was given to the ensuing power vacuum in a country that had been under the iron grip of Hussein since 1979. To be fair, none of this was a huge surprise to many senior figures in the coalition. Indeed, the extent of this miscalculation in planning for catastrophic suc-cess was laid bare to Richard when was working at the MacDill Air Force Base in Tampa, Florida, a year earlier, during the early stages of preparation for the invasion. Richard and another senior colleague had been asked to provide Donald Rumsfeld, the then Secretary of State for Defence, with an estimate of how many troops on the ground would be required to rebuild the infrastructure of Iraq, put good governance in place and reconstruct amenities such as elec-tricity and water. The number they came up with was 400,000, and that figure was duly presented to Rumsfeld. He said nothing for a few moments and then asked them to repeat the number. When they did so, they received a two-word response: 'Get out!' It transpired that the number the Secretary of State had previously been given by trusted advisors was 90,000. The subsequent chaos in Iraq and the surrounding areas is testament to the accuracy of the revised projections.

In business, it is tempting to focus everything on what is required for turning around a bad situation. It can be pretty daunting thinking about achieving only that. But what would happen if you get everything right? What if demand for your products goes stratospheric? In this eventuality, you would need to be able to meet that demand, and that would require having supply and production systems in place. Leaving things until the demand curve begins to turn north is too late. If you fail at the planning for catastrophic success stage, you may end up in a worse situation than before, with a larger number of disgruntled customers. Meanwhile, your competitors will seize the opportunity and move in to exploit the weakness. It is not an obvious action to plan for success, especially when everything looks so bleak, but getting the timing right on this is just as important as spotting and acting on the burning platform in the first place. It can be the difference between a successful future and weighing up whether to leap back into a raging sea from the seemingly ever-alight platform.

STEP 2. ANALYSIS AND DETERMINATION OF THE MISSION TARGETS

A well-defined mission is the foundation of effective leadership. Without a clear objective, it is impossible to set out a credible plan, and still less so to know when you have achieved the goal. Step 2 is about making sure you embark on this process with a detailed and achievable mission. It is a step that is often ignored, or certainly not given enough attention, to the detriment of all else that follows.

In the context of the military, the idea of missing out on setting clear mission targets seems unthinkable, but it does occasionally happen. When Richard's unit was deployed to Bosnia in 1995, settling in a position sixty-five miles behind enemy lines, there was no defined mission. Rest assured, though, the unit immediately fought to obtain one, getting straight onto the phone with the force commander, General Sir Rupert Smith, to ask for precise details about what needed to be done. After some deliberation, the response was that the priorities were to safeguard the civilian population, as far as it was possible to do so in a war. This was, as Richard concedes, an intent not a mission. Nevertheless, it was a crucial development that gave Richard's unit much-needed focus.

Business leaders need to push hard to get precise details of the mission too. It is not always a given that the person who entrusted you with this turnaround challenge will have a crystal-clear goal in mind. This 'sovereign' (to use the words of Sun Tzu) – whether they are a company founder, the board of a public company or a private equity firm – may initially simply define the mission as 'turning things around and getting the organization back on its feet'. If this is the case, or indeed if the scope of the mission is in any way uncertain, now is the moment to insist on complete clarity. After step 1, where you defined the 'why', this is the 'what'.

By this stage, you will have spent the past few weeks inside the company, getting to know the team and finding out more about the issues being faced. To return to my earlier restaurant analogy, you, the new chef, have by now fully inspected the kitchen and have gotten to know the existing team there. You will have the benefit of more data on the situation after having spoken with a few people at different levels of the organization, although right now the information you have will not yet be quite deep enough to allow you to see the full picture. It is now time to sit down with the business owner – or the private equity firm or the board that appointed you – to determine exactly what it is that they want you to do. What is the mission? This, of course, requires that the leader fully understands who it is who has the authority to define the target. Are they talking to an entire board, or to just one person? Are they getting their information from one level above them, or is it two?

If understanding a mission is the only way to ensure success, what do we mean by 'mission'? If you were to break it down, the mission is a summary of the problems that need to be fixed, which will, in turn, give you clarity on what needs to be done to resolve them. The mission might centre around an organization's perilous financial situation and what caused the current losses. The focus might be on the rise of a competitor who has snatched away the business's core customer base. Perhaps the new kid on the block has come up with a fantastic new product that has taken the whole sector by surprise. Or maybe the company has simply failed to keep up with even the most gradual shifts in the market. There may be entirely unexpected external factors such as the Covid-19 pandemic, which changed the trading market for so many businesses almost overnight. The mission is about taking stock of the current situation, where the organization stands within it, and the severity of the decline. Is it a total collapse, or are some aspects of the business doing OK? Is the organization entirely responsible for where it finds itself now, or were there external factors that were entirely beyond its control? The aim here is for clarity that will allow a leader to have complete focus when subsequently setting out their priorities.

Richard's experience in Bosnia notwithstanding, understanding the mission is a process that the military generally pays a great deal of attention to. Indeed, he cites General Sir Rupert Smith as someone who is particularly effective at this. General Smith, who served in the British Army in East and South Africa, Arabia, the Caribbean, Europe and Malaysia before commanding the British 1st Armoured Division during the Gulf War, underlined the importance of a clear mission by making sure that his staff spent at least 70% of their time understanding the problem, with the rest of their time spent on coming up with a solution. Key to this process was the commander clearly conveying their intent to everyone around them, so they were in full possession of all relevant facts. After all, unless everyone really understands the what and the why, they run the risk of getting it wrong or of constant meddling from exasperated superiors who are frustrated that their mission is not being pursued correctly.

The military process of mission analysis centres around the following big questions that need to be answered:

- What are my superior commanders' intents one level up and two levels up, and what is my part in them?
- What is my mission and therefore my tasks, both specified and implied?
- What are the constraints?
- What if the situation changes and how could it change?

The simpler the goals, the simpler it is to complete the mission

Where the military and business situations often differ is that in the corporate world, a CEO may have many paymasters, and this can muddy the waters. Unless a leader is working for the founder, or the owner, of a private company, where they can get a straight answer to the question 'What is it you want me to achieve and how will you measure it?', it is quite likely that they will need to take into account the views of multiple stakeholders. Take private equity as an example. Many of my past appointments have been made by private equity firms, which have brought me in to sort out troubled businesses. Private equity is, of course, primarily concerned with investor returns, or money multiples and the internal rate of return. Where it gets complicated is that these organizations are governed by a board and it is not unusual for different people on that board to have differing interpretations of mission targets. Yes, they might all want the company to get back into profit, but opinions can and do vary on priorities. Invariably, each individual will harbour some additional side goals that they firmly believe are vital to the main mission. These side goals may be improving market share, or net promoter score, or customer retention or any one of another dozen or so side goals. What it all adds up to is a far more complicated brief than you might find in a military situation. It can become even more complicated if you are a CEO appointed to turn around a failing public company. Now, as well as pressure from the board, who may harbour different goals, there will be a wide range of opinions from powerful investors to throw into the mix. This is why, very often, when you read the corporate reports of quoted businesses, they will include a dizzying list of twenty mission-critical goals or more. Alongside goals relating to productivity, profit and performance, there will be a host of additional goals involving corporate social responsibility, environmental social governance and increasing the share of women in management. Often, these additional goals will simply not make sense when measured against the trouble a business is in. Memorably, in one private equity situation where the company was in exceptionally dire straits, I was asked to make an employee satisfaction survey a priority. The board was concerned about whether everyone was truly happy. I had to gently explain that their concern was all very well, but if we failed to prioritize the turnaround these employees would lose their jobs altogether.

As you can imagine, it can get pretty complicated for a leader when they are trying to plug a £50 million hole but also have instructions to solve a whole host of other issues. It puts an added layer of pressure on a CEO, especially if the board holds them up to it at every meeting. You will be thinking to yourself: if I am supposed to be making the company profitable again, why am I chasing this, that and the other? This is why a leader's first priority should be to push hard for a crystal clear and succinct mission. Without that, it is almost impossible for a leader to work out what they stand for, or what needs to be done. Not only that, but a rambling, or ill-defined mission will be a constant distraction as you get into the thick of the action while still wondering what exactly it is you are aiming for.

Being asked to focus on an unwieldy number of goals can also raise another issue: the fact that many of them might actually be contradictory. Imagine, for example, that health and safety is highlighted as a significant issue that must be high on the list of priorities. How, then, would that fit in if another one of the key goals is to maximize profits at the earliest opportunity? While focusing on health and safety in factories is a laudable aim, the necessary adjustments can cost a vast amount of money, significantly eroding the chances of meeting the other key goal.

I often think that this is why the CEOs of public companies are perhaps a little jealous of those leading private ones. Private company bosses have the luxury of being able to focus on a small number of clear, crisp goals. It is the same reason why, in the military, everyone prefers to be out on operations. While operations are dangerous, life is simple. Commanders do not have to deal with all the BS – things like barrack inspections, or hosting the General Officer Commanding for a luncheon, or doing good works in the local community. This might all be important stuff, but it is relentless and time consuming. Out on operations there are just two or three key priorities for leaders to focus on: doing better than the enemy, keeping as many of your people alive as possible, and keeping morale high. That is much easier and more satisfying to get to grips with.

Prioritizing is key. In the armed forces it is expected that leadership will be entirely focused on the designated 'main effort' – that one activity that is essential to mission success. If there is an upcoming operation, it is perfectly acceptable for a commanding officer to say: we need to focus on X. Whether X is getting to grips with a new weapon, honing fighting skills or looking after the welfare of the families who are about to be left behind, these priorities are accepted without question. This is predominantly because it is easy to justify priorities against the potential loss of life. Even so, I try to be equally ruthless with my time when prioritizing. I do not mean simply in terms of putting things in order of importance; I mean in actually saying what I am going to do and what I am not going to do. I should add that it is never as easy, or as clear cut, in a business setting. You may be entirely focused on sorting out a £50 million deficit, but rest assured that every time you walk into the boardroom the first question you will be asked is: how are we getting on with that employee satisfaction survey?

It is certainly in your best interests to narrow down the mission as far as is humanly possible. The simpler your goal, the simpler your mission, and the easier it is for you to focus. Plus, it will be easier to convey to the team what needs to be achieved. A long list of goals increases the possibility for misinterpretation. You want a short list of meaningful targets that can be easily communicated and understood by everyone. Empowerment and objective delegation is also crucial, so that everyone can focus on the 'main effort' and give substance to it.

Is the mission achievable?

Once there is clarity about the extent of what you have been asked to achieve, you can begin to properly interrogate and quantify the goals to ensure they are realistic and achievable. It helps to break the mission into qualitative goals, which are relevant to financial performance, and those that are not relevant to financial performance, and it is also important to get a feeling for their timescale: whether they are short-term, medium-term or long-term goals. This is the point where question three of the mission analysis featured above really comes in handy. What are the constraints? Is there a hard time limit? Does it have to be done in three months? Is there a financial resource constraint? Is there anything that may impede the successful execution of the mission? This is an important and oft-neglected step that leaders frequently ignore when setting their mission.

Mission goals may sometimes initially seem straightforward but in actual fact, upon interrogation, it is revealed that they bring with them a number of unspoken, implied goals. For instance, perhaps you are challenged to make the business more innovative, or to lead the way in new technology. The implied goal here is that you would need to invest a considerable amount in R&D. Alternatively, if there is a stated goal to grow the international business as part of the recovery line, this also means that a big investment will be required to enter entirely new markets. In both cases, this would be challenging if funding is tight.

The equivalent in the military context would be where the mission a unit is tasked with is taking 'Hill 125'. When the commander looks at the map they will see that this involves laying down significant and effective suppressive fire, which in actual fact means that the unit will need to take the north spur before tackling Hill 125.

To get to the bottom of whether or not there is an implied goal, or goals, business leaders can use the tactic deployed by the military, which is to repeatedly ask: 'So what?' Every time a mission is discussed, the question is repeated. So what? If we do this … so what? In other words: what is the deduction from that? The resulting answers can be mapped out in three columns, so using the above example of Hill 125, the 'so what?' response would look like this:

- The task: to capture Hill 125.
- The factors or constraints on that task: enemy fire concentrated from the south.
- The actions needed to achieve the task: take the north spur to lay down suppressive fire.

Uncovering the implied goals is an important part of understanding exactly what it is you are being asked to do. You can only get to this stage by thoroughly analysing the task you have been given.

It is always wise to be wary of sweeping goals to take a bunch of costs out. Once you cut out something, it is very, very difficult to reintroduce it at a later date – certainly not without incurring a whole lot more expense. This is something that is common to both the military and business. We often see examples of this in the armed forces following Strategic Defence Reviews. In the 1990s, a particularly stringent round of cost-cutting in the UK military saw a large amount of headcount cut, along with a few regiments. Not long after, the country found itself having to commit to operations in the Balkans as well as Northern Ireland and realized it was significantly under-resourced. Lessons were not learned, though, and a further round of cuts was carried out, this time right before the UK became involved in fighting a war on two fronts: in Iraq and Afghanistan. In just one example of how damaging these exercises can be, the country had to buy early-warning airborne systems from the American military (at considerable expense) having got rid of its own earlier. For a short-term gain, huge amounts were squandered.

Similar things occur regularly in business, particularly in a turn-around situation, where the natural inclination is to cut costs sharply at the earliest opportunity. While it may be tempting to nod these cuts through, particularly if a business is in clear financial trouble, thought must be given to what happens if it all goes right, as detailed in the previous chapter. When I initiate the cost-takeout exercise that is necessary to stabilize the business and create financial head-room, it must be done while considering these viewpoints. If, for example, a mission is mooted to close a bunch of factories, thought needs to be given to how this action might seriously hamper your future production capacity. If, as is hoped, you turn things around, how will you service the renewed growth? With fewer factories it will be impossible to keep pace with a revival in demand, and setting up new facilities will be a very costly exercise indeed. Likewise, if the stated goal of any restructuring programme is to reduce headcount, how does that fit in with future plans for growth? There is another very important reason to question job cuts too, before just executing them. As a rule of thumb, if you want to save £1 million in head-count costs, you may have to spend at least £1 million in severance payments and other types of directly related costs. If an organization is already in a perilous financial situation, personal layoffs may push it over the brink even if they are necessary to stop the financial bleed-ing: a classic Catch 22 scenario. Cost and capacity adjustments must be made with all these considerations in mind – including, as already mentioned, the fact that some of those structures (people, factories) may be needed again down the road, once things get better.

Beware, too, of any suggestions from the top that an acquisi-tion will greatly improve a business's chance of competing. Are the associated costs really necessary? Are they even justified? Tim Col-lins tells of an initiative from the Special Boat Service, who were keen to introduce a very innovative new craft. On paper, it sounded impressive. This long, super-slim vessel could go so fast that it simply sliced through the waves, even in very rough seas. The cost was significant, though.

'Why do we need this?' Tim asked the representative of the Special Boat Service who was touting the idea as an essential purchase.

'Because it is very fast and can cut through waves, even in very rough seas.'

'Yes, but why do we need this?' Tim pressed.

There was no answer. Everything has to be fully accounted for, necessary and thoroughly thought through. Just because it sounds good on first hearing, it may not stand up to later scrutiny. CEOs (myself included) often succumb to the temptation to try to M&A themselves out of growth problems.

Timescales are another important factor to consider here. Clearly, it is possible to be far more measured in your objectives if you have more time to execute them. Privately held and family-owned companies usually offer the luxury of looking to the medium to long term, whereas private equity and public companies err towards the short term. The medium-term or long-term horizon is easier to plan for and manage than the short-term one. For the effectiveness of looking to the medium to long term, you need look no further than Amazon. Jeff Bezos was fully prepared to lose money for years because he was focused on the long term. In fact, in his 1997 letter to shareholders he stated: 'It is all about the long term.' He wrote:

> We believe that a fundamental measure of our success will be the shareholder value we create in the long term. The value will be a direct result of our ability to extend and solidify our current market leadership position. The stronger our market leadership, the more powerful our economic model. Market leadership can translate directly to higher revenue, higher profitability, greater capital velocity, and correspondingly stronger returns on invested capital.[9]

Even if the mission is ruthlessly orientated to the short term, it is possible, certainly for an experienced leader, to keep one eye on the medium to long term at the same time. The idea is to constantly check that what you do today does not impede plans and priorities.

Thus, while sorting out a financial black hole, you will also spend time planning for a future in which you are in recovery mode. How will you regrow the business? If there is too much pressure on the short term, though, it could damage the chances of mission success.

Sometimes it cannot be done

It may be that, on reflection, it transpires that the mission is simply not realistic. This was certainly the case with one company I joined, which had been going downhill for some time. I was given the mission of securing some fresh money from the firm's banks in order to kickstart a meaningful restructuring programme. The company's financiers were, quite understandably, cautious to lend any more after a prolonged period of losses. Once I began visiting the various satellites of the business with this mission firmly in my mind, it quickly became apparent that many of them were so far gone that there was almost nothing that could be done to revive them, even with a substantial fresh injection of capital. Competitors were simply better, and they were capturing the more profitable and attractive business, leaving just the crumbs for us. Nevertheless, I made a restructuring proposal and the banks were persuaded to give the company fresh money.* The situation was still volatile, though, and the boss who hired me was out and a new one was brought in. The second boss was not up to the near-impossible task either, so, just as I had anticipated, the business went into bankruptcy and was broken up, with all the unprofitable parts sold off. In my view (one that I very clearly relayed to the original CEO), this was what should have happened in the first place. If we had adapted the mission earlier instead of wasting time chasing what was clearly a suicide mission, we might have embarked upon some feasible goals.

It is at times like this that I remind myself that the military, with all its checks and balances, does occasionally slip up and sign-up for clear suicide missions too. One of the most well-known from World

---

* It should be noted that while my proposal was as compelling as I could make it, banks are often willing to throw good money after bad, with the hope of somehow recouping their losses.

War II was Operation Market Garden, the failed airborne operation fought in the Netherlands in September 1944. The idea behind this mission was to bypass the formidable German defences along the Siegfried Line by crossing the lower part of the River Rhine, liberating towns and villages and then driving into the industrial heartland of northern Germany. Yet, a series of controversial decisions about the mission meant the initiative was doomed from the start. The British landing zones were too far from their target and, thanks to a limited number of transport aircraft, forces had to be dropped into Arnhem over a three-day period. To make matters worse, a combination of poor weather and broken radios made communications among the scattered troops almost impossible. Perhaps most unforgivably, the Allies completely underestimated the strength of the German forces, and even when they were informed that two well-equipped German SS Panzer tank divisions were in the area, they went ahead with the operation regardless. Although Operation Market Garden liberated some parts of the southern Netherlands from Nazi occupation, thanks to the courage and determination of the Allies, it came at a high cost. Some 7,900 out of the 10,600 Allied forces who made it north of the Rhine were killed, wounded or taken prisoner. If it had succeeded as planned, the war in Europe might have been over by Christmas 1944. Instead, the conflict dragged on for five months beyond that date and the Western Allies were beaten to Berlin by the Soviets, an event that had a profound impact on post-war Europe. This is an extreme example but one that is well worth reminding yourself of if you are given an impossible brief.

Very often, younger leaders do not have the experience or foresight to understand when a mission is hopeless or simply unachievable. No degree of planning or oversight will change the situation. Of course, few leaders ever want to say that something cannot be done. Doing so does not sound like the gung-ho rhetoric leaders are supposed to deliver. It certainly does not seem like a sure-fire route to a glittering leadership career. But it can sometimes be prudent and, presented in the right way, may lead to an adjustment to the mission that will have a positive outcome for all. Richard describes an instance from 2003, where a very ambitious brigade commander was told that a brigade he had just taken over was about to go to Iraq. A week later, the brigade commander had to go back to his divisional commander and say: 'This is the worst thing I have ever had to do, but I have looked at my brigade and, in my assessment, they are not ready to go on operations.' He did not lack enthusiasm for the mission, he just knew it could not be done with that formation. Coming out and saying that took a lot of moral courage. In fact, it is hard to think of a stronger example of courage. His superiors obviously felt the same, too, because he was promoted shortly thereafter. In most cases, a new brigade commander would have said, we have a few shortfalls, but we will be fine. This example clearly shows that a reality check can pay dividends. You have been appointed to a leadership role for a reason. If you do not feel something can be done, have the courage to say so and to suggest alternatives. It is better for all concerned.

Selling the mission

Analysis of the mission is just half of the job. Now it has been clearly defined, you need to sell it to the team. Just as you explained to everyone in step 1 *why* something needs to change, you now need to engage them in the *what*. This is where the team gets involved and paves the way for steps 4 and 5, where they begin working to achieve that mission.

The way you communicate the mission within the organization will vary according to your judgement of what is most appropriate. Even in the military, where process is generally far more defined than in business, commanders have some degree of flexibility over their briefings. In the simplest model, a platoon commander might give briefings to their section commanders, who would then get their reports in and pass the orders on. In other situations, though, such as on a bespoke operation where an ambush or fighting patrol involves the whole platoon, the platoon commander might take the opportunity to gather everyone together and deliver orders to everyone at once. It saves time and generates the tempo for the task ahead. A so-called oner (communicating to all levels) like this has the added bonus that it assures the commander that they have got their plan across to everyone in the same way. The important element here is to find the most effective and time-efficient method of getting everyone involved and on the same page.

The other factor at play here is the number of people you brief. You may choose to speak to a small group of direct reports, one level down, or to a larger group, two levels down. In the military world there is clearly a tradition of caution about telling too many people the plan, too soon. If the details of a mission are leaked to the wrong people, it can have disastrous consequences. The same goes for business, especially today. Industrial espionage is a very real threat and instances are growing all the time. Somehow, you need to walk the tightrope between telling as many people as you need to in order to begin to get the job done while not telling too many people, meaning details will leak out causing harm to a business that is already in bad shape. It is a question of keeping careful control over information.

My approach is to brief everyone that is going to be integral to fulfilling and succeeding in the mission. This in itself can be a bit of a juggling act, particularly when one is new to an organization. You will not have had time to make any changes to the structure yet, or indeed to come up with a plan, yet you also need to have gone some way towards identifying the important people who will be key to adding value to achieve mission success. Something I always do at this point is to go over the key points of step 1 again. When discussing the what, or the mission, you need to reiterate why you are doing this. What is the benefit for you and for the stakeholders, whether that is customers, suppliers, employees or shareholders?

If you had not already done so, this is absolutely the moment in which you will realize the importance of making sure that the goals are realistic. You will be the person standing in front of everyone declaring: 'we're going to break even' or 'we're going take this company to an EBITDA of $100 million'. If the mission is complete BS, rest assured that everyone, to a man and woman, will be thinking: *What is he talking about? There is no way we are going to achieve that!* You will be made fully aware of whether your target is ambitious or just plain silly in the eyes of your team.

There is, of course, always a fine line in this respect. By its very nature, a turnaround is ambitious. The business is in real trouble and things need to change – that is why you are there. But if you set the bar too high, the team will be defeated before you even start.

Jack Welch, the chairman and CEO of General Electric, once one of the world's largest corporations, had a ruthless management style that entailed setting the bar very high indeed. The aim was to get his team to jump as high as possible. Nearly everyone knew that they were not supposed to achieve the actual target but they needed to try to get as near to it as possible. Those that did not get close were culled in an annual clearout of the bottom 10% by performance. While Welch's style was lauded by many, history has not looked upon him kindly. Indeed, his approach has been cited as the reason for General Electric's decline.[10] If a target is completely unrealistic, no one will take it seriously.

To make sure the team fully understands the mission, use a 'back brief'. This is a military technique in which the person receiving the summary is asked to give back a synopsis of what they have been told. Ideally, as in the military, you will give team members time to go away and digest the briefing, so they can fully analyse and digest the information they have been given. This is not just to give it time to sink in, but also to allow them room to properly drill into it. They may well come back and say they need a bit more of this, or a bit less of that. They may think of constraints you have not yet considered. Or they may tell you why they think the mission is, in fact, unachievable. Do not forget, the people who work within the company generally have their feet on the ground in respect of what can be done.

Think carefully about how you set up the back brief process. Some people find it difficult to ask a question in public and it is your challenge to create an environment in which they feel comfortable doing so. Richard always says to his team that there is no such thing as a stupid question. And he is completely right, too. We have all experienced the scenario in which someone asks a question and there are probably half a dozen others in attendance who are nodding their heads, with the clear implication that that was what they would have asked. You need to ensure that everyone feels able to speak this freely.

Revisit the mission

Despite all the work that has gone into analysing and then briefing the mission, the task is not done. In fact, it is never done. What you do now will not be set in stone. In fact, it is highly likely that you will revisit the mission definition several times. Things will change. To use the earlier example of storming Hill 125, it may well turn out that the location is more heavily fortified and defended than first thought. If that is the case, the original mission may not be such a good idea after all, and it will need to be redefined. A business equivalent might centre around, say, a priority to 'fix a subsidiary'. It may subsequently transpire that the subsidiary simply is not worth fixing, and that it would therefore be foolhardy to go on trying to turn it around. The only realistic option is either to sell it or to close it. This is why, when briefing the team, any leader should always put in the caveat that as new information becomes available, the mission may need to be revisited. It is crucial to have the flexibility to go back to your mission and, if necessary, change or rewrite it.

In the military, the constant vigilance over the changing nature of a mission is known as a 'question four moment', named after the fourth question of the mission analysis: has the mission changed? It is important to keep asking this question over and over. The mission might not have changed now, but it may well do so in the future. Going back to Richard's story with which we opened the chapter – where his unit essentially had to create their own mission in Bosnia – he experienced a massive question four moment when the Serbs attacked their carefully defended safe haven. He had contingency planned against this from the outset and was able to thwart it but he had to go back to the mission and reassess. In fact, the mission changed six times in six months, as many of the initial tasks that were set ceased to be viable.

There is, of course, an element of luck involved in responding and adapting to any changing situation. Richard and I both know people who are lucky, in business and in the military. But, there is also an element of making your own luck. The way Richard used to explain this to his young officers sums it up well. You have to seize the initiative. Imagine there is a ball that falls between you and your enemy. Whoever takes the initiative and reaches out first to grab that ball will gain an advantage. Even if the mission changes, it is possible to take advantage of the change if you quickly reach out and grab the ball. This is why it is so important that the team understands your overall intent. Where is it you want to be? Knowing the answer to that question will enable them to see the end game and go for it.

My own early experience of seizing the initiative in a rapidly changing mission occurred during one of my first jobs as a sales rep with Hewlett-Packard. I initially sold expensive technical products, such as printers and plotters, to customers that mainly comprised small, specialist corner shops. Then, along came the company's laser jet printer. These printers, which were housed in large unwieldy boxes, were nothing like the laser printers you see today, and Hewlett-Packard had modest expectations for their success in the market. They certainly did not understand that their generally quite cultish following would be particularly interested in a laser printer. Our sales targets (our mission) were set pretty low. The future of laser jets was not lost on me and my sales colleagues, though. We could see huge potential in them – but in a different market. Instead of our usual contacts in the corner shops, we approached distributors of general printers. Our hunch was right. They could not get enough of the laser jets, which despite being bulky were better than anything else on the market. Within a short space of time we were all making very handsome commission indeed, smashing our targets by more than 400%. As you can imagine, our Hewlett-Packard paymasters moved fairly quickly to adapt the mission targets!

While many businesses have suffered thanks to Covid-19, we have also seen some very innovative mission pivots too. Unilever, under chief executive Alan Jope, prioritized its packaged food, surface cleaners and personal hygiene brands over other products, such as those related to skin care, where demand had fallen. Numerous restaurants have switched from their eat-in model to takeaway and home delivery. Spotify, the global leader in music streaming, started offering original content in the form of podcasts after the advertising revenue that had previously supported the free user base plummeted. CEO Daniel Ek is now being praised for his innovative thinking: the platform has artists and users uploading hundreds of thousands of podcasts per month, and exclusive deals have been signed with celebrities. This shift in strategy means that the business, which was showing signs of maturity, is now emulating the successful Netflix model in which copyright owners enjoy healthy margins.

Interestingly, one group that has shown great flexibility in changing its operating model since the pandemic is the criminal fraternity. While their intentions are wholly unpalatable, it cannot be denied that crime syndicates moved at a dizzying rate to seize the initiative, adapt their mission and make money out of the economic and health crisis. The authorities have struggled to keep up with the ways in which drugs rings have adapted their county lines distribution model; at the same time, online scams targeting the vulnerable have rocketed during lockdown. Of course, drug dealers and scammers are not beholden to the law, and they do not feel constrained by health and safety rules, but there is no doubt that they have adapted quickly to the situation they faced.

If you are not clear about the mission in the first place, it will be very difficult to react to changing circumstances. Change, though, is inevitable. It is your task, as a leader, to adapt and keep moving.

STEP 3. COMPREHENSIVE EVALUATION OF THE ENVIRONMENT/ THEATRE OF OPERATIONS

What separates the truly great leaders from the merely good ones is that the former never, ever underestimate the competition. Everything they do is focused on keeping one eye on the enemy and maintaining the edge over them. They are always very close indeed to their market and customers.

The Palace fashion brand, which is famous for its 'streetwear' hoodies and T-shirts that carry the brand's oversize logo, has exploited this advantage perfectly. Despite the fact it is positioned in one of the most competitive and unforgiving markets of them all – fast-moving fashion – it has, in a short space of time, carved out a niche for itself that makes it stand out from the crowd. Since its launch in 2009, Palace has become a cult brand on the back of a 'treat 'em mean, keep 'em keen' strategy.[11] To achieve this, Palace has eschewed the normal practice of producing seasonal collections and instead produces entirely new looks every week. Then, just to make the brand even more compelling when measured against its slower-moving competitors, Palace only produces a limited run of each design. Founder Lev Tanju has devised a system that cleverly anticipates demand and keeps supplies below that level. The strategy keeps fans queuing up outside Palace's four stores or religiously checking back with the website each week. Once the mad scramble to secure stock has ended, the individual pieces are worth more than their ticket price, adding further to the brand's cult status. The aura around the brand, which snubs the traditional way of doing things, is heightened by Tanju's quirky product descriptions on the Palace website. Each narrative ignores practical considerations – details about fabrics, say – in favour of provocative statements: for exampe, a bomber jacket is listed as '112% gully', which means 'authentic' and 'street' to the uninitiated. Interestingly, Palace was not the first streetwear brand to do this, with the team readily admitting they took inspiration from the American brand Supreme when they were looking for an innovative way of delivering their slick brand message to a new audience. The brand has gone on to make a massive mark on the sector thanks to a strategy that cleverly exploits the highly competitive nature of the branded fashion business by creating a fresh new angle on the traditional 'must have' allure of their designs.

The cost of ignoring the competition is always high. We can look to the military for what is perhaps one of the most famous examples of a disastrous outcome resulting from underestimation of one's opponents. For all the valour and skill of World War II RAF pilots, the Battle of Britain was also lost by the German forces because they both completely underestimated their enemy and overestimated their own abilities. Those in charge of the Luftwaffe were confident that many RAF pilots were not sufficiently skilled, because they had not had enough flying hours, and that communication between them was often difficult since some of the Polish pilots who had joined barely spoke any English. They also believed that aircraft manufacturing was woefully behind schedule. Initially, German confidence did not look misplaced, and the Luftwaffe came close to overwhelming the RAF several times – especially when German bombers successfully attacked vital radar masts at key airfields in August 1940. Yet, in the belief that they had the upper-hand more than they really did, they failed to stick with a single strategy. Frequent changes let the RAF off the hook time and again. When these changes culminated in a switch to daylight bombing raids, it gave British forces valuable time to regroup. The climax of the battle on 15 September (now known as Battle of Britain Day) saw the loss of sixty German planes to Britain's twenty-six, leading Hitler to postpone his long-planned invasion.

Step 3 is the moment to pause and look closely at the competition, or your enemy, as well as at the market. As Sun Tzu says, the five constant factors that are key to ensuring a military victory are moral law, Heaven, Earth, commander and method/discipline. Here we are concerned with Heaven (night/day, temperature, seasons and times) and Earth (distances, danger, security, terrain, chances and life/death). In other words, this is what would be described in business terms as the market/customers and competitors.

While there are a number of factors to take into account when planning a military campaign – such as the ground, the enemy, the time and one's resources, all of which will shape your plan – Richard says the number one criterion has to be to focus on the enemy. If you understand your enemy, what their options are and what they prefer to do, then you are in a better place. You can begin to think like your enemy. No wonder there are (probably apocryphal) stories of famous commanders setting up pictures of their opposite numbers on their desks and 'talking' to them on a daily basis. Whether or not the stories are true, there is much merit in getting under the skin of the competition and learning from what they have done in the past to help shape your view of what they might do in the future. If you understand what your enemy thinks, you will not go far wrong.

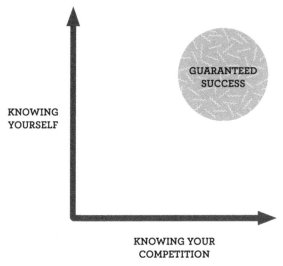

Know yourself/your competition. (© Pepyn Dinandt.)

In a business setting, a CEO would need the equivalent of two, three, four or five portraits on their desks, because there will be many different 'enemies', or competitors. While physical framed pictures are perhaps taking things a little far, every leader should definitely adopt the mindset of considering the strengths and weaknesses of each of their business rivals. Not one of them should be underestimated. In my experience, far too few CEOs make a point of going through the intellectual effort of really getting to understand the sectors they are in and the environment in which they operate, preferring to stay in their ivory towers, surveying things from afar. Now is the moment, though, to ask yourself: what kind of leader are you? Are you an involved one, or not? The answers to these questions will shape much of what comes after.

In a crisis situation, more so than in any other, it is not enough to say: we did some research into the market last year and the data looks pretty much up to date. Even if you have access to acres of recently produced stats from the marketing department – or even from a dedicated market research unit – it is not enough. There is no substitute for first-hand knowledge of the full facts, and this requires getting out to speak with both customers and, if possible, competitors. Who is buying your products and services and from whom? In the military it is often said that you learn the most about an enemy when you are nose-to-nose with them, fighting. The closer you are to the enemy, the more you will learn about them, and this knowledge is crucial if you are seeking to unbalance them.

The same goes for the business world. In a world where there are multiple sources of data, one of the most important is 'contact information'. If you lose contact with your customers and competitors and do not know what they are doing, they are likely to surprise you. This is why you need to retain 'eye contact' with them at all times. All leaders should make a point of interacting with 'real' customers and listening in order to understand, not simply to respond.

To fully understand a market, a leader needs to seek out the unfiltered insights of everyone involved in it. As Richard says, one of his earliest recommendations to any young new officer is to walk around and listen to experienced soldiers talk about their experiences. It is in this way that these new officers will garner some of the most important lessons – ones that will stand them in good stead for years to come when they meet the enemy. The trick is to let everyone talk freely and without interruption. Richard jokes that experienced soldiers 'love to tell you how good they are', but to be fair, this is true of most people. We all like to be asked our opinion and to feel our answers truly matter. And they do. Whether in the military or in a civilian setting, honest conversations are key to leaders better understanding the capabilities of their staff/subordinates and of their organization. If you listen – really listen – it is always to your advantage, and (again) listen to understand, not merely to respond.

Of course, the wider you spread your net, the more you will learn and the better placed you will be to understand what it is you are dealing with. This process is deeply ingrained in the military. On operations, officers are always encouraged to weigh up and explore all the variables, because they need a sightline across the various domains that they control, as well as those they do not. In a Multi Domain Operation, commanders will gather intelligence on the land, sea, air, cyber and human domains, all of which will have an influence on the outcome of that operation. They are expected to work effectively across all these domains while simultaneously discouraging any silos: that is, mindsets where team members can only reflect on their own sphere of influence. This is exactly what a CEO should be doing in any organization today: looking across all those various parts of the business and putting the information together to create a bigger (and more considered) picture.

My step 3 starting point is to talk to customers themselves directly: all the reports in the world are no substitute for interacting with real people. I do not ignore the data – indeed, I always read it carefully – but I place far more emphasis on verifying it. I speak with customers from all parts of the spectrum too: past and present, happy and loyal, as well as those who are distinctly disgruntled. They are not hard to find, if you look. My goal is to build up a fair and accurate picture of my organization's place in the market and what everyone really thinks of it. In some situations, I failed to do enough of this and then regretted it later on.

The second stage of this step is to broaden the scope of the investigation to look at competitors more deeply. There are many useful sources of information here, over and above the data you will receive from your own in-house team. A potentially useful resource is the appropriate trade association for organizations in your sector. Many industries have associations that gather bespoke data that can offer a very comprehensive analysis about market volume, developments in the competitive environment and market share. Not all markets are so well served though. Certainly, when I worked for Hilding Anders (a leading bedding and mattress company), there was very little general market information available. In circumstances like this, a leader will need to collect what data they can themselves, and there will, on occasion, be a degree of estimation in the numbers.

Trade associations are not the only possible sources of intelligence about the wider market: you can also get people in the know to do some of the work for you, which can be very productive indeed. This process is nothing new. Indeed, Sun Tzu wrote an entire chapter on spies in *The Art of War* and was very sophisticated in structuring his own spy network. He observed that when it came to gathering valuable intelligence, the best spy was the converted spy. These are the enemy's spies who are brought over to your side and used for your own enlightenment. This principle of recruiting covert human intelligence endures in the military even today. Indeed, Richard says that the best informants during the thirty-year conflict in Northern Ireland, which began in the late 1960s, were not those who did it for money – it was those who passed on vital information because they *believed* in what they were doing. Very often this was because something bad had happened to them within the organization that they were working for, or they had witnessed something they strongly disagreed with. Their distaste for the incident was strong enough for them to switch sides and become passionate about helping the opposition. Their level of belief meant they were prepared to take enormous risks.

The truth is, despite all the films that show hackers shouting 'We're in!' triumphantly from behind their laptops, most information leaves companies on two legs. It is just that it is often politically expedient to *blame* cyber hackers for any information leaks. One of the most well-known cases of this was in 2010, when car maker Renault accused Chinese hackers of stealing information about the company's electric-car programme. Even Nicolas Sarkozy, the French president at the time, weighed in, ordering an investigation into Beijing's cyber activities. The investigation revealed that the espionage was far more two dimensional, leading to the firing of half a dozen senior Renault executives, including the company's COO. The truth is, however sophisticated anyone's technology and listening devices are, there is no substitute for human interpretation of what is really going on in a given situation. Otherwise, it is rather like hearing one side of a phone call: there is no real context and not everything will make sense. It is much better to have someone on the inside.

The military has a process for spotting the most likely source who will give up information. It is called BEANS: an acronym of beliefs, emotions, ambitions, needs and status. Beliefs is fairly self-explanatory. These are people who do not agree with the path their organization is taking and will take any steps they can to disrupt it, including divulging information to a sympathetic ear. Emotions are a powerful force – as Tim Collins says, if there were no such things as sex and violence, there would be very few informants. When it comes to ambitions, people are often motivated by having been passed over for promotion, or if they feel that they do not sit in the right place in the hierarchy. If you get them onside, it might be possible to motivate them by proffering an alternative channel for their talents. Offer them a job elsewhere, but not until they have completed their current project. When it comes to needs, some people simply want a better, more comfortable life and will be open to offers. And finally, status, which is important to everyone to varying degrees. People want to feel recognized and valued.

In business, there are, of course, strict anti-trust laws that dictate what you can and cannot do in seeking out data about individuals and about your competition, but this does not completely preclude you from recruiting converted spies. There are certainly many former employees of competitor firms who may be able to help you fill in a good many blanks about the market. I have always made a point of trying to hire some of the best people from my competitors. It does not even need to be someone with a grievance. The principle is the same: if you want to want to know why the other person is better than you, the best thing to do is to try to hire someone from within that company. Obviously, the proviso here is they will have had to sit out a notice period and observe any confidentiality clauses. Even so, it is worth it: the best insights about your enemy are likely to come from somebody who used to be with the enemy.

I should add here that I have been made aware of a rather sneaky variation on this theme – a technique pioneered by a company that I will not name here for reasons that might become obvious. The management board of this highly successful company makes a point of regularly advertizing very interesting senior leadership roles within their organization at *very* attractive salaries (i.e. paying well over the odds). The chief executive in question routinely receives a pile of applications from a selection of the best executives in the sector, who also just happen to work for rival firms. The applicants are invited for interview and, in a bid to impress their potential new employer, invariably fall over themselves to share their comprehensive understanding of both the sector as a whole and their experience of it from their current vantage point. A valuable source of intelligence indeed.

A final point to note about the concept of spies is that, while the above information is all very useful when it comes to finding people to help you understand the competitive landscape better, BEANS works both ways. Leaders need to ensure that their own teams feel valued, motivated and driven or they could well find themselves vulnerable.

The other source of market intelligence that many CEOs naturally reach for, often as a first resort, is that provided by consultants. While not wishing to denigrate the often-great work that consultants do, I would not recommend rushing to bring one in to tell you all about your competitors. These same consultants* will also, very probably, be working with your competitors and telling them all about you. They are, as Sun Tzu would say, buyable spies, and everyone can buy them. The question any leader should ask themselves is: to what extent do I wish to share important confidential information about my business, particularly at such a sensitive time? The other reason for caution is that you may not even get the level of data you expect. Consultants often rely on open-source material and could well quote back to you data you already know. You will not have an advantage over customers if you do nothing beyond getting the

---

* Obviously not the same people, as all top consultants observe strict Chinese walls, with different teams for competitors, but the same consulting firm.

same information that everyone else has. To be clear, this is not to dismiss the value of consultants; it is merely an observation that this is not the best task to give them and is not in your best interests at this stage. I have no qualms whatsoever about bringing in consultants for a specialist job: advising on a cost-takeout programme in a factory, say; or to help with a project to make savings on purchasing costs; or even in collecting publicly available data if you do not have enough research resources. And if a sector or geography is new to you and your business, certainly use consultants and draw on their deep expertise. So, in these instances, it is often prudent to bring in specialists from the outside. However, at this point in the turnaround, a CEO needs to be a leader, to do their own homework and to understand their own territory themselves.

Solid information beats assumptions

Contact with customers and competitors will reveal much about how your organization has reached its present circumstances, and it will build a much clearer picture of how perilous your situation really is. It will also help shed more light on the market sector in general and possibly even begin to reshape your thinking about your mission. It may be that the reversal of fortunes in your organization has thus far been blamed on a shock to the market – something like the Covid-19 pandemic, say – and this may well be true. However, any such assumption needs further scrutiny. The market you operate in may have halved in terms of sales, but if your business's market share has significantly reduced too, this fact should have an impact on your thinking because things are clearly worse than you first thought: the business is clearly already in decline and would have been in real trouble even without the extenuating circumstances. The opposite may also be the case: maybe you have seen a precipitous drop in income but your market share has actually increased. This is an indication that the prevailing circumstances have weakened your competitors more than they have weakened your business. Your organization may actually be reacting really well to the new circumstances, and, if this is the case, more thought needs to be given to what it is that customers think you are getting right. Keep on doing whatever it is and you could greatly improve your chances; you might be able to push even more weaker players aside. Market intelligence will reveal who those weaker players are and will provide ample clues about how you could pick them off.

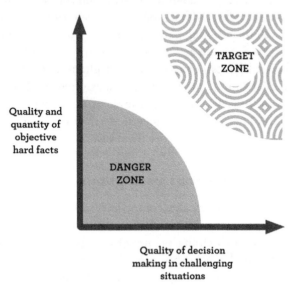

A matrix of good decision making. (© Pepyn Dinandt.)

The real threat to the business may not be the shock to the market or trading environment – it could be the rise and rise of a competitor who has come along and changed the game. There are disruptors in every market: firms that develop, grow and push out all their competitors by either inventing something new or by markedly improving upon what came before. It may be early days, and the customer shift towards the new product or service may be barely discernible, but it is there if you look for it. The more adventurous among your customer base – the innovators and early adopters according to the theory of how individuals gravitate to the new[12] – may have already drifted away. Alternatively, things could be worse than that: the disruptor could already be attacking your previously solid customer base. Combine this scenario with a market downturn and one can clearly see that the situation is desperate.

At this stage, it is a question of the more detail the better. Finance is an obvious starting point, since the amount of profit a company is generating is an obvious shortcut to seeing who is doing well and who is not. Find out who, among your competitors, is making money and, in particular, which businesses are the most profitable. More generally, consider what drives competition in your sector. To return to the fashion business for a moment, this is a sector in which businesses have a clear market proposition and yet the strengths and weaknesses of brands are entirely intangible. The things that attract people to shop at a chain such as Primark are completely different to those that bring customers through the gilded doors at Prada. Primark is all about price; a designer brand like Prada is all about image. The fact that some shoppers will not bat an eyelid at spending $1,000 on a Prada handbag may be an intangible strength of the brand, but it is certainly a strength and it is something that needs to be protected. It is also what differentiates Prada from its competitors. In other industries, while the differentiation is not always so acute, it will be there. There is always a logic to competition, whether it is pricing, mass differentiation or segment differentiation.

Different industries also operate at different intensities. Is your business operating in a sector in which the price of/barriers to entry is/are high? Maybe getting started would require an investment of £100 million or more to build a new factory? In this case, the implications of 'return on invested capital', where there is a need to make a decent return to justify such a substantial investment, makes competitors less likely to take any chances, or do anything too foolish. This strengthens your hand if you are planning to make any bold moves to recover market share. Alternatively, if the entry barriers are very low, like they were in my former appointment in the mattress sector, almost anyone can set up a company. This makes for a highly aggressive and dynamic business environment and it means that significant investment in any new innovation needs to be carefully thought through. If it works, or even if it just looks like it might work, everyone else will pile in very quickly.

Do not overlook the people who run the businesses that compete with yours. Perhaps they are individuals with a super-successful track record? Or maybe you can see evidence that they are inexperienced and are running their businesses down? Undertaking this exercise will help you pinpoint your most dangerous enemy. Ultimately, this turnaround will come down to general versus general. It is, after all, the general who decides how successful any campaign is. Bear in mind, too, that your competitors will also be looking at you in this way. As you make plans, so are they. No one is going to sit back and say: 'I've lost half my market, but that's OK, I can live with that.' They are scheming and planning their attack, just as you are. This is why you need to work out the better, more considered, plan – and fast.

Look inward as well as outward

It is very easy to get bogged down in the sheer quantity of information you can gather once you begin looking for it. Avoid being the type of leader who demands ever-more-comprehensive weekly reports with a plethora of key performance indicators. They will quickly become noise and a distraction. You need to focus on priorities and what it will take to make sure your business remains stable. You need to concentrate your energies on working out what it is that your customers really want and whether you, or your competitors, are delivering that better.

It is here that owners/founders often hold an advantage: they find their strength and then they keep building and building upon it. Take the example of Heinz Hermann Thiele, who in 1985 acquired a majority share in Knorr-Bremse, a German manufacturer of braking systems for rail and commercial vehicles. The company, which was almost a century old at the time, had somewhat lost its way and needed a radical restructuring programme.* From the beginning, Thiele made it his business to be well informed about every aspect of the company, in every geographic location, and he went out into the business to speak directly to the people who were dealing with

---

* A funny anecdote. When Thiele took control, under the previous ownership, top management consultants had undertaken a restructuring strategy project and had made recommendations about the way forward. He ignored these and did the *opposite* – and the rest is (successful) history.

specific issues. While his word was always the final one, he made his decisions after listening carefully to the people on the ground. This ensured his decisions were always made on a completely informed basis.

One of Thiele's first acts was to invest millions in developing the Chinese market. China was hardly on the radar at the time, and even businesses that were eyeing possible future developments were incredibly reluctant to make any meaningful moves there. Yet, after carefully researching the market, Thiele did not hesitate: he went all in. You might say, with reason, that that is easier to do in a private company, where there are no highly vocal investors watching your every move, but even so, such a move took a huge amount of courage. Thiele was only able to be courageous because he was so well informed.

There is much to be learned from the owner's/founder's mindset. Leaders like Thiele started from scratch and therefore they were the ones selling themselves and their products or services from day one. This means they have developed a leadership style that focuses very clearly on getting things exactly right when it comes to the customer. It pays to approach any situation – whether it is day-to-day business or balancing a crisis – from the customer perspective. The success or failure of a business comes down to really understanding what one's customers want and need. If someone somewhere else does it better, customers will vote with their feet.

To be most effective in this step 3 exercise, you must look inward as well as outward. Like Thiele, leaders should spend time speaking with their team, getting their views on how their organization measures up against the competition. Having a clear understanding of your organization's strengths and weaknesses is important: you want to protect your own strengths and attack your competitors' weaknesses. If you are able to make an informed assessment of both these things, you will be able to answer the crucial question of where to apply your strengths to take greatest advantage of your enemy's weaknesses. You are, after all, preparing for a fight, and you need to know what you are dealing with.

Your market share is a reflection of your strengths and weaknesses compared with the competition. But what is the story behind that brutal reality? To understand this, you need to consider what your organization's current place in the market really says about it. If your organization is number three in the sector, your weaknesses are probably greater than you care to admit and your strengths are probably not as good as you hope they are. It is difficult to admit that someone else is doing a better job than you, but if you fail to find out why or how, you will be unable to move to correct the performance gap.

Every circumstance comes with challenges. If a business is highly complex – a conglomerate, working in many different sectors, say – a leader has to really understand every part of the business. They have to be really involved and immersed in the detail. If your organization is number one in the market overall, you face a tough battle because every other business in your sector will want to attack your position. Even if you occupy the number three position, things do not get any easier. If anything, in fact, it can be more complicated. Your business will be under attack from those in the fourth and fifth positions (if those companies are well led) and you should be planning an assault on numbers one and two. In the constant of a VUCA world, the intensity only ever increases.

When taking a viewpoint about where you are relative to the competition, you must also think about timing. If you have been brought in because revenues have dropped significantly, are they still falling precipitously relative to the competition or have they stabilized? This will, again, have an impact on the planning process. There is little point making a plan based on current revenue or market share if things are still heading downwards at speed. By the time you begin to enact your plan, the business will probably already be in a significantly worse position. This might even make your entire plan obsolete. Granted, it is difficult to pinpoint when a business will hit the bottom, but this is something that needs to be uppermost in your mind.

Resources will be an issue when you come up against competitors. If you convince yourself that you have *just about* enough to go up against your competition in the current environment, then either you are going to have to come up with a very good plan indeed or you will need some ideas for a really good surprise attack, otherwise you will lose. In the military, as a rule of thumb, one always aims for an attacking ratio of a minimum of three to one against what they estimate the strength of the enemy to be. This is because you are at your most vulnerable when moving and on the attack. You must assume that your enemy is well prepared, so the factor of three to one is essential in terms of resources in order to have a viable attack plan.

A leader may sometimes need to make a tough decision if they are light on resources. Richard recalls one impending attack in Afghanistan where he was told just two days before an operation that was set to last six weeks that he would be down an entire squadron of armoured vehicles. It was a sobering moment, he says, since he knew that timing was absolutely critical to the operation. He knew he had to go ahead, come what may, and the only option was to go back to the drawing board and work out how to carry out the mission with the reduced resources.

It is for this same reason that this analysis of the competitive environment – analysing the strengths and weaknesses of one's competitors – is crucial for any business, particularly those that are under-resourced or at some other disadvantage. The more any leader knows about the competition – how their businesses and others are perceived, and the available resources for an attack – the better their chances. Remember that, in a contracting market, the competition is doing their best to work out the same things about your business.

Is the vision still viable?

The findings from step 3 may well mean that you will need to return to step 2 once more. Having uncovered some more ugly facts about the business you lead and where it sits relative to its competitors, the mission may now seem less viable than you first thought. To return to the Hill 125 example, there might now be a requirement for additional elements to the mission to smooth the way in light of new information that has been revealed about the enemy. Storming the hill will not be successful with the resources you currently have, particularly when it is against an enemy with superior strength.

It could be that you were led to believe that the business you lead is number three in terms of market share, but you have found that the position is not as clear cut because you sell several different product ranges. In some cases, your true position may be worse; in others, it may be better. It might transpire that you only really have a chance of winning in two out of five segments, say, because these are the only areas in which customers really rate your output. Perhaps the battle has already been lost in the other three but no one had realized before. This knowledge helps you become more rational and to understand the level of danger. It also means that you need to revisit the mission and possibly even change it.

This will be one of many times when you need to go back to the mission as new information comes to light. This is why it is so helpful to build in a loop, so that you can quickly and easily return to the sovereign with your findings. This is not an uncommon process in the business world, where, once targets are set, there is an opening to go back up the chain to discuss the mission again. Be prepared though: it may be that once a leader explains that the mission cannot be achieved with the available resources, the ultimate boss says to go ahead anyway. In this case, they will be duty bound to try, despite failure being pretty much certain without a change of plan.

STEP 4. WHO DARES WINS/ STRATEGY AND TACTICS

I n the run up to writing this chapter, Richard shared a document
with me that sums up much of what you really need to know
about strategy. It was a copy of General Montgomery's plan for
the D Day landings of June 1944: one of the most complex military operations ever undertaken. There are many remarkable things
about the document – which spells out history's largest combined
land, air and sea operation, involving around 160,000 Allied troops
– but perhaps the most amazing is that it is scribbled out on one
single sheet of paper. And, just in case the message is not clear, the
sheet concludes with a note that says: 'The key note of everything to
be SIMPLICITY.'

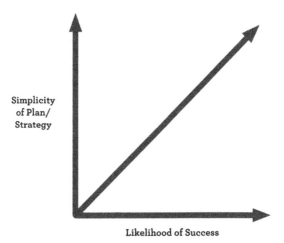

The simpler the plan, the more likely it is to succeed.
(© Pepyn Dinandt.)

The simpler the plan

The best, most effective strategies are simple and easy to execute. While there are many weighty books, guides and documents about creating the perfect strategy (and I have written a fair few weighty strategic documents myself, particularly while at McKinsey), strategy does not have to be hugely complex. In fact, it should be pure common sense. If you had to boil it down to a single key point, a good strategy is one that builds on a set of one's strengths that are considered to be better than those of one's competitors, be it a better product, an improved route to market or a more compelling positioning. This is what will give you an advantage and help you to attack competitors' weak points.

In recent years, there has been a tendency to over-complicate strategy, and we have even seen evidence of this in the military too, despite the shining example of that D Day page. Richard was provided with an operational plan in excess of 250 pages when he was deployed to Kosovo in 1999 on a multinational operation. The annexes alone went from A to Z, and the appendices AA to ZZ! Richard recalls that his (perfectly reasonable) reaction was: who is going to read this? Yes, the situation in Kosovo was complex – there were multiple domains to take into consideration, and troops are very much held firmly accountable today for their actions in the field – but it nevertheless seemed over the top. Certainly, the powers-that-be had strayed a long way from the ideal of keeping it short and sweet – or KISS, for keep it simple stupid, as the acronym goes.

Over-complicating strategy with unwieldy documents is self-defeating because, even if they are read in full, they have a negative impact on tempo. As Richard says, by the time you have waded through them, the enemy is likely to have already outfoxed you. Too much detail can also act as a constraint on initiative, thanks to an excess of guidance and detail.

Businesses suffer from a similar tendency to over-complicate when it comes to mission statements, and this has just as much of a negative impact as it does in the military scenario. If a corporate strategy cannot be summarized in seven points (or a maximum of ten) on a single page, no one is going to read it, let alone understand it, let alone live by it.

So what is the perfect, succinct strategy for your particular situation? This chapter will not be able to tell you that, but what it will do is help you begin the thinking process to work that out for yourself. Using a combination of the information acquired so far in this process, it will help you focus on your organization's strengths in order to attack competitors and gain the advantage.

In the previous three steps we asked ourselves whether the situation has changed, looked carefully at the current environment and scrutinized the mission. In step 3, you collected data that gave you a clear, honest understanding of your organization's strengths relative to your competitors. Now, in step 4, we will look at how to adapt this information and design a strategy for the way forward. The end goal is to answer the question: what is the big idea? To do this properly, there needs to be rigorous scrutiny of the facts. You also need to be 100% certain that the strengths that have served the business so well in the past are still, in fact, as strong today. Similarly, you need to be sure that whatever strategy you choose, there are enough resources available to fight your way through and, ultimately, regain market share by dislodging competitors.

The goal of step 4 is to create a strategy that plays to your strengths while being as simple as possible: the business equivalent of Montgomery's one-page plan. You will be using the combined might of all the data you have gathered to date to say: this is what we are going to do. If you come up with something that is too ambitious, or overly complicated, you will only succeed in confusing your organization. If you get it wrong, your big idea is going to fail.

Deciding on the approach

Ask most people to visualize the SAS in action and they will probably picture some sort of variation on the theme of mysterious men, dressed all in black, freefalling from 22,000 feet with Heckler & Koch weapons coughing out death as they land, before they leap into a speedboat and zoom off into the darkness, James Bond style. In actual fact, while such scenes make great fodder for action movies, they would be very unusual in real life. The 'average' day for an SAS soldier is spent on the ranges, or on the training area, practising and rehearsing, making sure they do the basics really well. In fact, hour upon hour is spent researching and understanding the whole landscape, so that when the operation does begin their actions and reactions are instinctive.

When designing your own strategy, you need to think like this. (The latter scenario, not the leaping into the abyss one!) Every potential variable needs to be fully weighed up and considered. Getting the basics right with your strategy is the foundation for all that follows. If you are going to announce to the team, and possibly even the wider world, that you are going to do something, you need to make sure you can realistically achieve it.

There are a number of strategy approaches open to you, and each is based on an assessment of the data gathered so far. For example, the previous steps might have indicated an opening in the market to create an entirely new product or service, and you may decide that your business is in the right position to be the first mover. Alternatively, a competitor might be selling a product that is crying out for improvement: the customer base likes it but would like a better version even more. Or perhaps there is an opening for a product that improves on the last iteration but at a more compelling price point. The most appropriate strategy for your organization may even be a hybrid of all of the above.

A useful way to begin looking at the potential possibilities is via Porter's model for strategies: a useful tool to apply to any organization. It was first set out by Michael Porter in his 1985 book *Competitive Advantage: Creating and Sustaining Superior Performance*.[13] The generic strategies identified by Porter are listed below.

- *Cost leadership*: becoming the leader in terms of cost in your industry or market. This can be achieved by increasing profits through taking costs out while charging industry-average prices. Alternatively, there is the option to charge lower prices and increase market share, with the onus being on ensuring there is still a reasonable profit on each sale despite the reduced price tag.
- *Differentiation*: creating uniquely desirable products and services. This may involve adding new features, functionality, durability or support to existing products, or it might be working on creating

a more favourable brand image that customers value. This strategy requires the organization behind it to be perpetually agile, because they risk constant retaliation from competitors. As soon as something new comes out that captures market share, rivals will be onto it.

- *Focus*: offering a specialized service in a niche market. To pursue this strategy you need to understand the unique needs of customers and develop low-cost, or well-specified and different, products for the market in question. Focus is not enough on its own, so it needs to be paired with either cost leadership or differentiation. The aim here is to build strong brand loyalty among customers through giving them something extra as a result of serving a niche.

Each of Porter's strategies are routes to gaining a competitive advantage: the edge that gets you the sale and, by implication, takes the business away from your rivals. Since the goal is to leverage your organization's strengths and attack competitors' weaknesses, a good starting point is a clear understanding of your company's strengths. Do you, for example, have a product that has thus far been really good in one market? Could you take it into another market? Perhaps you have fantastic infrastructure and could, therefore, launch a wider range of products. It might sound obvious, but it is no less pertinent for that: if you are successful in one area, you should use that success to create more success. The reverse is also true. Embarking on new ventures where there is no prior record of success is a very risky thing to do. The military parallel here is to always to fight a battle based on your strengths, ideally pitted against your enemy's weaknesses. If you do not do that, you are in danger of losing.

To better illustrate the thinking process behind working out which of Porter's strategies may suit your organization, let us look at the example of Audi, the German car brand. If we go back thirty years, Audi had a limited range of models and sales were falling after a series of product recalls following issues with acceleration. While the vehicle maker was grappling with static sales, the car market was changing all around it. High-end, luxury models were popping up on one side of it, eating away at its core market, while nippy, inexpensive city cars were attacking sales from the other side. Fortunately, Audi was by this time under the leadership of the visionary Ferdinand Piëch.

The grandson of Ferdinand Porsche, Piëch had begun his career at Porsche and had risen to become head of product development, but he had had to leave because of a company policy that no members of the Porsche or Piëch families could lead the company. Fiercely ambitious and talented too, Piëch was determined to prove his mettle by making Audi a worthy competitor to Porsche, as well as other leading brands such as Mercedes and BMW. He was acutely aware that, if nothing changed, Audi could easily find itself being left in the hugely dangerous and often stagnant mid-market (stuck in the middle), where it is easy to get lost among all the other brands that fail to move with the times. Under Piëch, Audi introduced a very successful differentiation strategy under the new slogan 'Vorsprung durch Technik', backing this up with unique innovations like the introduction of the concept of four-wheel drive for road cars (i.e. the Audi Quattro and many others). In the space of a few years, the company used this strategy to great effect to grow the business, producing a veritable banquet of new products that addressed all of the market segments. Today, we have the A series (1 through to 8) and the Q series (2 through to 8), not forgetting the R Range and the TT.* That is quite a list of different car types: ones to suit every palate and potential end use, whether it is nipping into town, cruising cross-country for a mini-break or being the preferred mode of business transport for a successful executive. Most importantly, each car in the extensive range retains Audi's positioning at the premium end of the market, with the emphasis on the latest technology. As already stated, the whole strategy is held together by Audi's core strengths and its reputation for quality and innovation, as defined by the company's now famous slogan: 'Vorsprung durch Technik' (progress through technology). The strategy closely follows the Porter model by building products in specific segments, or even a whole proliferation of segments, as the car industry now requires.

---

* Audi has now also added electric cars to its range, under the 'e-tron' label.

Elsewhere in the car market, we see a range of differentiation techniques working well for other vehicle makers. Toyota, Kia and Hyundai have been hugely successful at exploiting the low-cost segment, while Renault's very basic, no-frills Dacia brand dominates the entry-level car market by selling new vehicles with three-year warranties at used-car prices. Meanwhile, the top end of the market is dominated by supercars, from the McLaren P1, to Ferrari's LaFerrari, to the Porsche 918 Spyder. Each brand has pursued a strategy of carving out a definite niche that clearly differentiates it from the competition.

Contrast the Audi story with that of another major brand – one that failed to react to changes in the market and differentiate itself, becoming stuck, as a result, in the unprofitable mid-market, with customers questioning what it really stood for. Here we are looking at the once much-loved British food and clothing retailer Marks & Spencer. M&S, which first opened its doors in 1884, became a brand that once shaped how Britain shopped, yet it has been steadily losing market share for decades having seemingly completely failed to look at the competitive landscape and set a coherent strategy. In September 2019, the retailer lost its place in the FTSE 100, which must have been pretty humbling – it was, after all, a founder member when the blue chip index began in 1984. So what was behind this fall from grace?

The chain allowed itself to become firmly stuck in the mid-market, squeezed by fast-fashion discounters such as Primark, H&M and Zara below it and high-end brands such as Chanel, Reiss and Prada above. The chain's growing reputation for being old-fashioned and behind the times (never a good look for a clothing retailer) was emphasized by odd quirks such as refusing to take debit and credit cards until 2001. It even lost its way in food: a sector that M&S once dominated with its top-of-the range offerings. After years of bumper growth, M&S foodhalls are now lagging behind upmarket rival Waitrose and even discounters such as Aldi and Lidl, which have raised their game by selling the products M&S was once famous for.

Despite a succession of management changes and strategy shifts, M&S has simply failed to move with the times and differentiate accordingly. No one in leadership there seems to have worked out

that the consumer base will always bifurcate very strongly, meaning that all businesses need to look at where they are strongest and
work towards meeting the demands of that specific segment. It is
inexplicable that M&S has not capitalized on its strong following in
underwear: a third of Britons still buys their undies at M&S. Why
not remove some of the acres of unsold fashion and replace them
with a whole floor of underwear? On the face of it, this may seem
like a drastic solution, but it is responding to what customers want,
and that is the whole point of this strategic exercise.

Step 3 showed the way by highlighting the strengths and weaknesses of competitors and within the environment as a whole. As
you work to refine your strategy, it is crucial to keep returning to the
previous step to check your ideas against the facts. If you ignore your
findings, you will come unstuck.

For the final example of the penalties of ignoring clear customer
data, we will revisit the story of Nokia, which we briefly highlighted in step 1. As noted, the Finnish company held an enviable
40% of the mobile phone market in the early 2000s and yet it
somehow completely failed to see the threat of upstart competitor Apple until it was too late. It seems evident that the firm's
management, under then chief executive Olli-Pekka Kallasvuo,
must have entirely ignored step 3 and failed to properly evaluate
the competitive threat, which in turn had a knock-on effect on
step 4 because it was therefore left out of considerations in the
strategy going forward. In the resulting confusion, as market share
inevitably plummeted, Nokia adopted a desperate strategy: trying
a bit of everything to solve its problems.

Stephen Elop was brought in as a replacement chief executive
and made a grand announcement to staff about 'burning platforms',
declaring it was time to act. The Symbian operating system – which
had seen dwindling margins on the millions of devices of low-end,
low-margin phones being shipped – was replaced by a Windows
Phone operating system in a tie-up with Microsoft, Elop's former
employer. Microsoft was similarly keen to make its mark on the
smartphone market. Yet, too little thought seemed to be given to
the fact that there were already plenty of comparable and attractive smartphones on the market, developed by rival brands such as

Samsung, as well as Google's smart interface (Android). The media and analysts were dubious from the start, as demonstrated by the many headlines bearing variations on the theme of Nokia having leapt from the burning platform … to almost certain catastrophe. Their cynicism was proved correct: just three years after the announcement of the tie-up, Nokia exited the market altogether and sold out to Microsoft. Ignore step 3 at your peril.

Leverage strengths and attack weaknesses

It is at this point that I will put my hand up and admit to one of a small number of failures in my turnaround career, since it is crucial to learn as much from the things we get wrong as from our successes. In my position as chair and CEO of Hilding Anders (the global bedding and mattress group), we bought British furniture retailer Feather & Black out of administration in 2017. The idea behind the deal was to restructure the troubled business and establish it as a platform for selling beds and mattresses into UK homes. With the benefit of hindsight, I now see that step 3 was missed out of our strategic thinking process. (If I had had this book back then, I would have been in a better position.) We did not drill down deep enough into the customer base to really understand who our customers were so that we could leverage the strengths we had. As a result, we assumed that the brand was a lot more premium and upmarket than it really was. We missed the fact that, despite Feather & Black's historic positioning being at the top end, its upmarket credentials had been completely eroded by an extended period of discounting before we came along. In fact, as far as the bed- and mattress-buying public was concerned, Feather & Black was a business that was in near-permanent discount mode. This is not compatible with an upmarket, exclusive positioning, since the widespread expectation was of low prices.

Despite this strategic mistake, we managed to recover some of our position and began to grow revenue after hiring a crack commercial sales team that did a fantastic job. Unfortunately, and despite our best efforts, what finally did for this deal was the fact we were unable to sort out the supply chain side of things as planned.

The newly appointed supply chain team promised much but (literally) failed to deliver. In hindsight, we should have waited until that problem was properly fixed before expanding the business on the commercial side. The turnaround could not be completed and Hilding Anders eventually sold the business in early 2020. While other mistakes were also made, the error that had the biggest impact was underestimating Feather & Black's reduced position in the market. It was a brutal reminder that yesterday's strengths or weaknesses may not apply tomorrow. In a disruptive situation, avoid the pitfall of failing to recognize a changed environment and react accordingly.

The other mistake that is often made is to 'misinterpret' step 3 according to your own agenda. In setting strategy, it is not always easy to advocate a complete change in direction to focus on a strength you have identified, particularly if your organization has doggedly been pursuing another course for years. It may feel uncomfortable to look at an emerging situation, or it might seem like a lot of hard work to change strategy to meet it. Switching strategy requires a lot of emotional, psychological and physical effort. By this stage, an incumbent leader may be exhausted, or a new leader might be wary of upsetting a team that has been working hard towards their objective. *How am I going to tell them they need to start all over again?* The worst possible outcome is to put your head in the sand and hope the new details will simply go away. Once again, 'hope' is not a mission verb! You cannot use hope in your mission statement.

No one ever wants to admit that they have done a bad job in the past, or that they have got it wrong and need to change to focus on their strengths. In a transformation situation, though, this is invariably what is required. If you find yourself wavering, remind yourself of the penalties of inaction. John Maynard Keynes and Irving Fisher are widely thought of as two of the greatest economists of the last century. It was said they were able to predict the future – and, indeed, for a long time they both made a killing on the stock market. Right up until the Wall Street Crash of 1929, that is. What is most interesting, though, is what happened afterwards. While both economists were caught out by the fallout from the crisis and lost heavily, Keynes was able to recover and again become very rich while Fisher died a pauper. The difference was that Keynes was willing to change his investment strategy, refocus and start afresh. Fisher was not.

Keynes and Fisher originally had very similar approaches, based on timing the business cycle and then moving into and out of different investment classes according to the way the wider economy was moving. After the crash, Keynes adopted a new approach that abandoned macroeconomic forecasting and, instead, sought out well-managed companies with strong dividend yields and held onto them for the long term. (This is also the approach pursued by Warren Buffett.) Fisher, on the other hand, remained convinced the market would turn again, once the 'largely psychological' panic had died down. He therefore topped up his investments according to the original strategy, and as a result fell deeper and deeper into debt.

This is cognitive dissonance on a grand scale: an inability to see beyond what seem to be the true facts. Again, this is not something that is confined to the corporate world. There are plenty of examples from history where the armed forces have failed to learn lessons and repeated the mistakes of the past. We certainly saw this in France in May 1940, when the French army fully expected the impending German invasion to mimic the Schlieffen Plan of 1914 and positioned its forces accordingly. The foundation underpinning this strategy was a firm belief that the Ardennes region was completely impassable. Despite numerous warnings from intelligence agencies that there was a significant build-up of forces in the area under the command of General Gerd von Rundstedt, together with a large amount of bridge building, the French stubbornly refused to waver from their original plan and respond by shoring up their defences there. They had made their plans, decided which way things were going to go, and they would not change, despite a wave of new information coming in. History, of course, proved the French very wrong indeed. The resulting action was a debacle for them. Even the German troops and commanders were surprised at the speed and success of their invasion.

The key message here is that if you are not willing and able to change your views according to the latest available information, you will always lose out with your strategy.

Risk taking and assessment

You may have heard the expression 'culture eats strategy for break-fast', which was originated by management consultant Peter Drucker. It means that whatever course you want your business to take, it will be your culture – what the team believes and how it behaves – that will determine how it gets lived out in the workplace. Culture is not about ping-pong tables and 'dress down Fridays', it is beliefs and the habits that employees form, how they make decisions and respond to challenges, pressure and discomfort. However much leaders expect the majority of the workforce to act out the same set of beliefs, it does not automatically follow that they will do so. Culture can and does interfere with, or contradict, strategy, particularly if the new direction is very different from before.

STRATEGY   CULTURE

Culture eats strategy for breakfast. (© Pepyn Dinandt.)

In step 1 we touched upon the theory of architectural innova-tion, where countless businesses have floundered because they have become too comfortable with their old way of doing things and therefore missed out on making necessary and important changes. This is why culture is an important consideration in this context. If the strategy you settle on does not fit in with the culture of your organization, or is vastly different, culture will always win out. When you look at a strategy that appears to best suit your turnaround aspi-rations, and you begin testing it against the variables and the risks of it succeeding, consider it from the point of view of the scope of your organization. What are its capabilities relative to the strategy you have envisaged? While the strategy may look good on paper and take in all the key points from the previous steps, it might be 180 degrees away from the culture of your business.

Let us return to cars once more and look at another German brand that is pertinent here: the Smart car. Smart was conceived by the Swiss company Swatch, who had the idea of creating a tiny car that would be easy to park in Europe's crowded cities. Seeing that car-manufacturing expertise would be required, Swatch tried and failed to interest Volkswagen in the project before managing to convince the Daimler board, the makers of Mercedes, to go into partnership with it. Little thought seemed to be given to culture, particularly the fact that the Daimler team knew virtually nothing about small cars. This was a big mistake. The design, production and marketing of the vehicle were imbibed with the culture and brand values of its parent. The Mercedes teams that were assigned to the project were steeped in the culture of producing top-end, luxury vehicles, and they seemed to find it impossible to prioritize value over quality. The team was also very male dominated, which meant they did not seem to have the capability to understand how to position a vehicle that should have appealed greatly to female motorists. The resulting vehicle made no sense. Sure, the car was only 248 centimetres long, but people do not really buy a car with parking as their top consideration. A two-seater may have saved valuable space, but what if a motoring couple wanted to give a lift to a friend? The Smart was fuel efficient, but it was achingly slow too. Perhaps most unforgivably, Daimler completely overestimated the market. After building a new plant for Smart, the company needed to sell 200,000 a year to break even. Sales for two-seaters were half that at the time.

The entire team got carried away with what the vehicle was *supposed* to be, but ended up spending a fortune on a vehicle that failed to appeal to anyone, let alone the car-buying public. It was a leadership failure to find the right strategy and the Smart has not made money since its launch. In 2019, Daimler went into a 50/50 joint venture with Chinese vehicle manufacturer Geely that will see the next generation of Smarts made in China.

Culture is a powerful force in any organization. This does not mean that you cannot set a new strategy, though. That is, after all, what we are here to do, in order to effect a successful turnaround and transformation. However, you do need to be aware of ingrained cultural habits that could potentially lead to problems with executing your strategy. You need to ask the question of whether the business's existing culture will or will not readily enable the strategy. If you have any doubts, work will need to be done to map the way decisions and actions are taken within the organization, so you can begin considering how to change them. Alternatively, there may need to be adjustments to the strategy.

There will always be the question of risk-taking when you devise a new strategy. Every time you make a change you will expose your organization to risk. This is why it is important to weigh up the downsides of the new direction as well as its upsides. If you are able to pinpoint the potential weaknesses, you will be able to do something about them. And having done so, if the risk of failure seems too great, you can make a more informed decision about the strategy. As a general rule, if the risk is high and the reward is low, the strategy may not be worthwhile. The same is true if the rewards are negligible even if the risks are low too. Conversely, if the risk is low and the potential reward high, it seems like a no-brainer. A greyer area might be where both the risk and reward are high, in which case you might like to spread the load by getting another party involved.

Sun Tzu has some helpful advice here in assessing your appetite for risk and visualizing outcomes. In this case, he looks at nine varieties of ground to fight on:

> Ground which is reached through narrow gorges and from which we can only retire by tortuous paths, so that a small number of the enemy would suffice to crush a large body of our men. This is hemmed-in ground. Ground of which we can only be saved from destruction by fighting without delay, is desperate ground. ... On hemmed-in ground, resort to stratagem. On desperate ground, fight.[14]

Our version of the risk–success matrix can be seen below.

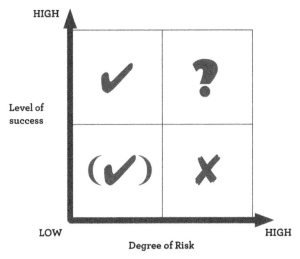

Risk–success matrix. (© Pepyn Dinandt.)

The serious question you need to ask is: how much risk are you prepared to take, and how much can your organization stand? Some leaders take risks that, in hindsight, are just gambles. You do not want to be in that position. This is why the basics are so important: if you get those right, then if the strategy is a risk, it is a considered one. If you understand that the risk is high, you may be able to lay the ground for it by setting out an iterative approach, rolling out the strategy step-by-step. That way, you can check on how each stage goes before moving on to the next. Your risk of failure is increased if the multistage strategy becomes too complex though, of course. Alternatively, even though time may seem of the essence in a turnaround situation, there is another option when it comes to reducing risk: learn from others. Let a competitor make a move and see how they get on. Learn from their successes and failures and then come out with your own new and improved version of the first mover's product. What this all boils down to is being smarter than your competitors.

Most importantly, if you are making a considered decision, you will be able to ascertain a safe cut-off point. This is the last moment at which it will be safe to pull the plug and protect whatever assets you have if the calculated risk is not playing out as you hoped. While no leader wants to be seen to be negative by saying they will pull out if things do not work, they also need to make it known that there are predetermined risk-mitigation strategies that are going to be regularly reviewed and commented on. They can tell the team that this is a worst case, and that this is what the worst case is.

The final point on risk is one that is often overlooked. Remember, if you are planning an ambitious plan of attack on your competitor, it is equally likely they will be considering the same strategy against you, particularly if you are seen to be a weaker player. If a competitor has gained market share against yours – hence the need for the transformation plan – they are not going to give it up easily. You need to take this into account in your strategy, and you may well need a defensive strategy as well.

Overall, as long as you give risk due consideration and give time to weighing up the basics, the idea behind strategy is simple. In the words of General Charles Krulak of the US Marine Corps:

> For strategy to be a success, you need to begin by getting the big ideas right, then, give clear direction on how to achieve them, supervise the execution and then have a good process for any lessons learned and for identifying best practice.

STEP 5. DETERMINING THE
BEST COURSE OF ACTION

There cannot be a firm in the world that would relish head-lines describing it as 'totally chaotic' or 'an utter farce'. Yet, this is exactly what security firm G4S experienced in the coverage around its role in the 2012 Olympics, one of Britain's most high-profile events for decades. Thanks to what appeared to be a complete lack of preparedness, G4S failed to fulfil its contract to provide the security around London's newly built Olympic Stadium and other sporting venues. At the eleventh hour, in a hugely embar-rassing moment for the British government and the event organizers, as well as for G4S, the police and military had to be drafted in to fill the void left by the private security contractor.

To understand a little about what went wrong, you would need to start by looking at G4S's business model, which centres around low-margin, high-volume security. After winning the tender to pro-tect the Games, the directors of G4S no doubt stuck to their usual tried-and-tested formula of hiring teams as and when they needed them. After all, if they hired them too quickly and began the train-ing process too soon, they would have to pay them in the months and weeks ahead of the Olympics. It seems that it was decided that this was not feasible, since G4S had cut its quote to the bone in order to win the competitive bidding process. While the just-in-time strategy sounds wise on paper, since it maximized margins, it did not translate well into reality.

In the crucial weeks before the event, stories began to emerge of complete chaos behind the scenes. Those guards who had been signed up reported that they had no schedules, no uniforms and no basic training on the X-ray machines that were sited at the entrance to each location. Others said they had been allocated to venues hundreds of miles from where they lived, while some came forward to say they had been offered shifts despite failing G4S's own supposedly strict vetting procedures. Eventually, just days ahead of the event, G4S bosses had to put their hands up and say that they could not deliver the number of trained staff that were required. Until that point G4S had enjoyed a decent reputation, but the PR fallout from this failure was enormous, with commentators lining up to slate their performance. The directors were hauled up in front of a House of Commons Select Committee to explain the failings (and that did not go well either).

At the heart of this excruciating episode is a very simple, yet hugely important, failing: the executives at G4S who negotiated the tender did not consult with the people who were charged with executing the job the firm had signed up to do. If they had, these operators would most likely have said: 'You need to start the process of recruiting and training now. This is a massive undertaking.' The operators would have known how long the process took and that it is not always possible to find all the right recruits straight away; they would have been able to tell the executives that a further time buffer was required between the date on which recruiting started and the date personnel were needed. The first day of an Olympic Games is not a movable feast, after all.

The G4S story is a classic example of step 5 having been broken. After being charged with a simple plan (i.e. provide security for the Olympics), executives at the firm should have worked closely with the people who would execute the plan to agree a realistic timeline, with key goals, milestones and objectives. This type of empowering leadership is at the heart of step 5.

In the context of business practice, step 5 is a stage that is often overlooked. Having looked at the market, weighed up all the variables and decided upon a strategy, the next logical step for many leadership teams appears to be to roll it out into the organization and let them get on with the plan, as specified. *This is what I want; make it happen.* As can be seen so vividly in the G4S example, this is not enough. Not by a long way.

Step 5 will entail a new way of thinking for some leaders. Opening up the strategy to the wider organization, inviting comment and perhaps even suggestions for change may not sit well with those who feel they have done all the hard work in steps 1–4: assessing the market and developing their plan in line with the stated mission. Surely it does not now need to be redone? Adding to their reticence is the fact that the transformation process does, by necessity, need to be moved along with some sense of urgency. Surely it cannot be prudent to pause and check what everyone thinks of it so far? It may also feel impractical to get everybody who is due to execute the strategy around the table, particularly when they have a day job to attend to during an uncertain period for the organization. The answer to these objections, though, is that it *is* worth taking the time, pausing for a moment, and seeing what the operators think. While the effort involved in step 5 is significant, leaders need to make the effort. This is very often the point at which transformational projects fail.

Becoming agile

Historically, the military had a reputation for being hugely hierarchical, favouring top-down thinking. Everyone knew their place, with the command coming from the person at the top of the pyramid, directing their armies to win battles by focusing a huge amount of resources on subduing a smaller enemy force. In the past, battles were often fairly static, with the main advantage gained through having more men than the opposing side. Famously, during World War II, the British General Montgomery called it the 'orchestra of war', with him as the conductor and his men as the instruments doing exactly as he instructed them to do. Things have changed a lot since then, mainly through necessity.

To stick with the British example for the moment, consider what happened nearly forty years later, during the Falklands War. By this point the British Army, like so many armies the world over, was considerably smaller. It could no longer rely on a numerical advantage to subdue its enemy. Even so, the deeply ingrained culture of top-down leadership endured. As a result, soldiers on the field waited to be told exactly what to do despite the fact that casualties could well have been avoided if they had used their initiative. At the end of the war, the British Army reviewed its approach and radically redesigned it, working towards empowering people on the ground so they felt able to make their own rapid decisions. A comprehensive review after the campaign recognized that many of the battles were won by small bands of non-commissioned officers and soldiers who just seized the initiative and refused to be stifled by 'directive control'. Thus, the British command philosophy of Mission Command was formalized. The idea was that by becoming more agile, it would be possible for a smaller force to defeat a larger enemy, by moving quickly and cutting through the decision-making cycle.

This agility has become increasingly important in modern warfare. Few nations have anything like as much strength in their armed forces as they did even at the time of the Falklands War. We often need to rely on 'coalitions of the willing', and even the most unpopular operations end up being multinational. This means that the way the plan is framed and communicated to all parties is more crucial than ever. The plans team at HQ therefore keeps the operations team absolutely at the front of their minds. Indeed, the norm is that they work together, bouncing ideas back and forth, so that by the time the plan of attack is handed over, everyone gets it. By standardizing the path of the operation cooperatively, soldiers are confident in making decisions and coming up with ideas. Equally importantly, they will have fully bought into the mission and understood the overall intent. A military mission is no longer a set of tasks: it is a dynamic situation with a specific purpose as its goal.

A business situation, particularly a transformational one, needs to replicate this way of thinking in order to be successful. Any leader that sees their team as a static group, waiting to be told what to do next, is wasting an opportunity and will inevitably come unstuck. Everyone from the ground up needs to understand what they are doing against the bigger picture of the backdrop of the 'what', 'why' and 'when'. Thus, if unexpected hurdles appear or new opportunities arise, they will know what the overall objective is and what the boss wants the team to achieve. They will know what needs to be done to increase their chances of success.

The G4S story that opened this chapter gives a very vivid example of what happens when the operators – the individuals who will execute the plan – are ignored. Unfortunately, this is not a one off, and it is a particular problem in a transformational situation: just the point when you absolutely want everyone to be pulling in the same direction. For some of the most extreme examples of what can go wrong when transformation plans are cooked up and presented to teams with zero collaboration, you need look no further than when two businesses merge. You may well be familiar with the scenario: two major corporations breathlessly announce a multimillion-dollar marriage made in heaven, but the reality frequently turns out to be pretty tumultuous and often ends in a messy divorce.

History shows us that most so-called transformational mergers are anything but. Indeed, according to McKinsey, roughly 70% either fail or do not come close to delivering what was promised.[15] The reason for this can be anything from a failure of due diligence, to inaccurate expectations. A key factor, however, is the failure of the merged organizations to properly integrate teams and get the best out of them.

'It's OK,' the merging parties will announce to often cynical investors. 'We have a post-merger integration (PMI) plan.' These PMI plans generally include pages and pages of process analyses, with 2,000 initiatives or more, outlining how the merger will succeed. Experience shows that these heavily top-down plans are invariably too complicated, or require resources that are scarce or non-existent. These factors are not made clear until the damage has been done though, because too little time is spent talking to the people who will actually do the job, in order to hear their views on the plans.

Throughout history, time and again, we have seen companies that were apparently perfectly suited to each other on paper coming unstuck because they clearly failed to listen to their operators either before, during or after a merger. Going back in time to 1994, there was the $1.7 billion merger between Quaker Oats and Snapple. Quaker's leadership declared its intention to leverage Snapple's existing relationships with supermarkets and large retailers. Somehow, though, they failed to realize that around half of Snapple's sales came from small channels like convenience stores.

Fast forward just over a decade and we see telecoms giants Sprint and Nextel celebrating their $35 billion union. Sadly, the no-doubt-weighty PMI plan failed to acknowledge that Nextel placed more emphasis on the business market while Sprint was more concerned with consumers and broadening data communications.

The $2.6 billion marriage between eBay and Skype suffered from a similar bout of tone deafness when it came to communication. Having declared an intention to integrate the two companies' technologies, so that VoIP could improve communications between buyers and sellers and improve sales, too little regard was paid to said buyers and sellers. It turned out that eBay purchasers far preferred the anonymity of email. Who knew? Well, apart from the people on the ground at eBay who moderate such communications.

For our final example of merger mayhem (there were many to choose from), we visit Yahoo, which celebrated a $1.2 billion link up with social networking platform Tumblr in 2013. Yahoo's then CEO Marissa Mayer even wrote a Tumblr post promising 'not to screw it up'. Investors were told that the rapidly growing social networking site would increase Yahoo's audience by 50%, putting it in the same league as Google and Facebook. The newly merged Tumblr and Yahoo sales teams did not concur, though. In fact, the unrealistic $100 million sales targets sparked an employee exodus. Yahoo ultimately wrote off $712 million in losses from the exercise.

In each case, the plans were overly extensive or complicated and were then imposed on teams to execute who had had little involvement in their development. And when theory met reality, deficiencies were exposed. The often-grandiose plans also neglect to take into account that teams have day-to-day responsibilities, too: the job they are employed to do, be it selling, or marketing, or taking care of production. This is what occupies them whether or not the company is embarking on a significant transformational merger. If leadership then appears and says 'this is what we are doing now', with the barest amount of detail or discussion, it is inevitable that the operators will have one overriding response: 'How am I going to get that done too?' Helping to execute the grand plan, which they may not fully understand, let alone buy into, will come on top of those day-to-day activities. It is little wonder that there is resource conflict and possibly even pushback over playing their part properly at all.

Pause for a reality check

As a general rule, the more ambitious the transformation plan, the more that leadership needs to involve the team from an early stage. Consider, as an example, a strategy that involves you laying off twenty people out of a department of fifty or sixty. This will entail some consolidation of activities and the taking out of some layers, but at the end of the day the remaining thirty or forty individuals will get by without their former colleagues. There is always a certain degree of slack in any organization.

However, if you are making a more significant move, such as closing a factory or merging one unit with another, that is when detail really counts. The vastly increased workloads that this will require will lead to inefficiencies, many of which leadership will not have thought about. The people on the floor will fully understand the nuances of sequence planning, or changeover times, or the whole topic of managing inventory and work in progress. A serious change like this will put pressure on all of these working elements and will inevitably highlight inefficiencies. It is quite likely that the calculations that have been done, pointing to savings from the move, will not have taken these complexities into account. If important details are missed, it may well dilute the targeted impact. Conversing with the team at an early stage and requesting impact statements from the line managers will give a leader an all-important reality check from the people that are actually going to execute the plan.

Experience tells me that this reality check is particularly pertinent with large organizations – especially those with a number of different business divisions or ones that span multiple locations across a wide geography. At a time like this, communication matters, and this includes taking into account potential cultural differences.

Over the years, I have done business in many different countries around the world. What I have learned through experience is that the realities of doing business in each geographic area are always very different from what one might expect, and it is easy to come unstuck if you fail to really understand the culture. Once a plan has been developed, it is crucial to get the native team that will be executing the plan into the room to present them with it. Even more importantly, listen to their feedback on it. If you do not do this, things can unravel very quickly.

A firm I once worked for wanted to close a factory in one part of France and move production to another part of the country. My experience told me that whenever I had been involved in closing a factory, there was always something that gets forgotten – a particular detail that is stumbled over. This case was no exception. The stumbling block here turned out to be a legal stipulation that the team at the new site could not be trained in the production of the goods they were taking over until *after* the announcement of the closure of the old factory. This created a huge problem for us. Not only would it take a while for the new team to get up to speed, but those at the factory earmarked for closure became increasingly uncooperative as they worked out their notice periods. Production slowed to a snail's pace, and the goods being produced were not made to their usual high standard. The entire timeline of moving the product range from one factory to another was seriously held up. If we had been made aware of the legal detail at the planning stage, more detailed discussions about a strategy to ensure consistency of supply could have been held before the process began. We could have spoken, in confidence, with shift leaders at the factory that was due to receive the additional production and asked how they would accommodate the extra work. What challenges did they expect to see? Did they have all the machinery that they required? Did the operators of all of the machines have the right training? Like many lessons, it was one that was only learned through experience. I am now very careful to explore all the legal criteria when closing plants in different geographies. Even in today's highly integrated world, culture matters. If you do business with Italians, French, Germans or Swiss, they each have a different way of doing things.

There is another very important reason for opening up that dialogue and making sure everyone is on the same page: if the team does not really understand what they are being asked to do or is not fully onboard, there is a risk that leadership can open themselves up to a situation in which everyone nods away, saying that everything is going well, when nothing could be further from the truth. This can produce the worst sort of reality check for leadership further down the line.

One of my earliest positions was with a large German conglomerate that was in the habit of producing regular, company-wide
improvement programmes. These were invariably created at head
office, although external consultants would also sometimes be pulled
into the exercise. The resulting strategies and initiatives were very,
very detailed – and very inflexible too. They would be rolled out
across the organization and it would immediately become clear to
anyone who looked that, despite the huge amount of detail the plans
contained, the strategies had very little, if anything, to do with the
reality of what could actually be achieved. Everyone apart from
those in head office could see that the plans were obviously written
by people that would not have to deliver the programmes.

Consider, for example, a plan centred around a quality initiative.
The goal of this initiative, which would be announced to investors at
the same time, would be to save €200 million across the group. Yet,
this figure may as well have been plucked out of thin air. What had
happened was that leadership had taken a couple of examples and
then extrapolated them to the entire corporation. They would say:
if everyone improves the quality of parts being produced by 5%, we
will save €200 million. The only problem was that the figures were
based on the data of just a small share of the corporation's factories.
At other sites, it was entirely unrealistic to expect a 5% productivity
improvement based on the same metric. Rolling out this one-size-
fits-all programme simply could not work.

There is more, though. When unrealistic pronouncements like
these are made and people do not understand the targets, still less
how to achieve them, how does the workforce react? It seems a lot
to ask to get everyone slogging away at targets they already know
they do not have a chance of achieving – and, unsurprisingly, fail
to achieve. Unfortunately, the unintended consequence of this
miscommunication is that sometimes teams say: yes, we managed
it! Certainly, when I was at the German conglomerate, there were
countless examples of teams telling HQ what they wanted to hear:
'lies to headquarters', as they were known throughout the company.
Yes, we are getting production efficiencies. Factories would fill out the
forms as required, tweak the numbers so they more or less fitted the
bill (and they did not get any hassle), and then get on with the day

job. It is not the best outcome for anyone, I am sure you will agree, but this is what you get when there is a huge disconnect between the people who write the plans and those who have to execute them.

This syndrome is not unique to the conglomerate where I once worked, either – I have seen it at many organizations. The reason we do not hear about it as often as we should is because it makes some very smart accountants out of operators. They will produce figures that show that, yes, they did produce the required productivity improvements, *however*, the full cost savings did not, sadly, flow through because of counter-effects that ate up most of the savings. It is a lose–lose situation for everyone. How much better would it be to produce compartmentalized packages that individual teams understand, so that they can then plan their own way to achieve the desired outcome? This may require a compromise between an aggressive target that will achieve the financial impact that is being sought and the operators' commitment to a more realistic plan, which may have less financial impact, but at least it will be realistic and therefore properly delivered.

Goal to create ownership/buy-in

While researching and writing this book, I had a conversation with Tim Freystedt, who has been working in senior roles at Amazon for the past nine years after being brought in to launch their Kindle e-reader device in Germany in 2012. I wanted to include some of what I discovered from Tim here because I believe Amazon has arrived at the perfect balance of involving its teams and achieving full buy-in to its strategy.

When Tim joined Amazon, the organization was still relatively small. Since then, it has grown into the multibillion-dollar giant we know today, boasting a broad portfolio of products and devices. Amazon's mission – to create the best customer experience on earth – is well known, but ask Tim what is behind Amazon's success in achieving this goal and he is unequivocal: it is the '14 Leadership Principles' that the organization is run by.* The principles span everything from obsession with the customer, to insisting on high

---

* Amazon's 14 Leadership Principles are all freely available online. Look them up: they are very inspiring.

standards at all times, to moving quickly. What underpins them all are Amazon's goal to recruit the very best talent and the strategies it has put in place to give the people they recruit free rein to use their talents.

'Amazon thinks big, thinks long term, hires the smartest people possible and then lets them do what needs to be done,' Tim says.

From the beginning, Amazon founder Jeff Bezos had the intention that everyone on the team would think and act as though they were an owner of the business. Thus, Amazon boasts a largely flat organizational structure as well as an unusual system of compensation for management at every layer. Everyone's base pay is relatively low, certainly compared with industry norms, but the overall pay package is boosted by shares. This ensures that everyone prioritizes what is in the best interests of the company (and therefore the share price) and that nothing is introduced that will weigh the company down with burdensome bureaucracy.

Everyone on the Amazon team has the opportunity to shine. When it comes to trialling something new, there are no debates that drag on for months. The team putting forward the idea is encouraged to try it out, even if at first glance it looks like it might adversely impact the core business. It is all about keeping on moving forward – almost like being in a constant burning platform state. There is no blame culture either if a risky concept fails to work out – as long as you do not make the same mistake twice! Likewise, if a new initiative does not seem to be working out, the team member responsible is trusted to 'kill it' even if the potential for failure is not at first obvious. One of Tim's projects was the Amazon Dash button: a small electronic device that was designed to be placed around the house and programmed to automatically reorder consumer goods before they ran out. Despite the idea being widely welcomed as a huge breakthrough, Tim quickly realized that the project was not working as billed. He advocated pulling the plug on the Dash in Europe and that is exactly what happened. The process behind this was straightforward, Tim explains:

> What makes it easy is there is rarely a discussion in Amazon based on opinions. It is all data driven. If you bring the data that proves something is wrong, they listen.

If there is a problem to solve, Amazon puts what is known internally as a 'two-pizza team' onto it. The idea is that the company does not throw hundreds of people onto a new topic when it is more efficient for a team of the size that could effectively feed off two pizzas to have a credible crack at it. And it works, too. The initial team that went on to launch Kindle in Europe was just this size. Many believe that it requires hundreds of people to achieve the best outcome, but small, agile and trusted teams that are dedicated to a topic are clearly effective.

Another system worth noting here, and one that has become part of the Amazon culture, is the question mark email. If anyone has an enquiry about something that does not seem right, or that may deserve further attention, they can forward an email outlining the issue to the relevant person on the team with a single question mark as the subject. This is enough to get things moving and see a problem resolved. And, as Tim says, a question mark email from Jeff Bezos always guarantees that day-to-day operations come to a standstill as everyone scrambles to resolve the problem.

The message here is that everyone has a voice. Things are not left to someone else to notice and sort out. There is an atmosphere of cooperation and open enquiry. Most importantly, Amazon fosters a culture of openness and ownership. The more delegated style, where it is clear that everyone's opinions count, means that individuals on the team are emboldened to make their own plans. They know the overall goals of the business but use their initiative to get there. This is something that you do not see in the many companies that are too hierarchical.

Listen to feedback

The central part of the SAS's Mission Success Cycle – with its stages of plan, brief, deliver, debrief – is to get everyone that will be involved in executing the mission into a room to make sure they understand the instructions. Once the mission has been briefed, each individual is given the opportunity to comment on the plan in a live 'back brief' session. This is the opportunity not only to be convinced that they understand the mission, but also to see whether they have any suggested improvements or variations that will make the plan even more effective. It is possible here to explore expected side effects and any unintended impacts too. Similarly, this is the time to overcome the common mistake of overestimating the available resources and underestimating the problems that may be encountered.

This feedback process was crucial to the success of the British defeat of guerrilla rebels in Malaya between 1952 and 1954. Field Marshal Sir Gerald Templer was appointed British High Commissioner for Malaya and was given a brief by Prime Minister Winston Churchill to 'deal with the Malayan emergency'. Sir Gerald initially refused the brief until he was given a more coherent goal. Churchill eventually gave him a complete brief, which centred around the firm aim to make Malaya fully independent by 1960. Once this was established, Templer knew he had no time to lose so he fleshed out the strategy, which would involve setting up a legitimate election process, reorganizing the civil service and winning the hearts and minds of the population. This clarification of the brief, based on Sir Gerald's feedback, meant the plan was successfully enacted and the emergency ended. Sir Gerald was subsequently honoured by the Malayan government for his contribution.

Listening to feedback on a plan – *really listening* – is a crucial part of the Mission Success Cycle and the step 5 process. Here, after working out the way forward, leadership will take the opportunity to slow down and think about their plan alongside all those that are involved. In a transformational operation, one should ask the following questions: Is everyone involved that needs to be? Are the instructions clear? Does everyone really understand what you want them to do? Is the plan feasible in its current form?

Tim Collins tells me about a Swiss company he was working with to deliver some leadership training. The predominantly young team he was helping operated out of London, and it transpired that the leadership back in the Zurich HQ was routinely despatching ideas to London on a Friday afternoon and then sending out inspectors the following Tuesday to see how things had gone.

'We've barely had time to figure out what it is we are trying to do,' the young team complained.

Tim introduced the team to the one-third/two-thirds rule outlined in step 1. This is where leadership devotes a third of their time to making the plan and the remaining two-thirds to their people. Once orders have been given, everyone needs time to think about how to implement the plan. They need to understand the plan, and they also need to know how they fit into it. The time when things start to go wrong is when leadership fails to allow enough time for everyone to properly consume and evaluate the strategy, leaving them to go off and do their best with the time they do have.

When you come down to the level of the trenches, or the operators, they may well have their own ideas on better ways to achieve the overriding goal. As Sun Tzu said, 'There are not more than two courses of action, direct and indirect, yet these two in combination give rise to an endless series of manoeuvres.' During discussions with operators, it may emerge that the plan is unrealistic, or maybe even that it is impossible to do everything you want to do at the same time. There may need to be phases or stages, where one depends upon another being completed. It is through these discussions and the subsequent planning programme that you will be able to decide upon the staging of your operations, from the early steps through to delivery.

The goal of leadership is to create an environment in which individuals feel emboldened to suggest a better way to the same destination. There may be an interesting parallel here with something that Richard introduced when he was running the Operational Training Advisory Group, preparing 45,000 troops a year to go to Iraq and Afghanistan. He started something he dubbed 'the good ideas club'. The message to the troops was simple. Richard told them what they were required to achieve and why, but the 'how' was entirely up to them. When Richard spoke with his troops, he acknowledged that they were 'living it' and were therefore technically far more capable of governing their part within it than he was. Granted, when he sat down with individuals and listened to their back briefs and suggestions, he would occasionally butt in and ask if they had thought about doing it in a different way, but nine times out of ten they absolutely had it nailed. Richard notes that everyone also relished the responsibility of being able to decide how to deliver what they had been asked to deliver.

Many leaders will find this part of the process difficult. In a failing organization there may be a view that everyone has got it wrong in the past and this is why the business is in trouble – so why listen to anyone now? Aside from the fact that this is a sweeping assumption and that things will never be that black and white, it would be foolish to ignore everyone in a bid to avoid all the 'bad' stuff. There will be a number of very solid operators within the organization who are well worth listening to. Give them the framework to contribute and you will be amazed at what they come up with.

The fact is, even though you are in a leadership position, you do not have all the answers and it would be counterproductive to think you do. Cognitive dissonance like this will always have severely negative effects. For an extreme example, let me share Richard's experience as part of the UN peacekeeping mission of 1995 in Bosnia, which went horribly wrong in the eastern enclaves. The UN headquarters in Sarajevo had put together what they believed was a very neat plan where things would move forward based on consensus from the warring factions and the political will to contribute troops. The problem was that they were unwilling to deviate from the plan even when it was very evidently unravelling on the ground quite quickly. Richard found himself sixty miles behind Serb lines when the Serbs attacked Gorazde, the town he was protecting. His soldiers fought them off, in the process abandoning the previously agreed impartiality to join with the Muslim forces, and managed to hold the Serbs back until they went away. The Serbs did not go quietly, however, clearly deciding they would try and cause as much damage to the town as possible, shelling it repeatedly. Every day, Richard would send a report up to the UN saying something along the lines of: 'Busy day in Gorazde, 500 artillery rounds impacted in town. Seventeen civilians killed, and three soldiers wounded.' Richard's reports would follow a well-worn path, being collated in Sarajevo before being sent on to the UN headquarters in New York and then redistributed back down the line to everybody, along with all the other reports being sent back and forth. Richard was well aware that the news he was sending was incompatible with the planned timeline and outcomes, but he felt sure everyone would want to know what was really happening. He was not prepared for the actual outcome of the process. It quickly emerged that his feedback was being transformed into something that was far more palatable to the central powers, fitting in with their vision of what they *wanted* to see. He read with incredulity the versions he received back that said things like: 'Gorazde, a quiet day.' The brief reports did not even come close to reflecting the reality of the hundreds of artillery rounds landing on the town and the people being killed. Indeed, it was a blatant misrepresentation of the truth that just happened to meet the leadership's single-minded interpretation of their plan.

Richard was, quite rightly, appalled. With few options open to him, both he and his commander secretly spoke with Martin Bell, then a distinguished foreign affairs correspondent with the BBC. It was a dangerous move, since the forces on the ground were banned from speaking with the press. However, Richard trusted the journalist and wanted him to tell the world what was happening. The response from the UN headquarters in Sarajevo was an even greater lockdown: they did not want the news that their mission was failing to get out, even though it was entirely obvious that this was the case to everyone on the ground and even to those beyond. Eventually, NATO had to intervene, resulting in the Dayton Agreement for peace in Bosnia and Herzegovina.

While this is, admittedly, a very dramatic example, this sort of cognitive dissonance and blind adherence to one's original vision for a transformation programme despite lots of incompatible information and evidence is not uncommon. We frequently see corporate leaders who have staked their reputation on a given process then being completely unwilling to show any sign of weakness, either in themselves or in the quality of their plans, despite the feedback from their very capable teams.

I too have been a victim of this in another of the turnaround programmes that I ran, this time for a roofing tile business. I had been appointed CEO of the business, and one of my first decisions centred on what we needed to do about an almost-new plant in France that had been built by the previous boss at a cost of more than €100 million. The entire strategy for this new plant had been badly thought through. Most unforgivably, it had been built in entirely the wrong place, seemingly ignoring the two key factors that are crucial to the success of such clay-tile-making facilities. The first of these is that one needs a good, accessible location, because clay tiles are heavy and are therefore expensive to ship. The second is that the plant needs to be close to a good source of clay, which can then be dug up out of the ground, processed and fired. This new plant was in a terrible location and the clay pit was substandard. To make matters even more bleak, it was nowhere near as good as the key competitor in the area.

As I got to grips with the company, it was clear that the problems were even worse than I had first thought. For a brief time my response was that we would get the plant up and running come what may. I became determined not to let it fail. It did not take me too long, though, to realize that I had fallen victim to the cognitive dissonance I described above. I should have listened more attentively to what I had been told: that there was nothing good about this plant, that many of the production processes were not working efficiently, and that these factors, coupled with the poor quality of the available raw components, were leading to a large number of quality defects. With the wonderful benefit of hindsight, I realized that what I should have done from the start was say: 'This was not money spent on my watch. The previous owner built it and it was a mistake. Let's close it right away.' Lesson learned. Since then I have been much more effective and efficient when deciding on, and executing, factory closures.

There is so much value in letting the team that is responsible for the execution do a lot of the thinking and then listening to their feedback. As a leader, give those people the guidelines and work with them to establish the best processes for a free flow of communication. It is not necessary to accept every suggestion they make. As the person in charge, you will get the final say over what everyone comes up with and over the context of their approach. Since you have the benefit of a 360 degree view over the entire business, the market and the competition, you will be able to judge whether certain things have been given too much prominence or whether people are trying to do too many things, or too few, at the same time. You will also have a good idea of the available resources. No one is invulnerable to making mistakes, though – and that includes you. It therefore makes perfect sense to fully involve the people who will be getting things done in the decision-making process. Genuine teamwork, agility and cohesion underpin every successful turnaround.

STEP 6. BUILDING AND MANAGING AN EXCELLENT LEADERSHIP TEAM

The firing of CEOs has long since become the norm when business performance dives. At a time when companies are judged by the valuation of their stock, investors have become notoriously impatient. Since chief executives are perceived to be the primary determinant of corporate performance, any period of decline, even a brief one, can see them heading out the door. And the same goes for the senior team, at least to a certain extent. When things turn sour, everyone in a leadership position is perceived to be potentially tainted.

It is easy to see why there is a temptation for any new leader who is entering a transformation situation, or even for an incumbent one, to have a substantial clearout and 'start again'. It is at this point, though, that I would urge anyone in a similar position to pause and take a deep breath. Bringing in an entirely new leadership team might seem like a decisive early action, but it is actually hugely disruptive, leaving deep and lasting scars on a company, which will in turn impact performance. Plus, in the race to rush through a swathe of firings, it is quite possible that crucial individuals will be lost and a lot of knowledge about the market will head out of the door.

While restoring confidence with a shake-up at the top might seem important, it should never be done just for the sake of being seen to do something and it should certainly never take the place of doing what is actually right for the business. It is for this reason that step 6 is concerned with a thorough examination of the quality of the existing leadership team. Although this is the sixth of nine steps, a leader needs to be thinking about this from day one. When I am working on a transformation and going through the other steps, I constantly observe the people around me. I am always conscious that for a plan to work properly, I need the right people at a senior level to help me execute it.

There is a high possibility that some senior people will indeed need to go, but a blanket clearout would be hugely detrimental. As a rule of thumb, I would recommend that no more than a third of the leadership team is moved on, and in some cases I have seen it has been significantly less. In some exceptional cases it may be the case that the share will be higher (when new skill sets are needed, for example), but this would be unusual. There will be some important issues to deal with going forward and the senior team that is already in place will have some very valuable insights gained through their experience with the business. Given the right environment and a little judicious leadership, they will step up. Indeed, they may well reveal previously hidden skills, be they entrepreneurial ones or commercial ones. After all, as we so often hear from the military, there are no bad teams, only bad leaders.*

There is another way of looking at this very transactional strategy of culling a substantial proportion of the leadership team. You may have decided that a large number of individuals are not up to the job, but are you equally certain that you will be able to replace them with recruits who are significantly better? It is rare for top performers to be willing to risk everything for a move to a troubled organization. Any rash firing decisions could seriously deplete the top team and leave gaps at a time when you need all hands to the pump.

The availability of potential new recruits to replace senior team members will also be somewhat dependent on the industry you are operating in. While with certain functions it is possible to easily bring in people from other sectors (e.g. finance or HR), if a business is in a very specialized industry – roofing, say, or automotive manufacturing or chemical processes – your recruitment options will be limited. Any new recruits with specialized skills will need to come

---

* There are quite a few variations on this theme. Napoleon said there are no bad regiments, only bad colonels, while Colonel David Hackworth, the author of *About Face: The Odyssey of an American Warrior* (Pocket Books, 1990), who was repeatedly given 'less than ideal' units to turn around, said there were no bad units, only bad officers.

from within your sector. It is unusual to find people from entirely different sectors that will have the right mix of skills, or enough of an understanding of the business to be of real value. This means that, when starting again, a leader will be fishing in a small talent pool – and it is a pool in which most, if not all, of your competition are also fishing for the best talent. Therefore, when any leader begins to weigh up whether or not to replace an existing person, one of the first questions they should ask themselves is whether or not the individual matches up to their equivalents that work for the competition. Are they better, the same or worse? The incumbent may not be 100% perfect, but if they are as good as everyone else, or better, this surely puts the onus on leadership to get the best possible performance out of them. This would be the best use of your time.

Just how much emphasis a leader places on this step will depend on whether they operate in an asset-heavy or asset-light business. The leader of an asset-heavy business, like a chemical plant that cost more than $100 million to build, say, will be pitched against competitors that also have plants that cost similar amounts. In this case, the most important factors to the business are both the plant and the senior team, so make sure you focus on the plant, too: without it, you do not have a business. In an asset-light business, e.g. retail, the cost of entry is far lower. In this case, one of the most important assets you have is your people. The quality of the team, and particularly the leadership team, is so much more important. In a competitive environment, you may win or lose on the strength of your leadership team in relation to those of your rivals. In this case, the skills and talent of each member of the senior team warrants very close focus. The wrong people, with the wrong mix of talent, can lead to a complete failure of the transformation plan. Perhaps one of the most famous examples in this respect comes courtesy of Blockbuster, the video-rental chain that was once a staple of every high street.

In 2000, when Reed Hastings (the founder of a then little-known company called Netflix) flew to Dallas to propose a partnership with Blockbuster, the company's then CEO John Antioco laughed him out of the room. At that time, Blockbuster dominated the video-rental industry with $5 billion in annual revenue, boasted thousands of retail locations and had millions of loyal customers and a huge marketing budget. As far as Antioco was concerned, there was little to interest him in Hastings's proposal that Netflix would run Blockbuster's brand online in return for the videostore giant promoting Netflix on the high street.

What was not clear at the time was that Blockbuster's model had a significant weakness – a weakness that went beyond the fact that all the signs suggested that, at some point, increasingly tech-savvy and demanding consumers were bound to value the convenience of having videos mailed to them at home (Netflix's early model) over heading down to the high street every time they wanted a night in with a movie. Blockbuster's critical weakness was that its profitability was based on charging customers late fees when they forgot to bring their videos back on time. The company had grown entirely dependent on penalizing its customer base. It is this fact that was perhaps behind Antioco's decision to ignore the danger of Netflix's subscriptions-based model, which rendered late fees obsolete, and instead double down on the high-street strategy. Blockbuster's response to the start-up competition was to open up more retail stores. By 2005, by which point the company had lost 75% of its market value, Antioco realized that the strategy was not working and tried to reverse it.[16] Although he convinced his board to back him in discontinuing late fees and investing in a digital platform, one of his lieutenants, John Keys, led a strong rearguard action. He argued strongly that the plan to drop late fees would cost Blockbuster $200 million per year and the same again would be needed to launch an online service. In the bitter row that followed, Antioco was ousted and replaced by Keys.

It is here where we can see the damage that can be done by having the wrong team in the wrong place at the wrong time, particularly when a crucial transformation is required. Keys, who had previously been CEO of 7-Eleven from 2000 to 2005, was a retailer through and through, and he surrounded himself with other retailers. By the time Keys took over, Netflix had powered on to have more than three million customers and had recently announced its new streaming service. Movie fans were raving about it and customer numbers were increasing rapidly. Keys's response? He introduced a new, technology-driven, *in-store* model – a strategy that hinged on improved customer service. This retail-centric strategy completely ignored the fact that people were less and less inclined to actually visit the company's stores, preferring to download movies. Keys also reinstated the hated late fees, infuriating even more of Blockbuster's customer base. The company filed for bankruptcy in 2010, by which time it was reeling under the weight of $1 billion in debt, and was subsequently delisted from the NYSE.

This story strikes at the very heart of step 6. When a new leader is appointed, as Keys was, they need to properly understand and relate to the environment they are entering. Keys was always going to prioritize a retail approach and surround himself with like-minded retail types, but this strategy was completely wrong at a time when the market was shifting firmly towards digital. What was needed was for someone to fully understand the context in which Blockbuster was operating and change direction, rather than doubling down on what was clearly a flawed strategy. The following telling comments from an interview with Bryn Owen, who was appointed as the CMO of Blockbuster's UK division in 2008, clearly show deep frustration at the strategy being pursued by the business's US bosses:

> I am sure 99 out of 100 people involved in Blockbuster would have told you the future was in digital downloads and online ordering, but the chief executive had a retail background and his priority was to save the high street business at all costs. Perhaps we would have benefited from a different perspective.[17]

If I had been on the Blockbuster board, I would have pushed hard for them to pursue a digital strategy and, ideally, hire someone from Netflix. I would also have allowed people like Bryn Owen to challenge an obviously flawed policy and I would have listened to their suggestions. The treatment of Antioco hints strongly that Blockbuster did not foster a blame-free culture, where free speech was encouraged.

Spotting leadership potential

An obvious response from any new leader when confronted with step 6 is to ask how it is possible, without having been in the organization for long, for them to know who has potential and who does not. There is a lot going on in a transformation situation, so it may not feel like there has been much time to make detailed appraisals of everyone on the senior team. There might have been only a brief moment for reviewing CVs and checking out the leadership team's background and experience, perhaps with a few face-to-face discussions to reveal their skill sets thrown in, but beyond that there will also be a certain amount of gut feeling involved. My starting point is to err on the side of giving people a chance. Not everyone will look 100% right at first glance – after all, who does? But there are many other useful pointers that can be picked up very early on.

When weighing up the performance of senior teams, it makes a lot of sense to review technical skills, and this is important of course, but I believe that it is also equally useful to look for signs of good character and exemplary behaviour. I have seen this brilliantly summed up by author and motivational speaker Simon Sinek.[18] He equated the technical side to the battlefield, where he would essentially be trusting the team with his life. The flipside to this was the broader trust required for off the field of battle, where he would want to trust the team with his money and his wife! The comparison might sound a little dated now, but the message is clear: a leader needs to be able to fully trust the people around them. It works the other way round too, as another military saying that has been attributed to various speakers illustrates: 'A man of character in peace will be a man of courage in war.' This is entirely the right balance: a leader needs to know their team will do the right thing on the battlefield, but they have to be certain that they are never going to take the easy option.

There are a number of other qualities that I give great weight to as well. With a tough job ahead, it is essential to be surrounded by highly motivated and energized leaders. It also helps if they are proud of being part of the team and excited about the challenge they face. I also look for humility. If people are humble, they will be more likely to see any risks behind the delivery of the chosen strategy. Rather than nodding away, saying 'yes, we can get that factory closed in time', they will be honest and raise potential barriers to success. A humble attitude is also very healthy because it means people are open to discussing failures and also to learning from others. Failures help people improve. I certainly actively try to learn and improve from my failures. It is very interesting to hear humble people talk about competitors too: they are generally very respectful, and this is the right way to be in my opinion.

Perhaps the most important quality to look out for, though, is a hunger for success. This trait was well articulated to me by the founder of Askona, one of the most interesting, successful and innovative companies I know. Askona is the single biggest bedding and mattress producer and retailer in Russia, with more than a thousand stores across the country, and it has strong ambitions for international growth. In fact, when I spoke with the company's founder, Vladimir Sedov, and its CEO, Roman Ershov, they were in the process of opening their first outlet in London. (By the time this book is published, they will have opened six outlets in the UK.) I wanted to speak to them while writing this book because of one of the aspects of their business that intrigued me most: the strength of their senior team. Many of the top team have been with Askona for years, helping to propel the business from revenue of 5 billion roubles in 2011 to almost 30 billion roubles in 2019.

Sedov told me that there are three elements that are key to Askona's success. The first is that they want to be the best in their industry, the second is that they do not simply promote the product itself but also the *benefit* of the product, and the third is that the leadership team must always be hungry for success. Here is what Sedov told me:

> We choose all our team members on the basis of whether or not they have a 'hungry' mentality. We like to push the targets and put in some crazy goals, to the point where they may not know how to achieve them at first. When we had our first strategic session in 2005, I introduced two targets. I wanted Askona to become the 'leader of the Russian market' and to 'gain 30% of the market share'. At that time, we were really a relatively small company, perhaps number three in the market and the leader of the market was much bigger than we were. Nobody on the team knew how to achieve that goal but that was the vision for the kind of company we are building. What was interesting was that I didn't define the exact revenue. I believe that when you set up the targets, like becoming

a leader, it is much more fun for management and more motivating than just saying we are going to 'grow revenue three times', or other financial goals. To become a market leader, when you're not a leader, is inspiring. It's a fight. It's a war and everything becomes about winning this war. That's what really motivates the team.

Now we have become the leader in our sector, we have set a new challenge. Our goal is to be the 'world's real sleep company'. Nobody knows how to achieve that, or what the components of the world's first sleep company are, but that's what drives our management. It is what keeps them always hungry.

It is important to fully support this passion for growth and success. Our HR strategy is to always grow internally and to only hire competence from outside the market when we really need it. Those that do come from the outside are usually only short term because they don't truly share the long-term passion and hunger that everyone has within Askona.

Once a year, Askona holds a strategic session, called the 'Next Big Thing', at which they agree what is going to happen over the next five years. People from Sedov and Ershov, right at the top, down through four levels of the organization meet and discuss ways to grow. 'It is,' says Sedov, 'a democratic discussion. However, as soon as the agreement is made, there is no longer a democratic approach. They get cracking to make it happen. They execute. That is what a hungry team does.'

Nurture the talent you find and allow those people to do what they do best. Companies all too often find the rising stars, promote them and then shuffle them away into a vacuum, losing all the benefits of the skills that were initially spotted. If you do find someone who shows natural promise, they will be far more valuable to you than people you need to coach into their positions. It is far easier to train people than to retrain them.

Tim Collins recalls meeting a very skilled linguist while he was serving in Anbar Province, during the Iraq conflict. The young lad, called Amon, was a tea boy who had volunteered his services as a translator and turned out to be entirely fluent in English, Arabic and Kurdish. He had learned his skills from watching TV shows.

He could translate in real time and type transcripts. In fact, he was infinitely more efficient at it than his peers. When Tim focused on what it was that made Amon stand out, he deduced that it was that the young man was a natural. His colleagues, who needed to be trained to be translators, always tried too hard to interpret their training, or they mistakenly tried bringing flair to the party – something that generally has a negative effect. Tim likened it to the situation where Iraqi soldiers are trained by Russians to infiltrate behind enemy lines, but stand out a mile because they turn up in leather jackets, sporting large moustaches, and adopt an unnerving habit of bumping into people and staring at them menacingly. As you might imagine, the enemy they are trying to infiltrate can spot them easily. The message here is clear: if you find someone who is naturally gifted, allow their talents to flourish. They will be a great deal more useful to you than people you need to train.

There is an interesting footnote to Tim's story. Despite immediately promoting this young man into an official translating position, Amon's career did not flourish until he was stationed in Baghdad. The team at the Anbar Province unit could never accept him as anything other than the tea boy. People occasionally resent talent, so it needs to be protected as well as nurtured.

Successful strangers are better than unsuccessful friends

As with any business decision, it always helps to look at things from the other side. What are the qualities you *do not* want to see in your senior team? Something I am always careful to scrutinize is the attitude of each member of my team towards achievement. I am keen to surround myself with a group that has a healthy attitude in this respect. People with this attribute are naturally focused upon improving their own professional abilities, but their primary driver is a desire to get the job done. Their goal is excellence. People with a particularly prominent drive towards achievement will often be strong-minded, independent types, and that can occasionally be challenging to deal with, but these are exactly the sort of people leaders need to surround themselves with. What no leader needs are those who are pathological in their achievement motivations. These are individuals who focus on self-betterment by any means possible, not caring how they achieve their goals. This single-minded approach makes for individuals that are not necessarily terribly committed to their organization. There are a lot of people like this in corporate environments and, ultimately, they make very bad leaders because they are invariably more concerned about their own egos and image. It means that their motivations to do things are skewed towards their personal aims, regardless of any potential damage to the strategic aims of their employer.

One of the mental checks that Richard always put himself through when going into battle is useful when trying to weed out people who may have this tendency. He describes a situation where, in the often-testosterone-fuelled atmosphere of the infantry, there is always a powerful desire for soldiers to prove their mettle, particularly since these soldiers have spent their lifetimes training for battle. As a result, and to guard against making selfish decisions, Richard always wrote the same note into the bottom of his plans. The note simply said: 'Do I *need* to do this, or do I *want* to do this?' He reasons that, if a commander is committing soldiers to battle, they have to need to do so and not simply want to do it to polish their reputation. It is a useful final check.

He cites as an example of how important this check can be the story of an SAS squadron that was ordered to clear out a group of 200 Serbs from a barracks in Bosnia. After the Serbs had been given a timeline to leave and had failed to comply, the elite fighting group had been called in. Malcolm Rifkind, the then Secretary of State for Defence, was present at the briefing for the mission.

'What do you think will happen?' the minister asked the SAS squadron commander.

To the squadron commander's credit, he looked the minister square in the eye and spoke from the heart.

'I think a lot of people are going to die over the next two hours.'

Rifkind cancelled the mission. In a later conversation with Richard, the squadron commander had a simple explanation for his candour.

'We didn't need to go in and do that,' he said. 'We were being told strategically to go in and do it. I was not going to say no to a mission, but I wanted to make it quite clear that a lot of people were going to die.'

There is an interesting footnote to this story. It transpired that the reason the Serbs had not moved out as agreed was because their trucks were completely out of fuel. Fuel was found and, three hours after the original deadline, all 200 Serbs left the camp peacefully. If the squadron commander had not stepped in, many, many people would have died unnecessarily.

Something else that I would recommend that all leaders guard against is hiring people because they seem 'nice', or easy to get on with. The aim of this exercise is to choose members for your team based on their professional competence. In the high-stakes business of a transformation project, it is far better to be surrounded by successful strangers than by unsuccessful friends.

Unfortunately, in the corporate environment, we often see relationships built up over a period of time. Promotions or hires are often done on the basis of familiarity rather than whether or not people are absolutely the right person for the job. An HR policy like this, however subconscious, inevitably means that leaders gather a trusted 'inner circle' of people they get on well with around them. This creates a really toxic environment for anyone who is not in that inner circle – people who will, perhaps rightly, be resentful that they did not get asked to join that hallowed central group. Large companies are, essentially, just large gatherings of people, so an element of politics and jostling for position will always be present. That is never a good thing, though, particularly not for businesses in a highly competitive and challenging environment. Leaders need the best people they can get, not those who are good politicians and fun to be around.

Select a range of talents

There is a significant flaw in most talent-selection operations, even in large organizations that have sophisticated HR processes involving all sorts of complex tests and methodologies to pick out the best possible candidates. That flaw begins with the leader of the organization. If they are not aware of their strengths and weaknesses, their recruitment preferences will be swayed towards their strengths. Like picks like – we all tend to gravitate towards people who are like us, even if we do not consciously realize that that is what we are doing. Leaders surround themselves with people who have talents that they like and admire because they are very familiar with those qualities. Their weaknesses – the bits about themselves they would rather ignore – are quietly forgotten, and personnel with strengths in those areas are passed over. What they should be doing, of course, is ensuring that they have a range of different talents on their team, and making sure that any perceived weaknesses are shored up by a member of the team having the required talent.

When there is a range of talents and competencies, people will think like individuals. Get them all together in the same room and discussion and entrepreneurial thinking are encouraged. If something does not work out as expected, it is more likely that a team with a broad range of strengths will have an idea of how to get things back on track. If, however, everyone comes at things from a similar viewpoint, it is very unlikely that there will be any changes. Indeed, the team may well be highly resistant to change or to trying something new.

Selecting talent on this basis may mean that a leader does not feel a natural affinity with every member of their team, but that does not matter. What is important is that all bases are covered. Achieving the right balance on a team begins with self-reflection. What are your strengths and weaknesses?

To properly assess the leadership team, it is also helpful to look at past selection processes. Who picked the members of the team and how was the selection process carried out? Look at past performance, too. The organization might be failing today, but many of the senior team will have been there when it was successful in the past. If that is the case, it indicates that the problem does not lie with the team members but with the previous leadership.

If it is clear that some sort of reshuffle of the top team is essential, avoid falling prey to the Peter Principle at all costs.* For those

---

* The term was coined by Laurence J. Peter in 1969, who said: 'In a hierarchy every employee tends to rise to his level of incompetence.'

unfamiliar with this term, it concerns the tendency to continue to promote people who are good at their job, so they rise from one level to the next level in rapid succession, until they reach a stage where they are no longer able to perform well. Just because there are good reports about the most productive worker in the organization, it does not necessarily follow that they will always be the best candidate to manage other workers. In fact, over-promoting someone like this may be counterproductive because the performance of their subordinates will decline *and* the productive worker will be lost to the team. Likewise, when a high-performing salesperson is taken out of circulation by being promoted to a managerial role, sales will drop *and* there is a danger that the sales team will begin to underperform if the manager is not up to their new role.

Weighing up whether to promote new senior talent from within an organization presents a challenge for any leader. The high-performing salesperson or the super-productive worker may be aching to take on the next role up the ladder – they may even see it as a rightful reward for their efforts to date – but it may be a step too far for them. It would be a mistake to over-promote those people at any time, if they are unsuitable, but it is definitely problematic in this sensitive transformation phase. A possible compromise might be to offer these high performers training to help them build up to these higher roles.

Organizing training is something that the military has always been good at. As a rule, anyone who is undertaking a new role must attend a relevant course first. Even if an infantry platoon commander has proved to be outstanding, they would still be asked to attend a course before they could become a mortar platoon commander. Additionally, on courses and in training, they are often allowed to carry out the duties 'one-up', to give them a flavour of life in command further up the food chain. The awful reality in battle is that they may have to step up at short notice, as casualties are inevitable.

This is quite different from what happens when people get promoted within a civilian company and are frequently expected to pick up the new role by little more than osmosis. At best they may get to understudy someone for a short period before stepping into their new role, but even that is unusual. New recruits often find a real battle on their hands if they request training. I will admit that, in the past, I have baulked at spending money on developing people's skills. Experience shows me now, though, that it is worth the investment; it is good to have task specialists on board who are good at what they do. Making this investment is not a waste of money: it builds strength in an organization.

One further note on training is that it is helpful in increasing the range of talents on offer. Again, there is a useful example from the military here. As Richard says, military leaders tend to get what they are given when they take over the command of teams that have been assembled by army HR in Glasgow. This can lead to a lack of diversity and experience that can really stifle creativity and means that the person in command has to work really hard to make sure they develop that team, because that is what they have got.* The onus is, therefore, on training people in rather than selecting them out. Richard's technique for doing this was to send individuals out to other branches of the forces and, in one case, to a sporting organization so that they could get experience of different planning cycles and different ways of looking at things. One of Richard's men was even deployed to a submarine that promptly went on operations at short notice. Richard did not see him again for four months, but the ploy played dividends because the individual became adept at working in very constricted spaces. That experience was to prove invaluable on his return when the unit subsequently went out on operations and had to establish a head-quarters in a small, ramshackle compound in Afghanistan. The man from the submarine deployment was entirely in his element. Setting up in a very confined space came naturally to him, and his experience was hugely beneficial to those who were more used to a traditional way of thinking: that an ops-room must always look a certain way.

---

* It is possible to fire people, or move them aside, if they are not meeting the requisite standard, but it would invite comment if a commanding officer began firing members of their battalion left, right and centre. As Richard says, people would perceive the problem to lie with the leadership.

There are clearly ideas that can be borrowed from this approach in a corporate setting. If one wants to develop a pipeline of senior talent, try to ensure they have experience in other parts of the business.

Developing the senior team

The early, transaction-orientated, days of reorganizing a leadership team will be disruptive, but this is, of course, a necessary step in the transformation strategy. Once that is done, it is equally important to stabilize what is left and to begin to create a tight-knit community among the leadership team. A key part of this goal will be empowering the team and letting them get on with it. Empowering them will help them build confidence in their abilities, so that you can all collectively achieve the mission using the strengths identified through the processes described in this chapter. This is something that is done very effectively by Johan Verstrepen, another of the CEOs we spoke to when researching this book. Verstrepen is the long-time CEO of the hugely successful Corialis Group, which designs, manufactures and sells aluminium profiles to window manufacturers for residential and non-residential properties across Europe. Verstrepen took over Corialis, which is headquartered in Lokeren, Belgium, twenty-five years ago, at which point it was a small business with an annual revenue of €7 million. Today, it turns over €600 million per year and has the highest EBITDA in its sector, double that of the number two business.

There is no doubt that Verstrepen is a very hands-on leader – one who is integral to the company's outlook and success. This is perhaps why he has remained CEO through no less than eight leveraged buyouts – something of a record. However, as he says, the growth of the organization can also be credited to its structure, which is in the style of a federation. Each of its eight different divisions are largely self-governing. For this to work well, Verstrepen is extremely reliant on the strengths and abilities of his senior team.

'We are a group, but we are not like a normal group, with a pyramid structure,' Verstrepen says. 'I hear too much rubbish about this. Everyone talks about "empowerment" but in reality everyone needs to ask the boss. Here, we have eight hubs, with eight leaders who all have ownership over what they do. We work as a federation with me as the *primus inter pares* ['first among equals'] and each hub operating as effectively a company within a company. That is the reason for our success.'

Consistency will also play a key role as a leader develops their style of working with the senior team. Everyone needs to be absolutely sure of what a leader thinks or how they will react to a given situation. There is nothing worse for morale, and ultimately for having an effective working environment, than a team needing to look expectantly at the boss each morning, waiting to see whether it is Happy Boss or Angry Boss that is in attendance today. Everyone knows that this will dictate how their day will be, possibly even their week.

Richard once came close to resigning from the army on the principle of consistency. A small group of his soldiers had returned from holiday and failed the compulsory drug test on their return. He had made it very clear from the start of his command that there were two things he would never tolerate or forgive within his battalion: bullying and drug taking. If evidence of either was discovered, he would always push hard for the perpetrator to be thrown out of the army – and this is exactly what he did on this occasion. Richard was summoned to a meeting with the Adjutant General, who urged him to take a slightly softer line. The counterargument was that the young men were under enormous pressure and also had to grapple with trying to fit in with their civilian friends, who were freely taking drugs. Richard's response was unequivocal. He had to be consistent and true to his word or the army would not be able to eradicate drug taking – indeed, it could actually become a serious problem. And not only that: Richard passionately believed that the people he commanded needed to be confident that when they were taking a risk on his part, they were 100% certain about what he would want. He felt so strongly about it that he threatened to resign. His decision stuck. It was not an easy situation, but this is a clear illustration of the seriousness with which he viewed the need to be consistent.

Developing a tight-knit leadership group is an ongoing process and one that will not be achieved overnight, particularly after an unsettled period during which individuals have left the company. It will require coaching, judicious feedback and empowerment. Get it right, though, and the senior team will become like an extension of the CEO, shoring up any weaknesses and giving the CEO more bandwidth for critical transformational activities that will improve performance dramatically.

STEP 7. TEAM AND ORGANIZATION STRUCTURE/MAXIMIZING BUSINESS IMPACT

Culture has been likened to the wind: you cannot see it but you can definitely feel its effects. A light breeze blowing your transformation strategy in the right direction is helpful. A heavy gale blowing against everything you are trying to do makes life a whole lot more difficult. While a transformation project relies on the innovation and creativity of leadership, it almost always also requires new behaviour from the employees who are going to make the strategy happen. That will mean a change in culture, or in 'how we do things around here'.

The dominant culture in most organizations – the one that has the biggest influence on a company's current behaviour and the outcomes it achieves – has often remained unchanged for years. In a transformation situation, it is highly likely that most of these behaviours are very different indeed from those that are required for the direction that the business now needs to go in. This is where the challenge begins. It is human nature to resist any changes in culture. By nature, we are creatures who prefer the comfort of the familiar. Once we have something that feels good, or even just OK, we do not readily change it for something that feels unfamiliar. Culture will be particularly deeply ingrained if a company has had a successful history in the past. Individual team members who were there for the good times will still see the business that way. There will be a deeply entrenched viewpoint that if they just keep their heads down and carry on as normal, things will go back to the way they were. This, of course, will not 'just happen' though.

We can learn a lot about culture from the military, where it is something that runs deep. Indeed, the regimental system is built on it, and most specifically on the *pride* people have in the culture of specific regiments, which all have their unique character. It has long been the goal of each regiment to ensure that the spirit and the sense of belonging to that regiment, and the belief that a soldier would do anything in its name, are stronger than they are in any other. As Napoleon once said: 'A soldier will fight long and hard for a bit of coloured ribbon.' It would be a very foolish commanding officer that took the attitude of 'follow me, chaps, and I'll show you where the Iron Crosses grow', but there is a lot of truth in the sentiment that the strength to be found in a powerful sense of culture and belonging will get you a very long way indeed.

It is this same strength of feeling that means that endeavouring to change an organization's culture is one of a leader's toughest challenges. If you think of culture as being the DNA of a business, this means that there is a requirement to change a vast interlocking set of goals, roles, processes, values, communication practices, attitudes and assumptions. Or, if you would rather picture it in more simplistic terms, picture a business filled with Frenchmen and imagine that you want to change them all to think and behave like Englishmen. Where would you begin? Your team may look largely the same but the cultural differences are huge. It is also very difficult to effectively forecast how long will be needed to shift things and how successful that process will ultimately be.

Although tough to change, the penalties for ignoring cultural influences are high. Many corporate failures boil down to an inability to shift direction and move with the marketplace, the story of Siemens being a classic example. The German conglomerate was once one of the big players in the mobile phone market, and its products were fantastic – great feats of engineering. The problem was that the market was changing around the company, and the direction of travel was towards cheaper, more fashionable phones, more akin to the fast-moving consumer goods sector. The engineers at Siemens and all the managers who were former engineers were simply unable to transform their outlook towards becoming a fast-moving, customer-centric organization. It just was not in their DNA. The struggling phone division was sold to Taiwanese company BenQ in 2005.

In my view, the most effective corporate culture is one that is entirely customer centric, where the customer is put in the middle and everything is looked at from the viewpoint of that old adage that 'the customer is king'. Begin from this point and work from there. The next most important element is to never, ever accept the status quo. Just because things are going well today, it does not follow that everything will be just the same tomorrow.

One of the interesting concepts we learned from our discussions with Tim Freystedt at Amazon was that of Day One and Day Two businesses. Day One organizations are those that are focused on keeping things dynamic and fluid, without a trace of complacency. Day Two firms focus too much on their historical successes. They become arrogant and underestimate their competition. Clearly, what all leaders should aim for is to keep their organizations in perpetual Day One mode. Things change quickly, and especially so in fast-moving industries like fashion or fast-moving consumer goods. No organization can afford to sit back and bask in their former glories.

The problem is that, culturally, a lot of organizations strive for Day Two status. Why? Because it is routine. It is familiar. Richard has a lovely expression to fight against this, and he often uses it with his soldiers: 'Routine is the devil's work.' In a military situation, routine is dangerous, possibly even fatal, because it creates opportunity for the enemy. If soldiers do the same thing, day in and day out, and become predictable, it will not go unnoticed and it will be exploited. Richard would not even allow the expression 'routine patrols'. He always called them 'framework patrols'.

As a general rule, smaller organizations with more flexible hierarchical structures are more accommodating of cultural change, whereas large organizations frequently fall into the lethargy of routine. For me, one of the clearest signals that this is going on is when a business has an 'organizational handbook'. If you are unfamiliar with these, they are usually weighty tomes that outline in minute detail how things are done. Although their spines rarely get cracked, they effectively document routine. If I am ever assigned to turn around a business that comes with its own organizational handbook, I always know that I will have my work cut out.

In some organizations, the platform may be burning so fiercely that a cultural change programme is the last thing any leader should be thinking about. Likewise with companies that have been around for many years and where the culture is too deeply entrenched. Here, cultural change should only be attempted if a leader has nothing else to do. In both cases, a leader may need to take a pragmatic approach: accept that culture change is mission impossible, take what they have and do their best with it. It may be possible to mitigate any negative aspects and then add to what is left by introducing a performance culture. This will involve telling everyone that they can keep their existing values but will be expected to orientate towards a few key measures that are important to the company, particularly anything involved with financial fitness. In an ideal world, though, leaders should always try to tackle the cultural aspects of their organization.

On the plus side, cultural change is much easier when there is dissatisfaction with what has gone before. In a troubled business, the team, from top to bottom, will be acutely aware that things are not as they should be, and they will not like it. From a purely selfish point of view, it means their livelihood is in danger. If the business fails, they will be out of a job. However, in order to buy into cultural change, employees have to believe that their leader is a person who is capable of turning things around. This may mean working towards a few modest wins to begin with, and then, when things look to be going well, you can gather momentum and scale as more people buy into the transformation programme.

Show, not tell: changing culture

The nuclear option when it comes to changing culture is to fire everyone and start from scratch! Obviously, that is neither practical nor particularly wise, as previously documented. Thus, the starting point should be to recognize that culture change will not happen overnight and that leaders need to take their teams along with them every step of the way. Shifts in culture are never achieved by a heavy-handed, top-down mandate. A leader can demand compliance, but that is never going to get the transformation over the line. Neither is plastering the walls with motivational slogans about the new strategy, or endlessly repeating it in all-hands meetings. For full buy-in, leaders need the trust and conviction of their teams, and that comes from rapidly engaging and mobilizing them to help set the new behaviours that are required. It is crucial to quickly set out your stall about the direction you wish to head in.

There is a good example here that arose from the turmoil that ensued when it was revealed in 2001 that a number of the UK's historic regiments had to go, thanks to swingeing cuts in the defence budget. Some of those regiments had roots going back 500 years. Unsurprisingly, there were many former distinguished and hugely successful officers who were fiercely resistant to change. Richard, who had just taken over one of the regiments slated for restructuring, worked at getting rapid buy-in from the younger members of his new regiment. He encouraged them to think about the exciting possibilities of their new situation: opportunities that would enable the regiment to be better and more efficient. He also argued strongly that the longer they procrastinated and prevaricated, the more vulnerable the regiment would become. Many of the older officers were never going to be able to accept it, and that is the reality of culture change. Not everyone will be brought along with you. The lesson here is that to be successful, a leader needs to make a decision, set the rules and run with it. If doing so requires you to also part company with members of your team, do so quickly, because the faster you move, the quicker you can start to rebuild.

Begin by speaking with the team and watching them in action in order to understand the existing culture. This will give you a great idea about what the current issues are and about how best to go about shifting things in a new direction. There is an element of care required here, because there will be some good parts of the culture that it is prudent to keep. This means that a leader needs to be surgical in their approach. Additionally, it makes a lot of sense to take at least a brief step back and consider things from the perspective of the team. No one wants to be told that everything they once believed in was 'stupid' or 'a waste of time'. It is a process that needs to be carefully managed.

Cultural changes need to be introduced with the 'why'. Why is it that the team needs to step away from the comfort of the familiar and embark on an entirely new way of doing things? If the why is not understood, decisions will never be readily accepted and executed as they are disseminated through the organization. Leadership needs to communicate accurately and persuasively why everyone needs to do this. Once that message has fully sunk in, then they can move on to the 'how'.

The corporate graveyard is littered with organizations that failed to understand the power of 'why'. The once mighty internet company Yahoo is a classic example. Back in 2002, Yahoo was making $837 million in annual revenue, against the $240 million a year being made by their upstart rival Google. Yahoo had the biggest share of search engine marketing, the highest number of site visitors and more cash than anyone else in the industry. It also had the pick of the most sought-after IT talent in the world. Today, Google – or rather its parent company Alphabet – is the fifth largest company in the world. After a string of terrible business decisions, Yahoo's core business was sold to Verizon for $4.83 billion. It is an impressive amount, but a fraction of its one-time rival's worth.

In the acres of analysis that exist about how Yahoo lost its impressive lead, one theme is returned to again and again: a lack of clear vision. Despite a number of leadership changes, no one seemed to be able to make up their minds whether Yahoo was a search company, a tech company or a media business. While Google's brand mission is well known – 'to organize the world's information and make it universally accessible and useful' – and is displayed front and centre on the company website's 'About' page, as well as regularly appearing in company communications, Yahoo never really had a brand mission at all. In fact, according to one piece of research, Yahoo's self-description on its press releases changed twenty-four times over twenty-four years. No wonder none of those talented employees understood the 'why'.

The purpose of step 7 is to maximize interest in the mission within one's organization: doing so will have a huge impact on the outcome. Once everyone has fully bought into the why, the most effective way to move towards the 'how' is to *demonstrate* ideas in action, rather than simply saying 'get it done'. The right framing is important. It is very easy for a leader to overuse their authority to mandate change. However, a bland exhortation to do X because X is what will get the business back on track will immediately experience pushback. The whole 'not invented here' syndrome will immediately kick in. Any team that did not come up with the idea will be suspicious of it – even resentful. This is a terrible start to introducing any new strategy. Much better to recast the initial brief so that the team feel that *they* are solving the problems.

There are two ways to overcome the 'not invented here' syndrome. One is to hire people and embed them into the organization; the other is to give people real-life examples of how things can be done differently. I have tried both and they are very effective strategies.

The first time I used the 'hire-in method' was when I ran the transformer division at Siemens. Siemens's transformers were very good products: they were robust, long-lasting, excellent pieces of equipment. The problem was that they were also more expensive than those made by our competitors and we made less of a margin. In my view, things needed to change. I looked at one competitor, ABB, who was doing a great job, and I realized that they were making more money because they were engineering their transformers with less of a safety margin. What this competitor had done better than us was to configure the exact right amount of material to achieve a specific performance, meaning that they spent less on supplies.

I had a discussion with an electrical engineer at Siemens and asked what seemed to me an obvious question: 'Why don't we do it like this?'

The response: 'This is the way we have always done it.'

I knew that I would never win this one if I *told* the team to do it the ABB way. Even if the team knew that the ABB way was better, they would not want to accept it because they had not come up with it themselves. They would find ways around it, or if there was a technical problem there would be a lot of finger-pointing at me for sending them in the wrong direction. I solved the problem by hiring a good electrical engineer from ABB and integrating him into the team. I asked him to show his new colleagues how they did things at ABB. Over time, I managed to get full buy-in from the Siemens team.

In another instance, when I was leading a business called Mannesmann Plastics Machinery, I went for the real-life-examples option.

We had a number of factories building injection-moulding machines and I became convinced that there was a better way of running the assembly line: one that would be quicker, more efficient and more cost effective. By chance, I then came across an ex-Toyota executive who was now a consultant. He was steeped in the Kaizen philosophy of continuous improvement pioneered by Japanese car giant Toyota. He explained that he had worked with another German company and had great success after introducing a Kaizen-style production line. I went back to my people: 'How about it?' I asked. 'Shall we give it a go?'

There was immediate pushback. We were a German company, they said, not a Japanese one, and we worked in an entirely different way. Unwilling to give up, I asked the consultant to put me in touch with the German company he had worked with before. I then contacted them to ask if I could pay them a visit to look at their newly installed production method – one that was a million miles away from the traditional method of assembling injection-moulding machines. They agreed and I organized a bus, filling it up with people from the assembly area in my company and with shift leaders, the production manager and representatives from the Workers Council. We went over to the other factory and spent the day looking at their system. When my people saw the effectiveness of Kaizen in a German factory, they began to open up to the idea that it might also be possible for us. After that visit, Mannesmann Plastics Machinery embarked on a project to introduce this new way of doing things.

Motivating your team during challenging times comes down, to a great extent, to personality, as well as to a bit of lateral thinking now and again. The final stage in getting any new initiative over the line is to get in among your people. Leaders cannot simply announce the strategy change and retreat to their office to wait for it to happen. As it is the team that delivers the strategy, everyone needs to be fully involved in the process. A footnote to the Mannesmann Plastics Machinery story above is that I embedded myself into the project team to show how important I felt the change was, and I also worked on the new production line personally in its early days. This follows the military philosophy that if you are going to ask people to take tremendous risks on your behalf, you cannot be 'in the rear with the gear': you have to be up there with them. This shows firstly that you are not daunted, secondly that you are clear on your objectives, and thirdly that you are fully prepared to share in the risk. And, as Richard said earlier, there is a moment in any situation when you need to (metaphorically) grab your team and get them to follow you. You then also need to motivate them and make sure they complete the journey.

None of this is to say that the team needs handholding all the way. A leader should certainly not be micromanaging, or constantly looking over their team's shoulders. Delegate the detailing of the concept to the team; give them the what and the why but let them actually undertake the project. After that, they can be measured against the targets that were set.

It may be prudent to give some thought to the process around how independent thought and ideas are encouraged to develop the 'how'. In a troubled organization there may be resistance to suggesting better ways of doing things: reticence based on an individual's own self-interest. People might believe that if their idea is too effective, they will talk themselves out of a job. I have seen organizations try to get over this issue by paying for good ideas. Unfortunately, this can be detrimental, because the tactic produces a deluge of hundreds – perhaps even thousands – of ideas, most of which have no hope of becoming realized. There are just too many. The happy medium is to make ideas part of the company's culture. Encourage everyone to believe that coming up with ideas is simply part of their job description. Part of the Standard Operating Procedure is to keep things under constant review, with one eye on making incremental improvements. This encourages engagement and, over time, it should elicit a good flow of suggestions.

A crucial part of engagement is to weed out naysayers: the people who will constantly snipe from the sidelines, no matter how necessary and impactful the strategy. Tim Collins recalls an issue he had with a quartermaster who was constantly undermining him. The quartermaster was an excellent recruit but his actions were negatively impacting the rest of the squadron.

'There is only one commanding officer in this battalion, and you are looking at him,' Tim told the quartermaster. 'If you are not happy with how things are done, leave now.'

It is essential to deal with dissent quickly in a crisis situation, says Tim, otherwise one individual can create a huge, disrupting diversion. People are either with the leadership or they are against it. If anyone is found to be against it, they have to go. The replacement may not be as good as the incumbent, but at least they will be on the right side of the strategy. That is what is most important.

As a final thought on changing culture, I would encourage any leader to think carefully about their own management style. In the previous chapter I mentioned that I liked to see some humility in my senior teams, and that works all the way to the top. An important part of engaging any team is for leaders to admit that they do not have all the answers, because they do not. Leaders need to make themselves available and put themselves in a position where they are approachable so that people can challenge their ideas, or suggest better ways of doing things. Then, if the new idea is better, admit it.

It is a measure of a good leader to value fully the creative abilities of all those around them and not to instantly dismiss any input. Always keep people informed about progress, highlighting what successes have been achieved so far or which are just around the corner. Equally importantly, talk about the mishaps too, and maintain a dialogue about what did not quite work out and why that might have been.

Strengthening structure

One of the big questions you will need to answer is whether or not you have the right structure to successfully execute the plan. The failure or downturn of many businesses can frequently be traced back directly to the company's structure. Often, they were simply too bloated or too stuck in their ways to respond when a younger, fitter opponent arrived on the doorstep, determined to eat their lunch. We have seen a lot of this in recent years with banks and fintechs. Most of the major traditional high-street banks recognized that online was an opportunity but then put little more than pale imitations of their bricks-and-mortar services into their mobile apps. It took fintechs such as Starling, Monzo and Revolut to completely revitalize and rejuvenate banking with their apps, which offered a host of new whizz-bang features to help banking customers manage their money better.

How did the established banks, with their much deeper pockets, allow themselves to get into a position of trailing so far behind? In a matter of just a few years, fintechs have signed up millions of their customers. The answer is, at least partly, that big banks are grappling with unwieldy, out-of-date technology that their teams have been working with for years. Some parts of some systems have roots going back to the 1980s, when technology was light years behind where it is today. For too long, the big banks failed to appreciate the need to completely change things, so they made incremental improvements that were barely noticeable. It took digital disruptors with an entrepreneurial viewpoint and smaller, leaner teams to see the real opportunity, and that is what led the innovation. Today, it is almost impossible for the big banks to catch up. They would have to scrap their cumbersome technology, completely restructure their teams and start again, all while continuing to meet their customers' day-to-day banking needs.

It may be that the structure of an organization that is in trouble is perfectly healthy. Many of the businesses that had difficulties as a result of the pandemic did previously have a healthy structure but were adversely impacted by the extreme changes to their market. The message here is: 'If it ain't broke, don't try to fix it' – particularly since a previously strong organization is likely to recover much more quickly. This is, however, the exception rather than the rule. It is more likely than not that the transformation plan will warrant some changes to the organizational structure, in order to be as effective as possible at delivering the best results. If there is any suspicion at all that there are flaws in the structure, a leader should look to make crucial changes.

While it is natural to want to look outwards, from inside your company, this process of reviewing structure should begin by looking at the competition and how they are structured. What does the way they are set up tell you about how you might be better structured? It may be that rivals' set-ups are much more effective for today's market. Something that the Covid-19 crisis very much exposed was that many retailers had yet to properly develop, or even launch, an e-commerce operation, despite the fact that established retailers had been perfecting their online capabilities for decades. With millions of people in lockdown, it was inevitable that online retailing would gain market share, and for many consumers it would become the new normal. Those potential customers may very well never return to the high street even when they are able to properly do so. This leaves some retailers vulnerable.

Prior to the pandemic, German discounters Aldi and Lidl, famed for their basic, low-price ranges, had grown considerably, and nowhere was this more true than in the UK, where they have outstripped the established chains in terms of sales growth. Aldi overtook the Co-op to become the UK's fifth largest retailer in 2017, and pre-pandemic it had a 7.5% market share, closing in on fourth-place Morrisons.[19] Yet, while the firm is a worthy – even dangerous – competitor in the world of bricks-and-mortar grocery stores, the discounter's lack of online capabilities has left it unable to keep making its steady gains. It would be easy to say that the pandemic is an exceptional situation – and, of course, it is. But there were already strong indications that the move to online shopping was gaining considerable momentum, and the health crisis will only accelerate this trend. The structural emphasis in any industry where online is the norm should be to set up a fully functioning e-commerce department. Without one, there is no chance of remaining competitive.

Overall, the goal for any organizational structure is to encourage independence, not dependence. This is why, whenever I join an organization, I always work towards quickly creating business units that are market- and customer-facing, with top-line and bottom-line goals. This breaks down the organizational structure into one that is completely focused on the relevant customer and also on the competition, rather than on all the other things that sap people's time and energy. My business units decentralize what have previously been very centralized organizations, and each unit runs as though it is independent. They are given a profit goal, told what their market is, and told that they need to earn X amount of money. Then they are left to get on with it. The targets that are set for the business units are obviously relevant to the mission and are directly related to serving the customer.

A big benefit of dividing a business into independent units is that it allows for creativity and rapidity. Sun Tzu worked this out more than 2,500 years ago when he said: 'The control of a large force is the same principle as the control of a few men – it is merely a question of dividing up their numbers.' He realized that creating small entities and letting them get on with the job was the best way to go about things. It engages people and gives them more power over outcomes.

Today, the military very much values empowerment as the means of structuring itself to enable soldiers to do their job. Richard says that the big benefit of grouping soldiers for independent action is that they then do not need to repeatedly come back and ask: 'Is it OK if I do this?' He would give them the 'why' and the 'what' and then let them get on with it. Of course, he also made it clear that if they needed to ask for any help, his door was always open. Equally, soldiers were encouraged to come back to him if there was an issue and they were unable to achieve their goal.

Richard saw real benefits of empowering small, tactical units when he was stationed in Helmand, Afghanistan in 2007. The challenge he faced was that he was in among the local community, who were effectively in the centre of the fight whether they liked it or not. It was essential to keep the locals onside but this was clearly not an easy situation. His solution was to 're-role' his snipers into tactical, psychological operations teams that were stationed in the communities on a daily basis. After a small amount of training he empowered his soldiers to go out and find repeated small 'wins' for their unit. They were also in exactly the right place to quickly report back if the unit inadvertently did anything that created local hostility. This was far more effective than the once-a-month meetings that Richard had scheduled with representatives of the Helmand residents, which clearly left a lot of space for things to spiral out of control very quickly. Handing over power to these small, tactical units proved much more effective.

Devolving power to individual units gives a team much more flexibility and room to be agile when responding to outside events. I often look at failing retailers, with their large head offices stuffed full of thousands of people, and wonder whether this is contributing a great deal to their problems. How much more effective would they be if they devolved some power to their individual stores, empowering those smaller units to make the changes that will most effectively serve their own customer base? The people who run those stores are there on the ground, seeing what shoppers in their community like. It must be infuriating to be given one-size-fits-all product assortments. And literally, in some cases: one British supermarket chain used to routinely send out supplies of suit jackets and trousers in a uniform range of sizes to each of its outlets. There would be four size 32 trousers, another four 34s, and so on. Each quarter, all of the smaller sizes would be routinely returned to head office from a number of stores, and it was always the same stores that returned them. It took a change of leadership, which devolved the ordering process to the stores themselves, to solve the issue. The stores in question were embedded in an area where the majority of suit buyers were on the larger side. There was no way on earth the smaller sizes would ever sell in numbers in those stores. Yet, because the decision-making process was largely centralized, those small suits just kept on coming.

Delegating power does not always sit easy with some leaders. Many like to be very hands-on, to the extent that they micromanage far too much, which is not only a waste of their time but a waste of all the talent around them. Yet, for a transformation to be a success, the way forward is to be agile, which is impossible if everyone has to wait for detailed instructions about what to do next. Everyone on the team needs to be engaged and to have fully bought into the 'why' and the 'what', so they can react quickly to new circumstances. Without this, competitors, particularly any quick-on-their-feet, new disruptors, will outmanoeuvre you at every turn.

Reducing headcount fairly

Any time a new leader joins an organization, they are, of course, presented with a ready-made team. Generally, if the person at the top is loyal to their people, the sentiment will be reciprocated. However, there may also be a need to bring in fresh talent – people who can help the organization see things differently. They will see areas where things have gone wrong and they may bring new approaches. These structural changes might well mean that a reduction in headcount among the existing team is necessary. While the business reasons to do this may be solid, I would always urge caution with this sensitive step, and with this in mind I will therefore finish the chapter with a few thoughts on how to ensure this process goes as smoothly as possible.

I have already spoken a little about not relying too heavily on consultants and this is the case again here – perhaps more so than with any other decision, I would keep things in-house as far as humanly possible. A reduction in headcount, or redeployment of resources, is the go-to strategy of most consultants. If you have any experience of this, you will probably realize that downsizing invariably focuses on the lower and middle ranks of an organization – very rarely are changes at the top seen. A cynic might say that a clearout at the top is never recommended because it is the leadership who approve and sign off on the large consultancy fees. Whatever the reason, when a bunch of outsiders sweep in and cut a swathe out of the lower ranks while leaving those at the top untouched, it causes a huge amount of resentment. Aside from the obvious them-and-us vibe, there is also the glaring fact that if a business is in trouble, it was someone at the top who led it there. This might be because they ran the business poorly, or because they failed to notice clear changes to the market – it could have been down to any one of a number of reasons. The point is that the people who are losing their jobs, and the colleagues that those people leave behind, will have had little to do with creating the problem. The aftershocks of this disgruntlement will echo through the organization for months, if not years, to come. Those that can will brush up their CVs and leave. Those that remain will work to the clock at just the moment when maximum effort is required from everyone.

Consultants can be used as 'warm body' support in the reorganization but they should never be the instigators.

If there do need to be cuts, start with the top management positions first and then move on to those lower down. In all cases, check back against step 5 and see what the execution team thinks about the plan. They may well have some constructive thoughts on whether it has gone too far in order to be able to achieve the strategy effectively. This is essential knowledge.

Even though it will not always be easy, it is crucial to create unity and a sense of purpose in a transformational situation. The strength and efforts of the team are central to the success of the mission.

STEP 8. CAMPAIGN DELIVERY

No army would charge into battle without a thorough understanding of the enemy and the terrain. That would be the equivalent of a mass suicide. Up until now, each of our steps has been geared towards gaining that understanding. Now that the analysis has been completed and the plan agreed, this crucial step is what everything has been working towards: the running of the battle.

Before sounding the charge, steps 1–7 all need to have been properly completed and the conditions met within each one. Only then can you move on to step 8. Leaders should beware of getting too carried away with their feelings of success as they move through those first seven steps, each of which can sweep them onto the next too quickly. Proper preparation is an essential part of the transformation project. As Benjamin Franklin is supposed to have said: by failing to prepare, you are preparing to fail. I know that in my early days of heading transformations, I was often tempted to try to do too much, too early, embarking on step 8 as soon as possible. I learned from experience that it is crucial to move through the stepped process to make sure nothing has been missed.

You could try visualizing what has been done so far and what is about to happen via a three-phase model similar to the one used by the British military in Afghanistan. Much of the operational design for the campaign there was based around three phases: secure, hold and build. In other words, individual towns were secured against insurgents and the positions held, and this in turn paved the way to build upon the success of the action. In the case of a turnaround, the phases would break down as follows: secure, stabilize, grow.

Phase one (secure) is where the future of the business is secured via the cost-takeout exercises already outlined, since most businesses in a transformation situation will have a significant cost overhang.

Fail to prepare, prepare to fail. (© Pepyn Dinandt.)

This phase should be undertaken with care, but it should be done as quickly as possible. The team that is left behind will need to be 100% focused on the job that is to be done in step 8. It would be hugely detrimental if one part of the business is grappling with lay-offs while another department is being urged to think outside the box and devise exciting new products in order to take on a powerful competitor.

In this initial phase I am always careful to ringfence the sales team because it is crucial that they keep doing their job effectively, otherwise revenues will fall even further. In phase two (hold), a key part of stabilizing the business is to tackle the sales team and put measures in place to help them do the best job possible, within the present structure of the organization. These are the first steps to rebuilding things and getting the business back on track.

Phase three (build) is where the new strategy is introduced; the equivalent of our step 8. If phases one and two have been completed correctly, this is where the transformation of the organization will begin. This is where the plan moves from the building stage into the growth stage. Today, whenever I am entering step 8, I always have this one–two–three approach at the back of my mind.

Delivery, delivery, delivery

Step 8 is all about delivery. It is also the step that the entire mission will be judged on and what a leader will be measured by. This is, after all, what it is all about: succeeding in the turnaround and transformation of a troubled business. It is for this reason that a leader needs to double-check, or even triple-check, the details of the plan.

In the final stage of analysis, check whether there have been any fundamental changes to the environment that will make the intended outcome unpredictable. Detail is important.

One of my first ever turnaround challenges occurred when I was a young McKinsey consultant and was assigned to Olympia, a German typewriter company that was a division of a large conglomerate. Sales of its once-popular mechanical typewriters were falling at a significant rate and I was tasked with the job of visiting dealers all over the world to find out what was going on before proposing a new strategy. I duly set off and visited all sorts of exotic locations around the globe. The managers of each dealership I visited all had their own thoughts on the issue of how to sell more typewriters, all of which I faithfully recorded to inform my subsequent presentation to the main Olympia board: a presentation that listed out the ways that revenue could be improved.

Looking back, with the benefit of thirty years of turnaround experience and a healthy dose of hindsight, I can now say that there was far too little detail in that report. Indeed, I omitted the most salient detail: that Olympia's mechanical typewriters were under threat from a new generation of electric typewriters that had emerged as a competitive force. Failing to take into account this important detail meant that there was no chance that the dealers could ever deliver the transformation strategy that Olympia's board craved. There was simply not enough substance to work with. The company was selling the wrong product and had no real ability to control the dealerships.

Sure enough, almost no one was able to deliver, and Olympia was later folded by its main shareholder. I am quite self-critical when it comes to this project, because I should have highlighted this obvious flaw in the company's strategy. I also feel strongly that the Olympia leadership was too far divorced from the reality on the ground. They did not need to bring in consultants. What they should have done is used their own people, who would have had detailed knowledge of where the market was going and understood the looming threat of more modern competitors.

Many of the concepts being put forward in this book may seem entirely logical on first reading, but the reason for documenting them in this structured way is because a transformation needs to be worked through methodically, otherwise things will get missed. During a transformation project there will be many things going on at the same time, each one vying for leadership attention. If a logical process is not systematically worked through, it is easy to forget an important detail.

In another instance of learning things the hard way, I will highlight an ambitious project in which I attempted to revive the fortunes of a firm by building an online business for one of its key products. Because we were so immersed in the long to-do list for enacting our new strategy, we failed to research one of the key distributors we were planning to work with closely enough. That key distributor was a little-known company called Amazon. If we had properly scrutinized the small print on our partnership agreement ahead of our launch, we would have been alerted to a number of hidden costs, known as 'added charges', that would put us at a significant disadvantage. The terms outlined that the more product we sold, the more these added charges would grow. In addition, our retail partner would have the final say over the price that we sold our goods at. As a result of this failure to check the small print, our revenue growth was much lower than projected despite the product selling quite well. Indeed, we found ourselves in the extraordinary and alarming situation whereby the more products we sold, the lower our percentage margin and profitability were. These all-important details had been missed because we had moved too quickly into the execution phase while working on too many initiatives at once.

Having reached this step, there is an understandable urgency to get on with it, because the longer it takes to get started, the more time it will take for the organization to catch up after a prolonged period in the doldrums. After all, profitability will continue to erode if you do nothing about it. Just be sure, though, that the detail of the plan has been checked and rechecked.

There is one further possible reason that you may need to hold back: it may be that as you prepare to press the 'go' button on the strategy, a competitor suddenly makes a move and begins to implement an ambitious new strategy of its own. If this is the case, it might be prudent to step back and see how they get on before enacting certain parts of your plan. Alternatively, even if your competitor appears to have every advantage, this might be an opportunity to revise the plan altogether to plot a well-timed counterattack. This is a decision you will only be able to take if you remain fully aware of your environment, right up to and beyond the launch of the strategy. Even if you have a firm plan, flexibility when it comes to timing and execution can give you a real advantage.

No plan survives first contact

There are plenty of variations on Helmuth von Moltke's eloquent pronouncement that no plan survives first contact with the enemy. Unsurprisingly, one comes from Sun Tzu, who said that to execute a successful campaign a leader needs the 'power of estimating the adversary, of controlling forces of victory and shrewdly calculating difficulties, dangers and distances – this constitutes the test of a great general'. The point is, from the moment the campaign begins, nothing can be taken as a given. If the transformation shows even the slightest signs of progress, there is no chance whatsoever that competitors will sit back and watch a once-troubled business take the initiative. They will respond.

It does not matter how straightforward and simple the initial plan might seem, there will always be unintended consequences. Say, for example, the sales team is charged with acquiring ten new customers. The current suppliers of those ten potential customers will fight very hard indeed to keep them. They may even go after ten of your customers too. This could culminate in a situation where there is a gain of ten customers, as planned, but a loss of ten others.

If that turns out to be the case, the revenue line will not have moved at all. Alternatively, a stronger competitor might go all out to win all of your customers at the same time and launch a compelling new product to get the strategy over the line.

You can also rest assured that customers will not react as they are expected to. If a new product launch is central to your strategy, it is quite possible that customers will adore it, and that is clearly a promising sign. But they may also completely give up buying one of your previous bestsellers because they have switched their spending to the new product. As before, this will leave your organization with no net gain at all.

Businesses must not underestimate the wide range of potential reactions to a plan, and by far the strongest kickback will most likely come from competitors. The enemy *will* respond because they have to, and a leader has to anticipate that they will be extremely agile. If you make a move in one direction, they will find a way to soften the impact or to turn things to their advantage. Richard likens this scenario to the one he found when he was stationed in Northern Ireland during the lengthy conflict there. The IRA had a routine of regularly using improvised mortars to bomb British bases. The British troops obviously could not just sit in the bases and be bombed, so they would move out into the towns in a bid to dominate the ground. This brought the added advantage that if they found spots where a mortar baseplate was being driven in, in preparation to attack a base, they would be able to intercept that activity. What happened time and again, though, was that the IRA swiftly changed strategy in response to the British shift. They would position snipers around the towns and plant improvised explosive devices in places they expected the British to go. This change in strategy had an understandably negative impact on morale among the British, so commanders would instruct their troops to go back to their bases. The IRA immediately switched back to mortaring the bases – and so the cat-and-mouse game went on.

Following this experience, Richard was much better prepared for the agility of the Taliban when he later fought in Afghanistan. The Taliban was very adept at quickly switching from fighting toe-to-toe in gun battles to more subversive actions such as placing improvised explosive devices on main thoroughfares. This was something that

Richard anticipated and warned his soldiers about – he had, after all, seen it before.

Your enemy will be agile, and it is crucial to understand this in order to stay one step ahead. This is why contingency planning in any hostile situation is crucial. Ahead of any action, the military will always wargame potential outcomes, and leadership will adopt a 'what if?' mindset. In other words, what will happen *if* the enemy responds in a certain way? What options will then be open to us? In other words: we act, the enemy reacts, we counteract. Therefore, once any plan is written, it is presented to another group and thoroughly challenged. This challenge group will often be made up of intelligence officials, who know the enemy better than anyone.

It is rare to find this sort of exercise in business, but it does happen. Richard had some experience of this in a corporate setting when he worked with the defence giant Thales, which would bring in ex-military officers to stress-test significant strategies. What made this work was that the Thales executives were completely open to criticism because they genuinely wanted to hear an alternative point of view. The exercise provided a crucial window into what the 'enemy' might think and do, which is not always easy to see when you are too close to a particular strategy.

As you might expect, the military is very methodical and measured in its wargaming approach. The many variable outcomes are plotted on a 'synchronization matrix': a visual representation of the various stages of a forthcoming campaign. Details about the enemy are recorded on the matrix, along with information about the terrain and the tasks to be achieved. Each element is reviewed against a number of possible reactions and the impact they may have on other elements in the mix. The tasks are also set against timelines, so it is possible to see clashes and where there are opportunities to put the enemy under real pressure by making even small adjustments to the plan. The synchronization matrix provides a very visual snapshot of what would otherwise be entirely unexpected actions and reactions. It also outlines the conditions under which the commander will be called on to make the key decisions.

If you were to do the equivalent in a business environment, crucial details could be plotted to expand knowledge about each step of the strategy. Thus, if one element of the strategy were to cut costs, it would be possible to plot out which departments would be put under pressure if headcount were taken out in, say, HR or marketing. This might prompt the leadership to discuss these outcomes with the relevant heads of department ahead of time and then take measures to smooth the way and cause minimum disruption.

Something that a synchronization matrix may identify is the fact that there are not enough people to achieve the plan. Organizations are understandably reluctant to invest in a higher headcount when times are difficult, but sometimes this is the only way to ensure the success of a transformation. I was briefly involved with a cosmetics brand that was losing market share after forty years in operation. The problem was quickly identified: its customers had grown older alongside the company, and no new ones were coming through. While it seemed logical to launch an initiative to attract a more youthful customer base, the brand had a small workforce that was already flat-out servicing the needs of the existing buyers. It was very difficult to convince the company leadership that they needed to bring in new people to focus on targeting another segment, but plotting out the programme on a matrix would have helped significantly.

One of the most effective uses of a wargaming matrix like this was in UK Sport's preparation for the 2012 Olympics. It is perhaps no coincidence that the man behind the meticulous plan, John Steele, had a military background, having trained at Sandhurst as a Royal Artillery Captain. UK Sport had a firm goal: to win the maximum possible number of medals at the home Olympics. It wanted to win at least forty-eight medals across twelve sports and to come fourth in the overall medal rankings. Steele set out a strategy where UK Sport's £292 million investment would be deliberately targeted at areas where it would gain the maximum number of medals. The timeline for the ambitious strategy started with UK Sport's opening conference, which was a thousand days out from the games. A comprehensive matrix of actions and counteractions was plotted, detailing timelines for each sport and the decision points for each one. Nothing was missed, from when funding would be required to the target number of medals that were going to be imposed on each sport. Each of the major decision points featured dozens of branch plans showing what to do if the initial plan failed to work. It was a massive document and a superb example of what can be achieved by setting up timelines and goals, as well as contingency plans and objectives in case something changed or funding was withdrawn. It proved effective too. The UK finished the 2012 Olympics with sixty-five medals – twenty-nine gold, seventeen silver and nineteen bronze – and came third in the medal table.

Once a transformation campaign begins, any leader, should, of course, retain the 'what if?' mindset. The military model that is used here is to constantly review *action*, which is what is being done to the enemy, *reaction*, which is how they have reacted, and *counter-action*, which is how to respond to their reaction. It also helps to run this alongside constant intelligence gathering, in order to stay one step ahead. What is the enemy doing now and what might it do next? There is a predictive element to any campaign that cannot be ignored.

Teamwork, empowerment, achievement and motivation

While the external reaction to any plan will greatly impact the outcome of the strategy, internal factors cannot be ignored. There are plenty of reasons closer to home for a plan not proceeding as expected. These factors are all dependent on the team.

When an SAS commander sends in a squad of Special Forces, they can be certain that everyone in that hand-picked, well-trained group will perform brilliantly. This is not a given in the business world. There can be hugely variable abilities in a team of just six to eight people. In a sales team of 100 or more, the range of skills and motivations will be huge. Some team members will be knock-it-out-of-the-park excellent, while others may be of more average ability. If just one or two of the less able team members fail to perform as expected, this may have a significant impact on the delivery of the plan. It may not even just be a case of ability either. The execution of a plan can be adversely affected by the absence of just a few team members due to sick leave. If key people are away at a crucial time, some of your momentum will be lost.

Leaders need to consider very carefully how much they load onto individual members of their team. If people are given too much to do in a short space of time, they may be unable to focus on their priorities and may even flounder. This, in turn, will make the execution of the plan less effective. For this same reason, it is crucial to make sure that members of the team have the capacity to devote to the new actions that will make up the plan. If they are overloaded by their ordinary day-to-day activities, they will be unable to give their full focus to the campaign. It is sensible to speak with individuals to check on their situation and, if they are not in a position to deliver the plan, reassign priorities so that they are. Question them about whether they have all the resources they require to meet the proposed timescale. Before a new product can be launched, for example, new paperwork and certification might be required. If there is any hold-up, it can delay the entire strategy.

When checking on the team, it is important to spread the net more widely than simply talking with people who have an immediate role. It is highly likely that others who are not directly involved will be impacted by the new strategy, so they need to be fully aware of what is happening. As an example, consider a plan that centres around a purchasing initiative to make the buying function more efficient. While it clearly makes sense to make sure that everyone in the purchasing department is fully on board, there may also be a crossover into production, which will need to deal with the new equipment. It is therefore important to set the scene by working closely with production, to ensure they have capacity to play their part.

Whatever the plan, it is highly likely that *everyone* in the organization will need to be a bit more flexible and adaptable than usual. In the best-case scenario, team members should be in a position where they are ready and prepared to change tactic mid-course if they need to. Ideally, especially with small course corrections, this move to a new direction will be something they can work out for themselves, without having to go back and check with someone at the top of the organization each time. This is the advantage of moving towards empowering your team, as was discussed earlier. Leaders need people who *think*, rather than just take orders. In a fast-moving transformation programme there is not always time for information to go all the way up to the top of an organization and then all the way back down again. After explaining the intent to everyone, a leader does need to step back and let them get on with it. Unless it is clear that the team is diverging from the plan in a way that will entirely change the intended outcome, leaders should not interfere with the way they achieve it, especially if they are proving successful. As Napoleon once said: never interfere with your enemy when they are making a mistake. The converse is true too: when your team are pressing on and doing well, do not get involved.

Leaders need to be tough but fair with their senior reports at a time like this. I am always sure to praise my teams – but never too much. That just raises suspicion! Richard makes a good point here too, adding that in a corporate situation it is not unusual for the big hitters, or the front-facing individuals, to get all the plaudits when something goes well. Yet, too little credit (or sometimes no credit at all) is given to the dozens of people who worked tirelessly in the background to make something happen. When something goes well, leaders should step back, take a look round and notice the unsung heroes. It makes a world of difference.

The other side of the coin is when members of the team need to be sanctioned. The rule here is to treat people how you would want to be treated yourself. Once again, leaders of international organizations are advised to think about culture. There is a world of difference between British, French, German and Italian workers. Some value directness while others require the message to be a little more nuanced.

Overall, the goal is to create a culture of honesty and mutual trust. Leadership need to be fully apprised of the progress of the strategy, and the only way to get a clear picture is via a clear line of communication with the team. If this culture of openness has not been established, a very one-sided picture might begin to emerge. It is not unusual for teams involved in these large-scale transformations to report back success after success, because this is what they believe the boss wants to hear. And they are right, it is, but it is actually more important to know about what is *not* going so well. Where are they *not* managing to deliver? A leader needs to get on top of any imbalance straight away.

The clear message to everyone in the organization is that if there is bad news to relate about the progress of the campaign, they must deliver it to leadership at the earliest opportunity. There is nothing worse than team members sitting on bad news, or delaying raising it while they try to resolve it themselves. (Logic would dictate that if this was indeed possible, there would not have been a problem in the first place.) Leaders need the bad news early enough that they are able to do something about it. This will happen much more easily if there is a culture of mutual respect in the business – and, of course, if a leader has laid the groundwork and is known to be forgiving of genuine mistakes.

The buck stops with you

When all is said and done, it is a leader's responsibility to make sure everyone has prepared properly and that the plan is pursued to its logical conclusion. The success or failure of a strategy is the responsibility of the leader. This is, of course, a challenge, since there are many moving parts and things that can go wrong. Sun Tzu eloquently describes six ways in which a leader might court defeat, with each one *entirely* down to the general in charge.

- *Flight*. If one force is hurled against another ten times its size, the result will be the flight of the former.
- *Insubordination*. When the common soldiers are too strong and their officers too weak.
- *Collapse*. When the officers are too strong and the common soldiers too weak.
- *Ruin*. When the higher officers are angry and insubordinate, and on meeting the enemy give battle on their own account from a feeling of resentment, before the commander-in-chief can tell whether or not he is in a position to fight.
- *Disorganization*. When the general is weak and without authority; when his orders are not clear and distinct; when there are no fixed duties assigned to officers and men, and the ranks are formed in a slovenly haphazard manner, the result is utter disorganization.
- *Rout*. When a general, unable to estimate the enemy's strength, allows an inferior force to engage a larger one, or hurls a weak

detachment against a powerful one and neglects to place picked soldiers in the front rank, the result must be rout.

It is the lot of a leader to always need to be in the right place at the right time to supervise the execution of the campaign and make the right decisions. Any leader that thinks it is now all down to giving orders and sitting back to wait for everyone to fulfil them is in for a big disappointment. A leader needs to take up a position in among their people and take them into battle to make the strategy a success. They cannot – as they say in the army – sit so far back that they have to send their washing forward. To ensure victory, they need to be on the ground, talking to the team.

As we wrote the book, we did a lot of research on leadership and we found many interesting examples where successful organizations such as Adidas and Nestlé were brought to whole new levels of financial performance by leaders with very hands-on styles – leaders who were always closely involved in implementation. I call this the Great Leader Effect (GLE), where such leaders create a positive level of performance compared with their peers and competitors purely through their level of excellence.

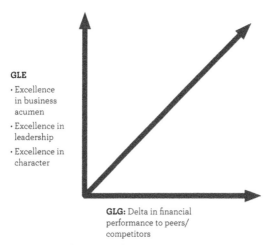

GLE
· Excellence in business acumen
· Excellence in leadership
· Excellence in character

GLG: Delta in financial performance to peers/ competitors

The Great Leader Effect (GLE) and the Great Leader Gap (GLG).
(© Pepyn Dinandt.)

Momentum and speed are key to the success of the strategy, and this means that an organization needs to keep moving through the various phases of the plan. No commander wants to be in a position where their subordinates complete phase one and then pause to await their next orders. There needs to be a smooth flow from one part of the plan to the next. At some point, though, there will always come a time when all eyes turn towards the leader. Everyone will want to know what to do next, even if they are fully briefed on the plan and the intent. A leader needs to be in the right place to rapidly make the decision that will influence the outcome.

Business leaders can learn a lot from the way the military do this, embedding commanders in among the troops. Too many organizations pride themselves on their heavily structured HQs, and speak glowingly about their super-effective lines of communication, but the reality is that if a leader is a long way away from the main action, how can they know if the transformation is really going as everyone is telling them it is? If a business has ten factories and one of those factories has been identified as the problem that is dragging down the whole company, it makes a lot of sense for a leader to position themselves in that troubled factory for a period of time. It is a clear signal that they have skin in the game and that the organization is delivering together. It is also extremely helpful to have the decision maker on the ground, so they can respond to events at the sharp end.

There are many advantages to a leader placing themselves at the centre of the action. At the simplest level, they have an important role to play in keeping up morale. My thirty years of turnaround experience has given me the benefit of a great deal of knowledge and experience. I have learned that while I relish the order and structure of the process, others who are in the midst of undergoing a transformation programme for the first time frequently find the high-pressure environment alarming and unsettling. The only way to deal with this is for a leader to adopt a calm and respectful demeanour while also ensuring that everyone is fully briefed and that the enthusiasm and momentum do not waver. When aspects of the strategy do not go according to plan – something that will always happen – it is crucial for a leader to remain cool and take the necessary actions to get things back on track.

There is never any room for complacency in a transformation project. While I have been involved in many significant turnarounds, no two cases are ever entirely the same. This means that each time I embark on the process, maximum effort, concentration and attention are required, otherwise things can and do get missed. Even when there are a number of elements to the plan, each one will require a leader's full attention. It is not an easy thing to do, but then this is not an easy task.

Making a succession of decisions under pressure is never easy. Nearly all of the key decisions in the delivery stage will need to be made under these circumstances, often because something has not gone according to plan. It therefore makes sense for leaders to prepare for such eventualities, so that they can keep a level head and quickly regain control of the situation. The basic military method of the OODA (observe, orient, decide, act) loop is just what is required when it comes to making rapid and effective decisions.

OODA was the brainchild of John Boyd, a USAF colonel who was a keen student of air combat. He was intrigued by the fact that, during the Korean War, USAF pilots flying F-86s were consistently beating the North Koreans in their MiG-15s. The MiG-15s were superior in nearly every way. They could climb and accelerate faster and had a better turning rate. The only thing that the F-86s really had going for them was that they were more agile. Even so, the US pilots were downing the North Korean planes at a ratio of 10:1. Boyd could easily have made the assumption that the US pilots were simply better trained, or were a little braver, but this did not properly explain that huge ratio. After doing some research, Boyd developed a theory called 'patterns of conflict', which centred around a series of decision-making cycles: observe, orientate, decide, act. OODA has since become one of the foundations of modern warfare.

At its simplest, the process goes like this. A threat is observed, we then orientate ourselves to deal with it based on our experiences to date, then we make a decision and then we act. This whole process is repeated as the action taken changes the situation. The idea is that the faster you cycle through the loop, the more control you will be able to exert on the situation. Most significantly, the environment will be changed as a result of undertaking this process, which will therefore blindside the opponent, who is still dealing with the previous situation. They will become unsettled at their inability to anticipate and deal with the new circumstances, and this will put them at an even greater disadvantage.

This model can be a very effective way of working through the sudden changes that may occur as the transformation plan evolves. Leaders can begin by observing the change in situation and then orientate themselves with it, decide on a plan to adapt the original course of action, and then act. It is a swift, effective way of taking advantage of the situation, and, if the change of plan has been influenced by competitor reaction, it is a useful way to put that competitor on the back foot. As Boyd deduced, the ability to observe and orientate oneself more quickly than your opponents can leads to faster and better decision making – and better decision making leads to wins. OODA provides a quick, easy way to reverse the odds, gain a competitive advantage and get your plan on an even better track than it was on before. In the heat of battle, as you enact the plan in step 8, this is the advantage any leader needs.

STEP 9. AFTER-ACTION REVIEW

To misquote Oscar Wilde: 'To go bankrupt once may be regarded as misfortune, to do so twice looks like carelessness.'[20] Yet, this is exactly what happened to US discount store Kmart. After a series of catastrophic leadership missteps the company filed for bankruptcy in January 2002, and then, having been rescued by hedge fund ESL Investments, under Eddie Lampert, the business found itself in the same situation again in 2018. It was a huge fall from grace for the once-formidable retailer – one with roots going back to 1899.

There has been much analysis of exactly what went wrong, and many of Kmart's problems were caused by the rise and rise of its rival discounter Walmart, which systematically gobbled up Kmart's market share. But this would be too simplistic a view to take. To really understand the root of the issue, you would have to travel back in time to the 1980s. At the beginning of the decade, Kmart was *the* place where young couples wanted to go to buy furnishings for their first home together. Everyone understood that the no-frills customer service meant that Kmart's goods were much, much cheaper than those of its rivals. The company played up the joy of hunting for discounts by placing a flashing blue light, with a siren, in the centre of stores. These would go off to attract shoppers to the latest deep discount at the same time as the store's loudspeakers would blare: 'Attention Kmart shoppers!' Some customers would hang around in the aisles for hours, just to be there when the big moment came. Then, not long after Kmart opened its 2,000th store in 1981, the company's management embarked on an aggressive acquisition strategy. In a matter of a few years, the retailer snapped up a series of big-box retailers, across all sorts of different areas. There was the Borders Group book chain, Home Centers of America (renamed Builders Square), Office Max and Sports Authority. Joseph E. Antonini, Kmart's chief executive, chairman and president (yes, he held all three top roles simultaneously), oversaw much of this unfettered acquisition strategy – a strategy that left many commentators scratching their heads. It was as if Kmart had decided it had invented discount retailing and therefore knew best what the market wanted.

Once any business believes it can dictate to the market and not the other way around, it is on a slippery slope. Fewer and fewer consumers were interested in Kmart, blue siren or no blue siren. Arguably, the company never recovered. The point of relating this story is to highlight a case where step 9, the after-action review, was clearly not followed. It is highly unlikely that Antonini or his successors spent much time talking to the people who worked in their stores, or to those in the back offices at Kmart's HQ, who were doing their best to juggle this aggressive expansion. If they had done so after each ambitious diversification, the leadership would probably have quickly realized that they were going down a very dangerous path.

Step 9 – an after-action review of the execution of the tactical plan and of how the results achieved compare with that plan – is an essential part of any business transformation programme. Yet, while this is something that is usual practice in the military, Kmart is not alone in failing to involve its team in this practice. Debriefs are very unusual in a business setting. It is very rare corporate leader who actively encourages a constructive review of business strategy, and it is still less common to see any active criticism of what has gone by from within a business. Yet, if you consider why the military follow this best practice – in order to continuously accumulate experience and improve the next time around – it makes perfect sense for a business leader to do the same. We can learn so much from our mistakes – as well as a great deal from what we get right.

The military action review process has itself evolved over the years. When Richard joined the army in the 1980s, he was presented with what he perceived to be a very antiquated debrief system. What concerned him most was that it made for a very one-way conversation. At the end of a mission rehearsal or a training exercise, or even an action itself, a commander would stand up in front of their direct reports and give their general thoughts on how it went and how everyone had done. The commander might finish up with a few recommendations of how they could improve next time as a group, or give their thoughts on what aspects of anyone's individual performance needed to change significantly. Those reports would patiently listen to the speech while taking notes, but they would not be asked to contribute anything. Richard recalls feeling very uncomfortable about the debrief system, and particularly the one-dimensional aspect of it.

After looking into several potential avenues that might have offered some improvements, Richard was exposed to the American military system of After Action Reviews (AARs), while on exercises in the US. The AAR is much more of a two-way conversation. Rather than a commander standing up and saying, 'this was my plan and this was how you did', the commander was put in a position in which they almost had to justify *their* performance to their soldiers. In addition, everyone was allowed to give input, which created a more rounded (and useful) feedback loop.

The AAR system is very direct, and the first time Richard tried it, while still on that exercise in the US, he admits that he found it quite brutal. After being encouraged to speak up, his direct reports remained polite but made some criticisms that were quite forthright. There were comments about everything from the speed at which the orders had been handed down to reflections upon the entire strategy being pursued. While initially taken aback, Richard quickly accepted that this was key to making his unit more effective. He told everyone present at that first AAR that he would take all their comments on board and adapt his behaviour and respond differently on the next exercise. He also made a promise that the AAR process would be repeated. It was not a one-off. Richard signalled that he fully expected everyone to come back and articulate whether or not they had noticed improvements and to say what else they felt could still get better. The response to this open forum was hugely powerful. The energy in the room was tremendous, he told me, and the AAR had a lasting impact. Afterwards, he overheard the platoon talking among themselves, and they were genuinely inspired by being given their say. He knew that the next time they did anything together, they would not just be carrying out *his* plan, it was now *their* plan as well. They had completely bought into it.

AARs proved so successful that they were subsequently migrated into other platoons, then battalions, and they eventually spread throughout the entire British Army. The process used today is very similar to the one that Richard first adapted from the American system.

With processes like AAR fully accepted as a normal part of the activities of the armed forces, it is ironic that most civilians picture the military as being very hierarchical – even dictatorial. The truth is that the military is set up to hear comments across the ranks, and its high command listens too. As Richard observes, he has seen many high-ranking officers brought up short by input from a private.

In reality, the hierarchical label is a far more appropriate description of most corporates. In a business setting, it is highly unusual to find a situation where people on the shop floor are given regular access to those on the executive floor in order to give their views, even though this would give leadership valuable insights into what is really going on. Indeed, on the rare occasions where we do see this happening, the process has often been introduced by an ex-military person who now works as a consultant in the civilian world.

This was the case when Richard suggested a debrief process to a major manufacturer he consulted for. This manufacturer relied on a highly structured bidding process for contracts – one that took its teams, step-by-step, through how to be effective when winning new work. What Richard discovered was that when a contract was won (or lost), the process simply reset to zero as the team began to work on the next bid. There was no formal process in place to assess what had been learned from the experience, despite the fact that such information could be useful for future bids. The team simply started anew each time.

A business after-action review process was subsequently inserted at the end of each bid. Everyone involved was invited to meet together to go over what they had learned. What were the issues they had overcome, and how had they done so? What would they do next time to make things go better? Today, teams embarking on new bids are able to access notes from previous bids, and this makes the whole process far smoother. There is no need to reinvent the wheel each time.

I have not yet worked for an organization where an after-action review is a fixed part of company strategy, but one other relevant example from my own personal experience comes via Askona, the bedding and mattress retailer highlighted during our discussion of step 6. The company has a practice of regular, company-wide reviews to go through everything that has been done and discuss what went well and what did not. This undoubtedly contributes to the firm's continued success and growth.

But beyond this one example, most corporate organizations I have come across completely sidestep the debriefing process once a project has been completed – this is a wasted opportunity. Reflecting on what has just happened presents everybody with a chance to learn and improve. This is a vital process because the takeaways from the experience will strengthen future missions. It prevents organizations from becoming stiff, inflexible and uncreative in what comes next.

After-action reviews do not solely make a difference to company-wide progress either: in a business setting, the process develops and empowers employees, encouraging adaptability and initiative. Individual team members who are given a voice and know that they have one are less likely to simply sit back and take orders from above. They will take ownership of the plan and be more receptive to trying something new next time – maybe even suggesting it – because if a strategy does not work, there will be a review and another opportunity to get it right. This is an essential part of a transformation: everyone pulling in the same direction to turn a business around. There is no point carrying on in the same way as before. That approach has already been proven not to work.

After-action reviews cannot be delegated

The after-action review process will only succeed if leaders fully immerse themselves in it and lead by example. This is not something that can be handed over to other senior team members: 'Have a meeting, see how everything went and report back to me.' If the CEO does not declare it is going to happen, set the process in motion yourself and keep on top of it – the debrief is likely to be kicked into the long grass as the organization moves on to the next thing. Or, as they say in the military, the AAR will end up in File 13: that is, the bin.

Apart from the fact that they will personally learn a lot from the after-action review, a leader's participation in it is a clear signal of how important the process is to the smooth running of the company. Can you imagine Jeff Bezos (or Andy Jassy, Bezos's successor as CEO) not getting involved if there were a major review at Amazon? It is already widely known that he takes a percentage of customer complaints to dive into personally, to see what can be done to resolve them. It is unthinkable that he would not get involved in any sort of after-action review.

None of this is to say that a leader has to get involved in the actual nitty-gritty of the organization or the logistics of the review process. Those things can be delegated to a 'chief of staff' (a political job title that is increasingly being used in the business world) or even to an external moderator, such as a consultant. In fact, if the debrief is an entirely new process for a company, it can sometimes help to have a moderator involved. Someone familiar with how after-action reviews work can set the tone and make the debrief more objective for any people who are not used to the process. The important thing is to retain momentum and ensure the review actually happens.

Many leaders will find the idea of an after-action review challenging on a personal level. Part of the problem is that a big title like 'chief executive' implies that leaders need to have all the answers. This may often be the case, but it is not always so. Presiding over a thorough debrief will present a true test of a leader's character, because properly subjecting oneself to such a process requires you to be strong, professional and competent. Leaders will need to supress any egotistical leanings they have, or the desire to constantly be seen to have made the best possible decisions in all circumstances. They will also be required to overcome any feelings of insecurity they have, or their fear of failure. Ideally, a leader needs to be humble enough to understand all of this and fully throw themselves into the process. To be successful, after-action reviews require total honesty from all quarters. If a leader does not want to hear what they are being told, or if they become overly defensive, the exercise will be a waste of time. Any leader who takes it personally, or feels insulted, is not going to get the full benefit, and nor will their organization.

A key point to remember here is that while after-action reviews are observant of ranks, they should also be classless. There are parallels here with the SAS, which has long made much of the fact that while it is not rankless, it is classless. An interesting illustration of this occurred during an SAS exercise in Latin America. It had been agreed that when the exercise was over, the squadron were to have a few much-needed days off to rest and relax. There was a clear directive, though, that they were not permitted to invite their spouses to join them. The squadron followed the instructions and no one invited their partner – no one, that is, except the squadron commander who had given out the no-spouse edict in the first place. Inexplicably, he was joined by his wife for the period of R&R. Unsurprisingly, the perception of double standards rankled, and a lot of ill-feeling spread within the squadron. When the commander got wind of the disquiet, he decided to tackle it head on. Gathering together his reports, his message was clear: 'I'm the boss and will not tolerate this backlash of disobedience.' This went down almost as badly as had the original sin. One of the squadron summed it all up very nicely.

'Sir, to disagree is not to disobey,' he said.

This response cut the commander to the quick. The entire episode summed up the fact that he was failing to exercise one of the founding principles of the SAS: humility.

To disagree is not to disobey is a lesson that any leader might like to bear in mind if a member of their team has something to say that contradicts their own viewpoint. Speaking openly about the specifics of the successes and failures of a strategy does not need to be seen as a direct criticism, but rather as a potentially constructive new piece of information. If people on the team feel empowered to speak freely, it is also a sign of the leader having created a sufficiently safe environment in which everyone is confident to offer suggestions.

Individuals who do find this final step challenging will need to find a way of overcoming any obstacles to this essential process. For those that are new to a senior role, and therefore not used to inviting such open feedback, it might be prudent to work with a business coach to help smooth the way. An experienced mentor should be able to help them identify best practice and put the necessary processes in place. Alternatively, more experienced leaders might like to view after-action reviews as a vital part of their ongoing self-development and continuous learning – an aspect that will greatly contribute to their future success as a leader.

Throughout this book, we have seen many glaring leadership failures, and these bring to mind a theory coined by a good friend of mine, the executive coach and author Stefan Wachtel.* Stefan believes that many leaders reach what he calls a career 'X' point: see the figure below.

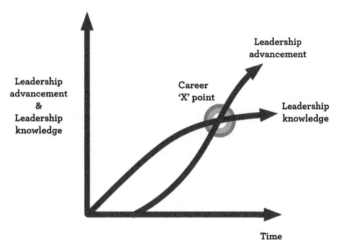

Career 'X' point. (© Stefan Wachtel and Pepyn Dinandt.)

One line of the X represents a leader's knowledge. They will have started to gain knowledge about the corporate world at school and university and will have expanded that knowledge as they become graduate trainees. Then, perhaps, they will be sent off on relevant courses to further their career. Throughout this process, the rate of learning is slowly decreasing as they are perceived to be able to do

---

* Stefan Wachtel is an executive coach and the author of ten books. His most recent is *Reversed Pyramid: The Punch Point Principle in Speech, Answer and Text* (Sinaveria, 2021).

their job and left to get on with it. There is a tendency for companies to cut training budgets to the bone, particularly for very senior staff, because it is seen to be an unnecessary expense.

The second line of the X is a leader's career curve. This begins at the bottom of the career ladder and steadily climbs as they move from their trainee position through their first managerial role and then on into the ranks of executives. At some point, more often than not, the two lines will cross. While the leader's career continues to advance, as individuals they will have stopped learning (or stopped learning much, at least). They may barely notice that this is the case, or alternatively they may have actively taken the viewpoint that because they have the title, they are sufficiently knowledgeable to successfully meet every challenge. Regardless, the result is the same: the sum total of their knowledge stays largely the same. The after-action review offers a valuable learning opportunity that will go on adding to a leader's skill base over and over again.

As previously noted, one of the big strengths of the military is that they actively manage personal and career development, no matter how senior an officer is. If there is ever a sense that the equivalent of Stefan's X point is looming, officers are always pushed towards another course. Each promotion is designed to push the X point further away. No one is ever considered to be the 'finished article', no matter how senior their rank.

There was a very clear demonstration of this in Richard's final army job, where, based out of Folkestone in Kent, he commanded all pre-operational deployment training. He adapted the process favoured by the 22nd Special Air Service regiment (22 SAS): holding quarterly cross-briefings. This meant that every three months, everyone (except those on operations) would get together and there would be a cross-brief of what they had all been doing. This allowed useful information to be shared in a very similar way to the AAR. Richard regularly invited all three elements of the Special Forces to take part: the 22 SAS (army), the Special Boat Service (navy/marines) and the Special Reconnaissance Regiment (a highly classified organization with people drawn from all over the services). On one particular occasion, he invited all of these elements to join the cross-brief that was preparing the regular army and the marines to go on operations

in Afghanistan and Iraq. The SAS and SBS were due to go on operations in Iraq too, and Richard reasoned that the Special Forces did
not have as much knowledge about improvised explosive devices as
the regulars had. As he told their commander, it did not matter how
special the Special Forces were if they stepped on the wrong piece
of ground. The result could be life-changing injuries, or death. The
cross-brief worked brilliantly well in a number of ways. It was hugely
motivational to the regulars, who saw their Special Forces colleagues
taking an interest in what they were doing, and it was very useful
for the Special Forces, who were getting the benefit of potentially
life-saving knowledge from people who understood the terrain and
knew more than they did about the situation on the ground. This
was a great example of the effectiveness of sharing information to
capture best practice. No one ever knows it all. We all benefit from
putting in processes so we can keep learning from our peers.

The perfect after-action review

An after-action review meeting should ideally be held in a group
setting, with each execution team being given the opportunity to
explain their role according to the previously agreed plan and then
to describe what actually transpired during the delivery phase. The
goal of the exercise is, of course, to highlight the positive aspects of
the mission and also its problems. As Tim Collins says, the closer
you get to understanding the truth of what *actually* happened, rather
than what you would *like* to have happened, the more likely you are
to learn lessons for future actions.

From a military perspective, it is all about understanding what
happened in an action in order to make sure you survive the next
one. One of the most important aspects of this is the removal of
hierarchy, so everyone feels free to speak candidly. For this to be
effective, representatives of all parts of the team should be involved,
regardless of their rank or title. Where possible, supporting data
should be introduced, since this is irrefutable and will provide a firm
foundation for any arguments used. Data is, after all, apolitical.

Some thought will need to be given to the size of the debrief
group. If there is a large number of people that should be involved

– thirty or more, say – it might work better to break the group down into a more manageable size: four groups of eight, say. Four different meetings can then be held, and the resulting feedback can be collated.

Alternatively, it is also possible to run the after-action review with a larger group remotely. It is not uncommon for military debriefs to be coordinated from headquarters, with various commanders and units 'dialling in' from around the world to give their input while the rest listen in. Today, of course, this is all done digitally, and the same thing can easily be achieved in a corporate setting. The pandemic has meant that many more people are now adept at working online and think nothing of connecting with their colleagues in this way to discuss company business, even in quite large groups.

One media company that Richard was working with opted to run its after-action reviews digitally. The person running the project under discussion opened the online meeting, outlining the aims of the strategies being adopted and the key results that had been achieved. Once he was done he opened the floor up to the more than sixty people who were on the call. It should be said that many people who had logged in were also going about their daily tasks at the same time and were simply listening in to the debrief. Being invited into the process ensured they felt involved, though, and if they wanted to contribute they were of course welcome to do so. Also, all the key people in the project – the marketing manager and her deputy, the head of sales and his deputy, and so on – were fully engaged. The whole event took some coordinating but it turned out to be a very effective and useful discussion.

As previously stated, the momentum behind the process is driven by the leader. Whether it is a battalion commander or a business CEO, the leader sets the ground rules and the tone of the discussion. However – and this is very important – this does not mean that the boss is in a position to immediately overrule everything they do not agree with. A good way to lead off an after-action review is, therefore, to state outright that you want full and honest comments.

If the feedback from the after-action review is completely honest, a leader may attract a few body blows. Someone might raise the fact that the message was not communicated well enough, say, or that it was too open to interpretation. Alternatively, it may emerge that the new product put forward by R&D was good, but not better than the equivalent one sold by a competitor. This is helpful information and not an insult or sleight to a particular individual. It is simply an indication that the communication side of things needs to be reviewed and possibly clarified, or that the R&D department needs to think again. Nothing being said implies that the team disrespects the leader – quite the opposite, in fact.

It is important that the after-action review is not allowed to descend into a free-for-all. While constructive, honest comments are invited (which is what an organization needs to capture), insults and petty point-scoring are not. The purpose of the process is to improve the performance of the team so that the business can get ahead of its competition. Thus, if it looks to be getting out of hand, or if team members get rather too enthusiastic, a leader must step in to get things back on track by reminding everyone *why* they are giving feedback. Only calm, rational comments that are not deliberately personal are required.

If it emerges that mistakes were made, that is fine. In fact, it is a huge learning opportunity that will help things improve next time. It is crucial that a leader does not punish anyone for making a mistake: that would stop people speaking openly in future, for fear of retribution. While a modicum of fear can be a motivator in some cases, pushing individuals to try something out of their comfort zone, being too heavy-handed can hinder people and force them to withdraw into themselves. There needs to be a blame-free culture in which everyone feels safe to criticize and offer suggestions.

It is equally important to give time to air successes as well. Messages of congratulations often go round when things go well, but no one really focuses on exactly why things went off so smoothly. What were the elements that contributed to this success? Leaders should expand the discussion by asking the team to think of three reasons why things went better than hoped. They can then follow up with a discussion of how they can be built into the Standard Operating Procedures, or SOP. Take care not to go overboard celebrating good results, though. This will invariably lead to one person, or a small group, receiving all the plaudits when, as noted earlier, many,

many people will have contributed to the success. If a 'them-and-us' environment is created, it will dilute the effectiveness of the review and possibly even of future activities.

Recording and using the results

An after-action review is not a symbolic exercise. A leader is not trying to simply be *seen* to do a debrief. It is not about *appearing* to be engaged, glossing over the triumphs and tragedies of a strategy before swiftly moving on. The goal here is to gain as much valuable input as possible: vital information that will contribute to framing future strategies. Leaders really need to get to the bottom of what worked and what did not, and they must give and accept criticism where it is due. Most importantly, these details need to be fully recorded and disseminated. If applicable, active measures need to be taken to alter the SOP so that the organization can improve its approach next time around.

Everyone involved with the after-action review will, clearly, hear the key messages, but these messages then need to be actively migrated across the whole organization (particularly to those who were not present at the debrief). They need to be continually reinforced thereafter too. People change, departments change, and if people were not exposed to the lessons learned, it is easy to end up in a situation where lessons need to be continually relearned. This is a waste of everyone's time, and it is hugely frustrating to many members of the team.

The final stage of step 9 is, therefore, to create a formal process for recording and relaying lessons to the whole team. Under the military system, there is an information exchange that is a good model on which to base a corporate strategy. Each new lesson learned from an AAR is fed back into what is known as 'the doctrine'. The doctrine are pamphlets produced by the military that are consulted before any unit embarks on an action, as part of the preparation for the operation.

Richard attests to the effectiveness of keeping these doctrines up to date with each new learning. His Kent-based operational training unit was in prime position to help keep these valuable sources of information current. It was in charge of training people to go out on operations, and there was always a routine follow-up on what had happened six weeks into their tour. It was another important part of the feedback process to understand the lessons learned almost in real time. These lessons were then carefully documented, and it was because of this that the operational training unit was, according to Richard, the most up-to-date training organization in the world. He recalls watching one of his instructors explaining to soldiers how to use a mine detector. He had just demonstrated the best setting to use in sandy conditions when he got a call from Helmand Province, in Afghanistan, that updated the instruction. The instructor immediately changed his recommendation to give the most up-to-date, accurate and potentially life-saving information to his class. This is a fantastic example of an organization that is 100% focused on improvement and committed to finding better ways of doing things and feeding them back in.

Richard has recently found himself pondering how the AARs on Afghanistan are going now, in the wake of the decisions by the US and the UK to withdraw from the conflict. I will let him explain his thoughts in his own words:

> There was, arguably, a flawed strategy, which changed three years into the campaign; over 450 young men and women were killed in action, hundreds more were left with life-changing injuries; and meanwhile thousands of Afghans were killed. Yet, we have just walked away.
>
> The decision to leave Afghanistan, firstly by President Biden and thereafter by Prime Minister Johnson, came in the same week as the anniversary of the death of my Regimental Sergeant Major Sean Dolan (KIA in Helmand in 2007). Sean was one of 12 men killed from my Battle Group during that bloody summer. I wonder how family and friends felt, after such sacrifice, to hear we were slinking away. I know how I feel.

In an ideal world, an after-action review creates a virtuous circle of activity – one that continuously pushes a business forward in a positive manner. Even if a turnaround strategy appears to have gone brilliantly, a leader should always be looking for the weak points: where could things have been done even better? A regular debrief process helps to hold in check any complacency and overconfidence that may creep in thanks to short-term wins.

Look back at some of the once-dominant businesses cited in this book: companies such as Nokia, Blockbuster and Kmart. They were all once at the top of their game: the undoubted, unparalleled leaders in their field, commanding a significant market share. How different would things have panned out if they had been enacting regular debriefs? It is quite probable that with this very analytical, company-wide approach, they would have identified the competitive threats a lot earlier than they did. Employees on the ground would have been more aware of what the competition was doing and where their organization fitted in in that competitive environment. If these companies had opened up a dialogue, it may have helped the company's leadership to think entirely differently – to reference the debrief material and change tactics to try something different. If an organization has the right attitude about what they do and how they do it – and, equally importantly, if it has a process in place whereby success is not allowed to go to its head – then it is better equipped to deal with threats.

The simplicity of an after-action review belies just how powerful one can be in delivering a rapid learning process, enabling leadership to innovate, grow and, just as importantly, avoid repeating mistakes. It also brings a team together, strengthens relationships and fosters learning across the board. Teams who regularly debrief will not simply be better informed, they will be more tight-knit than most and they will be fully aligned on the task ahead. With a background like this, the future of a transformation strategy looks much more solid.

AFTERWORD

B usinesses today face a host of threats. Many will have lost a large proportion of their income thanks to lengthy closures caused by Covid-19 lockdowns, and if they managed to stay open throughout the pandemic, there might still be a need to shed jobs or restructure in the ensuing tough economic environment. And even before the global health emergency, companies were faced with a rapidly changing trading environment that is increasingly embracing digital. Big businesses have been losing ground to leaner, fitter small businesses. Established businesses that dominated their spaces for decades have found that customers no longer care for their products as much as they once did.

There are few business leaders that have any experience of leading a company through a crisis, perhaps because full-blown crises are thankfully rare in corporate settings. Due to the havoc the pandemic has brought to the revenue lines of many businesses, though, leadership at these businesses do now have some experience of 'crisis'-type situations, but in most cases they were protected by state support programmes. For the armed forces, crisis is part of daily life. Because military leaders have always experienced significant challenges, it makes perfect sense, today more than ever, to learn lessons from some of history's most effective leaders at a time of pressing peacetime crisis. The military is, after all, well versed and well rehearsed in the techniques and practices that are needed to manage life-and-death situations. Terms such as tactics, strategy, exercising and wargaming are built into the training process. The principles of military leadership in a crisis can be transferred to business via our nine steps.

There is no point in deciding to just wait until things get better, or in trying to turn the clock back and replicate how things were in better days. A downturn will not simply stop happening. Businesses need to accept that and start making moves to resolve the crisis immediately. Strategy is at the heart of the nine-step programme outlined in this book, and business leaders need to look towards creating strategies too. Their actions need to be measured, though. It is very easy to fall into the trap of running around, trying all sorts of different things to bring back growth and profit, but being busy is not the same thing as being efficient. It is certainly not the way to achieve a successful turnaround.

Businesses need to tackle a crisis situation in its entirety. Military strategy shows us that in order to solve a problem, a leader first needs to evaluate what an organization stands for, what has changed to bring it to its current crisis state, and whether it is possible to reverse the damage. There needs to be a thorough assessment of the team: its strengths, its weaknesses and whether it has any untapped leadership potential. It is only once you know what an organization is all about and what it is trying to achieve that it is possible to devise a coherent strategy. Military leaders are obsessive about planning, and rightly so. The battlefield is an uncertain environment, which is why ideas need to be tested, retested and tested again.

Once a plan has been agreed, it is not a question of telling everyone what to do and waiting for them to succeed. A leader needs to be involved every step of the way to enact the strategy. The plan will almost certainly need to be re-evaluated and redrawn as circumstances change, and that process needs careful monitoring and management. Without a clearly defined approach, things will get forgotten or be missed. This is why the nine-step process is so powerful. It relies on the same tried-and-tested philosophy that has been followed by the military for decades – a multistage, stepped approach ensures that everyone knows where they need to be, what they need to do and what to do if things fail to go according to plan. As Dwight D. Eisenhower famously said: 'The plan is nothing; planning is everything.'

The nine-step process is underpinned by the agility and decisiveness of a leader, who will need to be highly visible within their organization, often during its most difficult moments. Great military leaders fight side by side with their soldiers. The Duke of Wellington was said to have observed that Napoleon's presence on the battlefield was worth 40,000 fighting men.

The nine-step process will require courage, which is a fundamental part of leadership, since it is crucial in earning the respect and trust of the team. This does not mean physical courage, which is usually identified with the armed forces, but moral courage. Moral courage is about doing the right thing, even when it is not necessarily the easiest thing. (Remember the last 'C' of the four Cs.)

During a war, both sides will be continually searching for an edge. Innovation will bestow an advantage, but so will constant change and evolution. This is the way to make a difference and out-manoeuvre the opposition. Success in a turnaround situation is never assured, but, as we have seen time and again throughout this book, doing nothing is not an option. Leaders who wish not only to survive but to transform the fortunes of their organization so that it thrives will need to establish clear leadership, analyse the mission and set the strategy. Equally importantly, they will need to work with and empower their teams to achieve the plan. Following the nine steps will enable the whole organization – from its leadership right down through the ranks – to adapt and have a clear understanding of the mission. Most importantly, those nine steps will help you quickly deliver and set you on the path to victory.

ACKNOWLEDGEMENTS

W̲e sincerely thank Teena Lyons for her eloquence as well as for helping us formulate our thoughts and understand them even better than we thought we did already. The encouragement of Tim Collins to get the project off the ground in the first place was extremely valuable. We would also like to warmly thank all those who contributed to the extensive research on leadership failures, including Djenet Djerourou, Sudhansa Torvi and Oleg Falkov. A special thanks in this regard goes out to Matthew Russell. Heartfelt thanks also goes out to some of the successful business leaders that let us interview them, especially Vladimir Sedov and Roman Ershov at Askona, Johan Verstrepen at Corialis and Tim Freystedt at Amazon. Henrik Thiele was also very insightful on the Knorr Bremse story.

From a professional inspiration perspective, there are a great many people I have learnt from throughout my career, starting with Heinz Schleef and Alexander Witzleben back at Tridelta, where I was given my first (almost impossible) mission by Lothar Späth. Some others who have been instrumental in my professional development as well as being great fun to learn from and work with are Johannes Huth, Gareth Turner and Karim Saddi, with special thanks going out to Sir Roger Carr in this regard. Warm thanks are also due to many of my other former bosses: Wolfgang Müller, Axel Eckhardt, Uwe Reinert, Jürgen Gerlach, Uriel Sharef, Heinrich Hiesinger, Ed Krubasik, Werner Paschke, Horst Heidsiek, Philipp Freise, Heinrich Weiss, Michel Paris, Mirko Meyer-Schönherr, Jean-Pierre Clavel, Fabrice Nottin, Winston Ginsberg, Jo Knoll and Mark Brown.

The teams at the many companies I have worked with – people who were instrumental in achieving lots of impressive results – must also be remembered. Individuals play the game, but teams beat the odds. The following list barely scrapes the surface of the many excellent people that I have had the honour to work with: Anton Margold, Norbert Passarge, Fleischmann Sr & Jr, Roland Philipps, Norbert Reinhard, Cornelia Schweiger, Tony Sansevero, Josef Maertl, Cornelia Menz, Georg Harrasser, Andrea Benincasa, Marco Righi, Frank Herrmann, Caroline Dildey, Joaquin Lozano, Wolfgang Marka, Ana Lluch Martinez, Bjorn Edwardzon, Klaus Erbismann, Peter Sturm, Toni Habertür, Jenny Appenrodt, Hans de Jongste, Geoff Gysin, JT Jensen, Elaine Davies, Musi, Ovi Petreaca and Ellen Palm (heartfelt apologies to anyone I have missed here).

For taking the time to proofread various versions of the book, many thanks also go to Joanne Bennett, Holger Engelmann, Graham Russel and Ranjan Sen. Thanks too to Richard Baggaley and Sam Clark at London Publishing Partnership, our publishers, who have been patient and helpful but who have also added much brio and insight to make our book even better. They do what it says on the tin: it really has been a partnership.

And finally, we both thank our families, and especially our wives Daniela and Jane, for putting up with us as we laboured through this project and probably drove them mad – at least a little bit.

Pepyn Dinandt, Munich, September 2021

There are many people who have inspired and helped me throughout my life and career. They know who they are, and they are too numerous to mention. This book would not have happened in the way it did without them. I hope that readers will find something useful to help them here. I enjoyed the chance to reflect on my career as well as discuss my observations and lessons with many different people. Certain patterns stood out even more clearly after those discussions than they did before. Despite all this kindness and help, all mistakes obviously remain my own.

Richard Westley, Hampshire, September 2021

ENDNOTES

1   Sergei Klebnikov. 2020. Tesla is now the world's most valuable car company with a $208 billion valuation. *Forbes*, 1 July (https://bit.ly/3neUSuf).

2   Department of Energy. Undated. Timeline: history of the electric car. Web page (https://bit.ly/2X66Z1K).

3   Dominic Rushe and James Ashton. 2009. The iPhone is giving Nokia a pain in the apps. *The Sunday Times*, 25 October (https://bit.ly/2VwiAXs).

4   Warren Bennis and Burt Nanus. 1986. *Leaders: The Strategies for Taking Charge*. Harper & Row.

5   Jocko Willink. 2020. *Leadership Strategy and Tactics*. Macmillan.

6   Nadine Schimroszik. 2012. ThyssenKrupp writes off £2.4bn over Steel Americas operation in Brazil. *The Guardian*, 11 December (https://bit.ly/2YHZ9ft).

7   Tony Wilson. 2011. The best legal advice is often an apology. *The Globe and Mail*, 1 February (https://tgam.ca/3yRKJpz).

8   Niccolo Machiavelli. *The Art of War* (various editions).

9   Nicholas McCullum. How investors can learn from Jeff Bezos's long-term thinking. *Seeking Alpa/Sure Dividend*, 14 May (https://bit.ly/3tqs4Qz).

10 Business Leader. 2020. Jack Welch: the GE titan who embodied the flaws in modern capitalism. *The Guardian*, 8 March (https://bit.ly/3nc1k5c).

11 Lauren Cochrane. 2016. How cult label Palace went from UK skate kids to hip-hop royalty. *The Guardian*, 3 May (https://bit.ly/3nfM1Iy).

12 Everett M. Rogers. 2003. *Diffusion of Innovations*, 5th edition. Simon & Schuster.

13 Michael E. Porter. 1985. *Competitive Advantage: Creating and Sustaining Superior Performance*. The Free Press.

14 All the options are very well illustrated in *The Art of War Visualized* by Jessica Hagy (Workman Publishing, 2015).

15 James McLetchie and Andy West. 2010. Beyond risk avoidance: a McKinsey perspective on creating transformational value from mergers. Report, McKinsey & Company (https://mck.co/2YAs19f).

16 Frank Olito. 2020. The rise and fall of Blockbuster. *Insider*, 20 August (https://bit.ly/3yWIxgq).

17 Thomas Hobbs. 2017. From iconic to punchline: Blockbuster's CMO reflects on how things imploded. *Marketing Week*, 3 July (https://bit.ly/3jSyKUm).

18 Simon Sinek. 2019. Performance vs trust. YouTube video, 10 November (https://www.youtube.com/watch?v=kJdXjtSnZTI).

19 Xan Rice. 2019. The Aldi effect: how one discount supermarket transformed the way Britain shops. *The Guardian*, 5 March (https://bit.ly/3yZOSHX).

20 The actual quote is: 'To lose one parent, Mr Worthing, may be regarded as a misfortune; to lose both looks like carelessness.' Taken from Act I, Part 2 of *The Importance of Being Earnest*.

INDEX

A

ABB, 133–4
achievement, attitude towards, 117
acquisition, 48
action–reaction–counteraction, 151
adaptability, 152
added charges, 146–7
AFCP (aim, factors, courses open
    (available), plan), xvii
Afghanistan, 24, 48, 148–9
after-action reviews/AARs, 15, 161,
    162
agility, 9, 93, 94, 102, 139–40,
    148–50, 176
Airbnb, 2
Aldi, 138
Amazon, 2, 22, 49, 100–102, 129,
    146–7, 164
    '14 Leaderhip Principles', 100
    Dash button, 101
    'two pizza teams', 102
Antioco, John (Blockbuster), 111–12
anti-trust laws, 65
Antonini, Joseph E. (Kmart), 159
Apple, 4, 82
Art of War, The (Machiavelli), 36
Art of War, The (Sun Tzu), 7, 64
Askona, 115, 163
asset-heavy versus asset-light
    businesses, 111
assumptions, 67
attacking ratio (in the military), 73
Audi, 79–81

B

back brief, 54, 102, 104
banks, 136
Barnes & Noble, 22
Battle of Britain, 60
Battle of Jutland, x
BEANS (beliefs, emotions,
    ambitions, needs, status),
    65–6
Bell, Martin, 106
Bennis, Warren, 8
BenQ, 128
Bezos, Jeff (Amazon), 49, 101–2,
    164
Black Hat, 18
blame culture, 101
Blitzkrieg, 6
Blockbuster, 111–13
Borders Group, 22, 159
Bosnia, 41, 43, 105, 118
Boyd, John, 157–8
brand loyalty, 79
Brexit referendum (UK), 11
broken telephone game, 29
Brooks, Vincent, 38
Buffett, Warren, 85
burning platform, 11, 17, 21–3, 32,
    37, 39, 82–3, 101
business coach, 165
business model, 91
business units, creating smaller,
    138–9
buy-in, 100

C

career 'X' point, 166–7
catastrophic success, 38, 39
Chandler, Colby (Kodak), 6
changed environment, recognizing, 84
Charge of the Light Brigade, 16
checklist, 19
Christensen, Clayton, 6
Churchill, Winston, 103
cognitive dissonance, 31, 85, 105–7
Collins, Tim, 9, 48, 65, 103, 116,
        135–6, 168
combat estimate, xii, xvii
competitive advantage, 79
*Competitive Advantage: Creating and
        Sustaining Superior Performance*
        (Porter), 78
complacency, 157
consistency of leadership, 124
consolidation (of activities), 97
constraints, 43
consultants, 66–7, 141
contact information, 62
contingency planning, 11, 38
Co-op, 138
Corialis Group, 123
corporate culture, 86–8, 127–9
    changing, 130–36
corporate reports, 44
corporate social responsibility, 44
corporate structure, 136–9
cost–benefit analysis, 10
cost cutting, 48
cost leadership, 78
cost-takeout exercises, 48, 67, 143
courage, moral, 177
Covid-19, 42, 56, 137, 175
cowardice, 8
criminals, 57
cross-briefings, 167–8
culture change, 129–32
cut-off point, 89
cyber hacking, 64

D

Daimler, 87
'Day One' versus 'Day Two' businesses,
        129
Dayton Agreement, 106
D Day landings, 75
decisiveness, 176
Deepwater Horizon explosion, 34
defensive strategy, 90
delegating power, 140
delivery, 145–6
devolving power, 139
differentiation, 78, 81
directive control, 94
disruptive innovation, 7
disruptors, 2, 68, 140
        digital, 137
dissent, 136–7
Dixon, Norman, 17, 31
doctrine, the, 171
Drucker, Peter, 86
due diligence, failure of, 95
Duke of Wellington, 176

E

early adopters, 68
eBay, 96
e-commerce, 138
Eisenhower, Dwight D., 176
Ek, Daniel (Spotify), 56
electric vehicles, 1
Elop, Stephen (Nokia), 82
empowering your team, 123
empowerment, 46, 139, 151
entry barriers, 69
environmental social governance, 44
environment/theatre of operations,
        12
Ershov, Roman (Askona), 115
ESL Investments, 159
estimate process, 9
execution of the plan, 14

F

Facebook, 96
failure, learning from, 83, 115
Falklands War, 93–4
Fallon, Walter (Kodak), 6
family-owned companies, 49
fashion business, 69
fast-moving fashion, 59
Feather & Black, 83–4
feedback, 102
fintechs, 136
firing of CEOs, 109
first mover, 78, 89
Fisher, Irving, 84–5
flat organizational structure, 101
flexibility, 152
focus
    as corporate strategy, 79
    on the enemy, 61
four Cs, the, 4–5, 177
Franklin, Benjamin, 143
Freystedt, Tim (Amazon), 100–102,
        129
FTSE 100, 81
Fuller, J. F. C., 6

G

G4S, 91–2, 94
Geely, 87
General Electric, 54
geographies, importance of
        understanding, 97–8
gig economy, 2
goals
    feasible, 50
    implied, 46, 47
    qualitative, 46
    realistic, 53
    simple, 43
    timescale of, 46
'good ideas club', the, 104
Google, 96, 132–3

Great Leader Effect, 155
Gulf War, 43

H

Hackworth, Colonel David, 110
Hastings, Reed (Netflix), 111–12
Hayward, Tony (BP), 34
headcount reduction, 140
Headquarters Special Forces, ix
Helmand, Afghanistan, 139
Hewlett-Packard, 56
hierarchy, removal of, 168
Hilding Anders, 64, 83–4
Hill 125, 47, 55, 73
Hitler, Adolf, 60
Home Centers of America/Builders
        Square, 159
honour, delicacy of, 8
humility, 36, 114, 136
    lack of, 34
Hussein, Saddam, 38

I

ignoring the competition, cost of, 60
impact statements, 97
improvement programmes, 99
incumbents, 7
industrial espionage, 53
initial address, importance of, 23–5
innovators, 68
intent, 43
internal rate of return, 44
investor returns, 44
iPhone, 4
Iraq War (2003), 38, 48
Irish Republican Army (IRA), 148–9

J

Jassy, Andy, 164
Jope, Alan (Unilever), 56
just-in-time strategy, 91

K

Kaizen philosophy, 134–5
Kallasvuo, Olli-Pekka (Nokia), 4, 82
Keynes, John Maynard, 84–5
key performance indicators, 70
Keys, John (Blockbuster), 112–13
Kindle, 22, 102
KISS (keep it simple stupid), 76
Kmart, 159–60
Knorr-Bremse, 70
know your enemy, 62
Kodak, 5–6
Korean War, 157
Kosovo, 76
Krulak, General Charles, 90

L

Lampert, Eddie, 159
lateral thinking, 134–5
layoffs, 97
leaders
    founders, 18
    highly motivated, 114
    visibility of, 29
leadership, 11
    empowering, 92
    establishing, 18
    failure of, 5, 8
    potential, spotting, 113
Leadership Strategy and Tactics
    (Willink), 13
leadership team
    firing or retaining, 110
    quality of, 109
Lidl, 138
listening, 33, 36
listeria, 35
Lombardi, Vince, 20
London 2012 Olympics, 91–2,
    150–51
looking inward (as well as outward),
    71

Lord Raglan, 16
luck, 55
    making your own, 55
Luftwaffe, 60

M

MacDill Air Force Base (Tampa, FL),
    38
Machiavelli, Niccolo, 36
main effort, 45–6
Malaya, 103
management team, 13
Mannesmann Plastics Machinery,
    133–5
Maple Leaf Foods, 35
market intelligence, 68
market share, 67, 71, 81–2
Marks & Spencer (M&S), 81
mass differentiation, 69
Mayer, Marissa (Yahoo), 96
McCain, Michael (Maple Leaf Foods),
    35
McKinsey, 33, 95, 145–6
mentor, 165
Mercedes, 87
mergers, 95–6
micromanaging, 140
    avoiding, 135–6
Microsoft, 4, 82
military
    hierarchical, 93
    strategy, 9
mission
    analysis, 11, 43
    definition of, 42
    pivots, 56
    revisiting, 54
    selling the, 52
    targets, analysis and determination
        of, 41
    unrealistic, 50–51
Mission Command, 94
mission-critical goals, 44

Mission Success Cycle, xvii, 102–3
momentum, 156
money multiples, 44
Montgomery, General Bernard, 75, 77, 93
Monzo, 136
Morrisons, 138
motivation, 151
Multi Domain Operation, 63
multiple stakeholders, 43
Musk, Elon, 1, 3, 15

N

Nanus, Burt, 8
Napoleon Bonaparte, 15, 110, 128, 153, 176
NATO, 106
naysayers, 135–6
Netflix, 2, 56, 111–13
Nextel, 95
Nokia, 4, 82
non-commissioned officers, 94
Nook, 22
Northern Ireland, 148–9
    conflict, 64
'not invented here' syndrome, 133–4
nurturing talent, 116

O

objectives, delegation of, 46
objective versus subjective, 37
Office Max, 159
Olympia (typewriter firm), 145–6
one-third/two-thirds rule, 103
online
    scams, 57
    shopping, 138
*On the Psychology of Military
    Incompetence* (Dixon), 17
OODA (observe, orient, decide, act)
    loop, 157,–8
open enquiry, 102

openness, culture of, 33
open-source material, 66
Operational Training Advisory Group, 104
Operation Market Garden, 51
operations team, 94
'orchestra of war', 93
organizational handbook, 129
organizational pyramid, 14
organization (units and subunits), 14
overload, 152
over-promotion, 121
over-solicitude, 8
Owen, Bryn (Blockbuster), 113
owner/founders, 70–71
ownership, 34

P

Palace (fashion brand), 59
'patterns of conflict' theory, 157
performance culture, 130
Peter Principle, the, 120
Piëch, Ferdinand (Audi), 80
planning, 13
plans team, 94
pontification, 31
Porsche, 80
Porsche, Ferdinand, 80
Porter, Michael, 78
Porter's model for strategies, 78, 80
post-merger integration (PMI) plan, 95–6
Prada, 69
praise, importance of, 153
price of entry, 69
pricing, 69
Primark, 69
principles of war, 15
prioritizing, 45
private company, 71
private equity, 43–4, 49
profit, as a sign of success, 69
promotion, from within, 121

public companies, 49
    failing, 44
pyramid structure, 123

Q

Quaker Oats, 95
question four moment, 55
question mark email, 102

R

racehorse phenomenon, 3
range of talents, 120, 122
reality check, 97
recklessness, 8
Red Team, 18
reducing headcount, 48
redundancies, 26
regimental system, 127
Renault, 64
resource conflict, 96
responsiveness, 9
return on invested capital, 69
Revolut, 136
Rifkind, Malcolm, 118
risk
    assessment of, 86–9
    neglect of, 32
    taking, 86–9
risk–reward assessment, 88
risk–success matrix, 88
routine, the danger of, 129
Royal Air Force (RAF), 60
Rumsfeld, Donald, 38

S

Sandhurst Royal Military Academy,
    33, 36, 150
SAS (Special Air Service), 20, 36, 77,
    118, 151, 165, 167
SBS (Special Boat Service), 48–9, 167
Schlieffen Plan, 85

seagull leader, 30
Sedov, Vladimir (Askona), 115–16
segment differentiation, 69
selection processes, 120
self-awareness, 34
senior team, development of, 123
sequence planning, 97
seven stage estimate process, 9
'shoot straight, run fast and drive on',
    24
side goals, 44
Siemens, 128, 133–4
silos, 63
simplicity, 75
Sinek, Simon, 114
situational awareness, 37
Skype, 96
'slate a mate', 33–4
Smart (car brand), 87
Smith, General Sir Rupert, 41, 43
Snapple, 95
Sony, 6
sovereign, 41
Special Reconnaissance Regiment, 167
spies, 64, 66
    buyable, 66
Sports Authority, 159
Spotify, 56
Sprint, 95
Standard Operating Procedures (SOP),
    135–6, 170–71
Starling, 136
Steel Americas project, 35
Steele, John, 150
Stirling, David, 36
Strategic Defence Reviews, 47
strategy
    approaches, 78
    culture's effect on, 86
    over-complicating, 76
    switching, 84–5
strengths
    intangible, 69
    levering, 83–5

strengths and weaknesses, 12, 14, 71, 79
stupid question, no such thing, 54
successful strangers versus unsuccessful friends, 119
Sun Tzu, 7, 8, 27, 32, 41, 64, 66, 88, 104, 139, 147–8, 154
    five factors, 60
Supreme (fashion brand), 60
Swatch, 87
Symbian, 82
synchronization matrix, 149–51

T

Taliban, 24, 148–9
Tanju, Lev (Palace), 59
tasks, specified and implied, 43
teamwork, 151
temper, hasty, 8
Templer, Field Marshall Sir Gerald, 103
Tesla, 1, 3
Thales, 149–50
theory of architectural innovation, 6, 86
theory of disruptive innovation, 6
Thiele, Heinz Hermann, 70–71
ThyssenKrupp, 35
timescale, 49
top-down leadership, 93
Toyota, 134–5
trade associations, 63–4
training, 121–2
transformational mergers, 95
transformation plan, 15
Tumblr, 96
turnaround, 18, 41

U

Uber, 2
UK Sport, 150
Unilever, 56
unintended consequences, 147–8
United Nations, 105–6

V

Verizon, 132–3
Verstrepen, Johan (Corialis Group), 123
vision, lack of, 132–3
VoIP, 96
von Moltke, Helmuth, 147–8
von Rundstedt, General Gerd, 85
Vorsprung durch Technik, 80
VUCA (volatility, uncertainty, complexity, ambiguity), 8, 9, 72

W

Wachtel, Stefan, 166–7
'walking the ground', 29
Wall Street Crash of 1929, 84
Walmart, 159
wargaming, 18, 149–50
weaknesses, attacking, 83–5
Welch, Jack (General Electric), 54
'what if?' mindset, 149, 151
who dares wins, 12
Willink, Jocko, 13
Windows Phone, 82

Y

Yahoo, 96, 132–3